895/47 6-2

ENZO FERRARI

ENZO FERRARI

50 YEARS OF MOTORING

BY PIERO CASUCCI

Greenwich House
New York

Copyright © 1980 by Arnoldo Mondadori Editore S.p.A., Milano
English language text © 1982 by Arnoldo Mondadori Editore S.p.A., Milano
Originally published in Italian by Arnoldo Mondadori Editore S.p.A., under the title *Enzo Ferrari*

A creation of Ervin s.r.l. Roma
Edited by Adriano Zannino
Editorial Assistant Serenella Genoese Zerbia
Illustrated by Maurizio Riccioni

Translated by Simon Pleasance
English language text edited by Kennie Lyman

First published in the United States by Greenwich House, New York, 1982
All rights reserved
Distributed by Crown Publishers, Inc., New York

Printed and bound in Italy by Officine Grafiche, Arnoldo Mondadori Editore, Verona

Library of Congress Cataloging in Publication Data
Casucci, Piero, 1918-
  Enzo Ferrari: 50 years of motoring.
  Translation of: Enzo Ferrari: 50 anni di automobilismo.
  Bibliography: p.
  1. Ferrari automobile. 2. Ferrari, Enzo, 1898-
I. Title.
TL215.F47C3813   629.2'222 [B]   82-6217
ISBN 0-517-38302-0   AACR2

CONTENTS

7 Foreword

8 Ferrari, His Life and Work

19 Ferrari, Through the Drivers Eyes

29 Ferrari, Talking about Drivers

41 Ferrari, That's the Way I Am

47 The Birth of Ferrari

55 **Formula 1**

88 The Ferrari Drivers:
A Hundred Men in Search of Glory

96 The Ferrari Racing Managers:
All the President's Men

99 The Ferrari Technicians:
Many Men, So Much Horsepower

121 **Sports Cars**

136 Formula 2 Ferraris

138 The Hill-Climbing Ferraris

139 The Ferrari Body Designers:
From Touring to Pininfarina

162 Index

167 Bibliography

167 Metric Conversions

FOREWORD

Much has been written about the "Ferrari phenomenon": Ferrari, the man, the engineer, and the "trouble maker," as he fondly labels himself.
As a subject, Ferrari is eminently topical. The wins chalked up by his cars hit the headlines. The name Ferrari has a sweet ring to it, both for the sporting enthusiast and for the man in the street. Now over eighty years old, with a shock of white hair and an air of dignity which does not rule out a keen thirst for argument, he follows the development of his racing cars on a day-to-day basis and with a persistent interest, which can, without exaggeration, be called pathological. He also takes it upon himself to ensure that engineers, organizers, and sporting bodies work as a team.
His total dedication to a cause can only inspire admiration. Throughout the world, the word Ferrari is synonymous with Italy, and, when people talk of Italian cars, the name that first springs to mind is Ferrari. Unlike other books which deal with this subject, this one takes a close look at every aspect of the "Ferrari phenomenon": the man, the driver, the engineer, the trouble maker, and the industrialist, forming an all-round portrait, which is not painted in other books about this leading twentieth-century personality. This book is therefore dedicated to Enzo Ferrari, in all humility. And it will not have been written in vain if it has managed to retrace—even if sketchily—the truly dazzling career of the man in question.

The author

HIS LIFE AND WORK

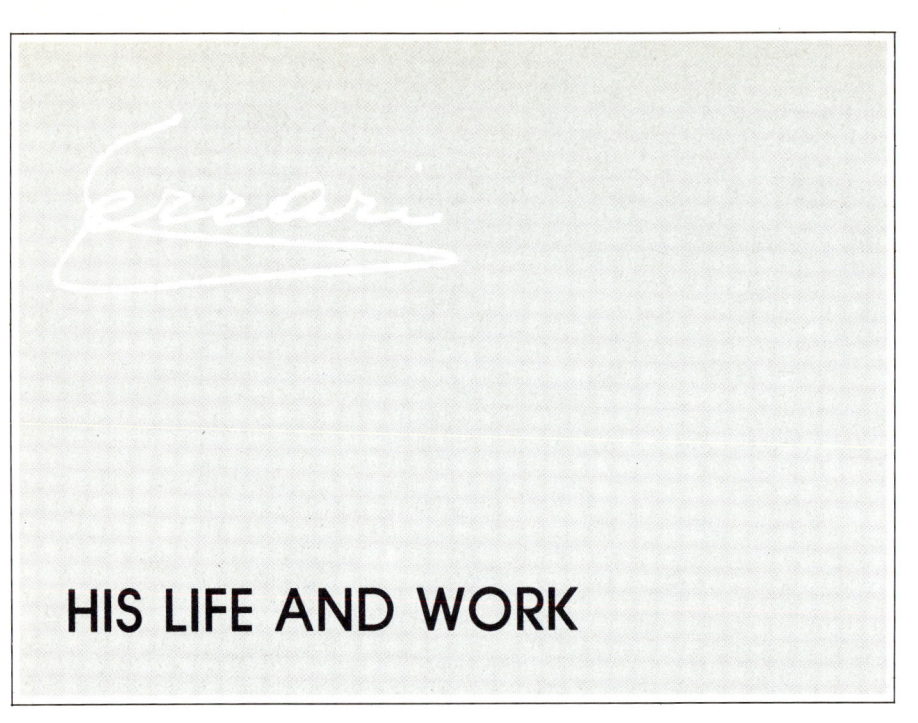

Enzo Ferrari was born in Modena on February 20, 1898. In fact, he was actually born on the 18th, but, as his mother was to tell him later, the snow that month was so deep that it was not possible to register the birth until two days later. His parents—both from Carpi—lived on the farthest outskirts of Modena in a modest home close by the factory where Enzo's father built axles and roofing structures for the Italian Railways. In those days Modena was a town of 50,000 inhabitants. Enzo and his brother Alfredo, two years his senior, shared the room above the workshop. Each morning they were awakened by the first blows of the metalworkers' hammers. Their father died of pneumonia in 1916. That same year Alfredo also died from an illness contracted during his national service. "I was left with a sense of terrible loneliness."

School was a real problem for Enzo: he

Two truly historic photographs: Enzo Ferrari, above, in an Alfa Romeo ES at the Mugello race track in 1921 and, in the photograph on the left, at the wheel of the CMN in the Parma-Poggio di Berceto race (October 5, 1919). This was his first racing event and he placed fourth in the 3000 cc. class.

sincerely hated studying, unlike his brother, who was very good in school. His father wanted him to obtain a degree, but Enzo's response to any such idea was: "What I want to do is work."

The first car with which he had an "affair" was a 1-cylinder De Dion. Later his father bought a 2-cylinder Marchand, and eventually he graduated to a 4-cylinder Diatto. This was the last car owned by the family.

As a boy Enzo's favorite sport was track and field athletics. Later he turned to target shooting: with Flobert he played havoc with many a clay-pipe. He was a regular visitor to the Panaro gymnasium with its poles, horizontal bars, parallel bars, and mats reeking of mold in the murky, dust-filled atmosphere. He also fenced and skated. But his first communion slightly dampened his athletic exuberance. On the Saturday before the service he received a heavy penance. It was his first proper confession. "And I don't think I've ever confessed again since."

As a boy Ferrari was attracted by the world of music, particularly the operettas then at the height of fashion, like *La Geisha*, *Eva* and *The Merry Widow*, but in one fell swoop the two deaths in the family changed everything.

Enzo entered the army in 1917 and was assigned to the Third Mountain Artillery. His knowledge of mechanics earned him a job in the smithy, shoeing mules. As a result of a serious bout of illness, he was moved to the hospital at Brescia and then to the Baraccano in Bologna, the last resort of hopeless cases. After two operations and a great deal of medical care, he was, once more, fit enough to go in search of work. With few means at his disposal, lacking in experience and educational qualifications, he nevertheless had a great urge to succeed.

Many years after those early days, he himself wrote these words: "I find myself once again in these parts and I can recognize some of the trees, some of the isolated cottages, some of the ditches, and the far-off silhouette of Mt. Cimone. But has my work changed anything? Maranello, for example, was a village with a population of 1,500. Today it's grown bigger: there are more than 11,000 inhabitants, there's the factory named after me, there's a professional institute named after my son

Dino with workshops and sporting facilities. Look a little further, over towards Fiorano, and you'll see a test track snaking its way through the green rolling hills. Today, strange cars streak round this track, along the same straights which I remember as dusty lanes with plodding oxen. Can I claim to have done anything? Can I look at you and say that I've achieved the dreams and passions I had as a boy?''
In effect the achievements and activities which have earned Enzo Ferrari fame and renown throughout the world have little to do with his boyhood dreams of being a tenor, a sports correspondent, and a racing driver. But is there any harm in detecting a tenor in some of the "theatrical" poses he assumes? And haven't his many articles in various newspapers perhaps made something of a journalist of him too? As for driving racing cars, this dream did come true, even though it was short-lived.

His first brush with the racing world happened when he was ten years old. His father drove him to see a racing event which took place on the Bologna race track and on the Via Emilia. He recalls feeling very emotional at seeing Vincenzo Lancia completing the fastest lap and Felice Nazzaro winning the day. The seeds of the future organizer were sown on that day, when he saw how the onlookers were kept at a safe distance from what was considered the most dangerous bend by a field flooded with a foot of water. In this way, the spectators were forced to keep a respectful 40 meters (130 feet) from the bend. This shrewd safety measure came back to mind on the day on which the man in charge of the Mille Miglia course, Renzo Castagneto, used bales of straw as a protective buffer between the cars and the public. Another racing event which Enzo Ferrari followed closely was the "record mile" which was held on the Navicello straight on the Modena-Ferrara road. "To reach that dusty straight (asphalt did not yet exist) I crossed several fields and the railway, because it was three kilometers (two miles) from my house to the timed track." Da Zara won at an average speed of 140.251 kph (87.437 mph).

By now, Enzo Ferrari had made up his mind: the automobile interested him more than anything else, but his first contact with Fiat, the firm where he was eager to get a job, was a total flop. "It was the winter of 1918-19; it was very severe; it hurts me to think about it. I found myself on the road, my clothes frozen to my back. I cleared a path through the Valentino park with my hands and collapsed on a bench. I was alone; my father and my brother were both dead. I sat on that same bench again, years later, in 1947, when Sommer won the Turin Grand Prix with the 12-cylinder Ferrari, the first post-war Grand Prix. The tears on that day tasted quite different."

It was, in fact, in Turin that he found a job in a factory where light trucks were turned into car chassis ready to be fitted with automobile bodies. Ferrari was responsible for testing them and then delivering them to the Italo-Argentina body works in Milan.

Enzo frequented the Bar del Nord at Porta Nuova, the haunt of racing drivers and many other people in some way associated with the automobile world. It was Ugo Sivocci who offered him the chance of moving to Milan. Sivocci had met Ferrari at the Vittorio Emanuele bar in the Lombard capital. He was working with CMN (Costruzioni Meccaniche Nazionali), and he and Enzo were close friends. CMN had moved from making four-wheel-drive tractors to mounting its engines on remaindered chassis from Isotta-Fraschini; and an independent production line was soon proposed. Ferrari became the test driver, but, before long, he moved to Alfa. Sivocci's death in 1923, while on a trial run on the Monza circuit at the wheel of an Alfa Romeo, was another tragic blow suffered by Ferrari. Sovocci has been a true friend, responsible for Ferrari's involvement with both CMN and Alfa.

Ferrari was a good driver. He made his debut in 1919 in the first Parma-Poggio di Berceto event (uphill), coming in fourth in the 3000 class. In that same year he took part in the Targa Florio. He went there with Ugo Sivocci. They reached Naples in the same cars—both CMN—with which they were to take part in that already famous race, after an adventurous journey highlighted by snow in Abruzzi. This, Ferrari said, was the first time that he sensed "the

Pescara, August, 1931: Enzo Ferrari receives the congratulations of the Duke of Abruzzi. Between them are Italo Balbo (left) and Giacomo Acerbo (center).

work there, at Alfa Romeo, when the surname of the Neapolitan engineer Nicola Romeo was added to Alfa, which stood for "Anonima Lombarda Fabbrica Automobili." In 1924, he won at Pescara with the RL and came in first again at the Savio and Polesine circuits. It is with particular satisfaction that he remembers the win at Pescara because he managed to beat the Mercedes entries in that race.

The man who was later to become the founder of the famous Scuderia and the builder of no less famous automobiles started to take shape while he was with Alfa Romeo. Ferrari started to prefer organizing and "trouble-making" (as he called it on several occasions) to the role of driver. The first step towards building up the racing division of the Milanese factory was when Luigi Bazzi, a brilliant technician and a natural talent, transferred from Fiat to Alfa Romeo. It was Enzo Ferrari who brought Bazzi to Alfa Romeo, and it was Ferrari who, at Bazzi's suggestion, set up another "kidnap," this time a truly sensational one: the man involved was Vittorio Jano. Jano had trained with Fiat and was from Piedmont. It was no easy task to persuade him to leave the Turin firm, but the operation was a stroke of genius, because Jano built truly exceptional cars starting with the P2. If Alfa Romeo has become a racing trade name par excellence, much of the credit must go to Vittorio Jano. Ferrari remained with Alfa Romeo until 1939.

In the meantime, in 1929, he had set up the Scuderia Ferrari, which gave birth to the Alfa Romeo 158 which was to become extremely famous in the immediate postwar period and remain so up to 1951. In 1938, Ferrari was summoned to the head office of the racing management of Alfa Romeo, but he left a year later, virtually slamming the door as he did so. Jano had also left, and his replacement, the Spanish technician Ricart, was someone whom Ferrari could not stomach. But a clause in the agreement he had signed with Alfa Romeo stopped Ferrari for four years from rebuilding his Scuderia and from being involved with the racing sector. "I was a leading and possibly a crucial character in two sensational clubs—Fiat and Alfa Romeo—by which I mean in the motor racing sector."

The Scuderia had been born over a supper in Bologna in 1929, and it remained alive for nine years. In 1932, by acquiring the P3s, which had dominated every race and which the Milanese firm no longer wanted to use on the track, it virtually replaced Alfa Romeo in terms of racing activities; but Ferrari remained in constant touch with Alfa. The initial plan of the Scuderia was to have its members race, but, before long, an official team was established with drivers of the caliber of Tazio Nuvolari, Luigi Arcangeli, Giuseppe Campari, Achille Varzi, Mario Umberto Borzacchini, Luigi Fagioli, Louis Chiron, Antonio Brivio, Guy Moll, Mario Tadini, and Carlo Pintacuda.

Ferrari's divorce with Alfa Romeo led to his permanent return to Modena. "I am attached to this land of mine, I confess, in a fierce way. This is particularly true today, for two tragic reasons which have to do with the fate of my family. This attachment did not exist in former times when I was working in Turin and Milan and Switzerland. They were all places which also told me much more about my own flat, monotonous, foggy birthplace, with its baking hot summers, where there are no lakes, no beaches, and just a few hills on the skyline. But I don't know if I'd have been able to achieve the same results if I'd stayed put there. In my return to Modena there was a sort of moral revolt; because when I left Modena, in my youth, I was just a rather strange lad with a passion for cars and sport, and I doubt if anyone saw any special abilities in me. By going back to Modena, after twenty years, to change from being a racing driver and the organizer of a scuderia into a small-time engineer and manufacturer, meant for me not only the end of what I would call an almost biological cycle, but also the attempt to show other people and myself that with Alfa Romeo, where I had been for those twenty years, I had not lived only off reflected light, so to speak. I wanted to show that the level of notoriety which I had reached was a legitimate and hard-earned outcome of my own hard work and of my own aptitudes. The time had come to make it known where my energy could lead to."

From Modena, Ferrari moved to Maranello late in 1943, in accordance with the law to do with industrial decentralization which had been imposed on all factories. In Modena he had a work force of about forty. In Maranello the numbers rose to between one hundred-forty and one hundred-sixty. The new firm was no longer a corporation, but a one-man show. Ferrari went to Maranello because he owned a plot of land right by the present-day factory. As a result of the commitment he had made with Alfa Romeo he did not become involved with automobiles to begin with, but with aircraft engines for training aircraft, which he manufactured for the Compagnia Nazionale Aeronautica of Rome. He also pursued the idea of making refacing machines of various types for the manufacture of ball bearings. The Maranello factory was not immune to bombardments, but it did not take long to put it back together again.

For Ferrari the end of the war also meant the end of his bond with Alfa Romeo, and it was natural enough that he should immediately start thinking about automobiles. He discussed things with a certain Gioachino Colombo, who had designed the Alfa Romeo 158 at Scuderia Ferrari. There was agreement to moving in the direction of a V-12 engine. Ferrari had always admired the automobiles used by American senior officials, having had a chance to look over the Packard V-12. He was also spurred on by the fact that, at that particular time, only one factory was building V-12 engines, and that firm was Packard. Ferrari remained stalwart in his conviction that he had chosen the right distribution of cubic capacity, even in the face of initial stumbling-blocks and criticism. He drew some comfort from the moral support given by Raymond Sommer who, like Ferrari, was a V-12 enthusiast. The design work started in 1946 and Gioachino Colombo drew out the first cross-sectional drawings of the 12 cylinders on wrapping paper, because the paper suppliers had run out of the right paper for the job. The car was called the 125 GT. The V was set at 60° angle, the bore was 55 mm and the stroke 52.5 mm, with a cubic capacity of 1496.77 cc. The 125 made its debut on the Piacenza Circuit, driven by

presence of death on racing circuits."
In this race, incidentally, he had a strange mishap which he describes as follows: "I had my share of bad luck; the fuel tank started to wobble in the very first lap, and I had to stop to repair one of the braces which held it to the body. I lost forty minutes and slipped down to the end of the field. I managed to regain some of what had been lost, despite a few reckless moves towards the end of the race, but then another curious stroke of fate convinced me to postpone any dreams of glory until the next race. I was about to reach Campofelice. Two other cars were quite close on my tail. Suddenly three policemen standing right in the middle of the road flagged me down. You never say no to policemen, so we politely asked why we had to stop. 'It's not an accident,' the Benemerita policemen answered, 'no danger, don't worry. You'll just have to be patient while the President finishes his speech.'

"A few yards further on, round a bend, the road was seething with people and blocked right up to the main square: the Sicilians had turned out en masse to applaud Vittorio Emanuele Orlando, the President. We mouthed a few cautious protests, but to no avail. The President's speech was quite a lengthy one, and, even when he had finished, I was still not permitted to drive on. After a lot of insisting we were eventually allowed to join the presidential procession. We drove slowly on for a few miles along with the black De Dion Bouton sedan and were only allowed to race on towards the tape when the President's car turned off the main road."

When Ferrari arrived at the finish, the timekeeper was a policeman with an alarm clock. Next day, the quick-witted Vincenzo Florio said to him: "So you're complaining. You were delayed. You didn't run any risks, and we're even going to give you a place." Ferrari came in ninth.

The following year he took part in the Targa Florio again, with the Alfa 4500, this time he came in second. He had started the season with an Isotta-Fraschini. The prize in this Sicilian race was considerable for the times: 10,000 lire. Ferrari's involvement with Alfa started in 1920 and he continued to

Tribune di Cerda, 1923: Enzo Ferrari at the start of the Targa Florio. On the right, Alfa Romeo's engineer Rimini; King Constantine of Greece is between the two.

Monza, August, 1923: Enzo Ferrari (on the right) with engineers Nicola Romeo (in the center with the stick) and Giorgio Rimini.

The souvenir of a convivial banquet after Enzo Ferrari's win in the Coppa Acerbo in 1924. On Ferrari's left sits mechanic Eugenio Siena.

Franco Cortese, but had to withdraw two laps from the end, when the car was in the lead, because of a blockage in the fuel pump. With this car, the Ferrari company established a system all its own for naming the vehicles which it produced. In this specific case the "125" corresponded to the unitary cylinder capacity of the 12 cylinders. This formula changed in 1954 with the 306, where the first two numbers indicated the cubic capacity of the automobile and the third figure referred to the number of cylinders (thus 3000 cc and 6 cylinders).

The 1500 cc F1 did not turn out to be a good car, and it was with the arrival of Aurelio Lampredi, who took Gioachino Colombo's place, that the Ferrari company underwent a decisive change with regard to the F1, using induction engines rather than super-charged engines. The first F1 of this type was the 3322 cc 275 F1, again a V-12. It was followed by the 4101 cc 340 F1 in 1950 and in the same year the 4493 cc 375 F1. This car reached the top end of the formula then in force, which permitted 1500 cc engines with a compressor or non-supercharged 4500 cc engines.

The history proper of Ferrari, the engineer, started with the 375 F1 in as much as it was with an 375 F1 that Froilan Gonzales won the British Grand Prix in 1951, beating the Alfa Romeo entries for the first time. This victory, which had been so longed for and worked for, caused Ferrari to write: "When, in 1951, and for the first time in the history of our direct rivalry, Gonzales and his Ferrari left the 159 and the whole Alfa Romeo behind him, I wept for joy; but my tears of optimism were also mingled with tears of sadness because on that day I thought, 'I've killed my mother.'" In that same season, Ascari won the German Grand Prix at the Nürburgring and the Italian Grand Prix at Monza. Fangio managed to secure the world title with Alfa Romeo, but it was a very close finish, and the Milanese firm realized that the undeniably excellent 158, which later became the 159, had reached its zenith, and it was withdrawn from the race track.

To have brought Alfa Romeo to its knees in 1951 was a tremendous achievement for Ferrari, and the world championship titles won by Ascari in 1952 and 1953 consolidated his renown as an engineer. The story of the 2000 cc 4-cylinder model is well enough

Top: the first true Ferrari automobile. In accordance with a clause in the contract which still bound Ferrari to Alfa Romeo, it was not called Ferrari but simply bore the number 815. Alberto Ascari (at the wheel here) took part in the 1940 Mille Miglia with the 815. A second 815 was driven by Lotario Rangoni.
On the left: the first Ferrari to bear that name, the 125. It made its debut at the Piacenza Circuit on May 11, 1947, with Franco Cortese at the wheel.

known. But its main features deserve repeating.
The Formula 1 (1500 cc supercharged 4500 cc induction) should have remained in force throughout 1953, but the withdrawal of Alfa Romeo at the end of the 1951 season and the unsatisfactory performance of the BRM had reduced the number of entrants in the Grand Prix events qualifying for the world championship to such a meager number of cars that the race organizers, with the assent of the International Sporting Committee, were forced to resort to Formula 2 cars. Furthermore, the Formula 1 planned for the 1954-1960 period required the use of 2500 cc engines. Enzo Ferrari believed that a 4-cylinder model would not only gallantly defend the racing colors of his Scuderia in the F2, but would also provide an interesting experiment, precisely in view of the new F1. The engine for the 4-cylinder model, which was called the 500 (once again referring to the unit cubic capacity) was a mechanical miracle in terms of reliability; this was fully demonstrated in the two years in which it was used. It was also remarkable for the extraordinarily short time required to build it. Alberto Ascari literally walked away with the Grand Prix races in the period in question (fifteen in all, of which eleven were won by the Milanese driver and the remainder by Taruffi, Hawthorn, Farina, and Fangio, the latter at the wheel of a Maserati which thus chalked up just one win against Ferrari's fourteen). At the end of the 1953 season, Alberto Ascari and Luigi Villoresi, the official drivers of the firm from Modena, moved to Lancia. It was a sensational move, perhaps only paralleled by Niki Lauda's withdrawal from Ferrari even before the end of the 1977 season.
Ferrari had started his fully-fledged activity with a GT, the 125, which, in reality, was a racing car in disguise. But the real Gran Turismo cars, des-

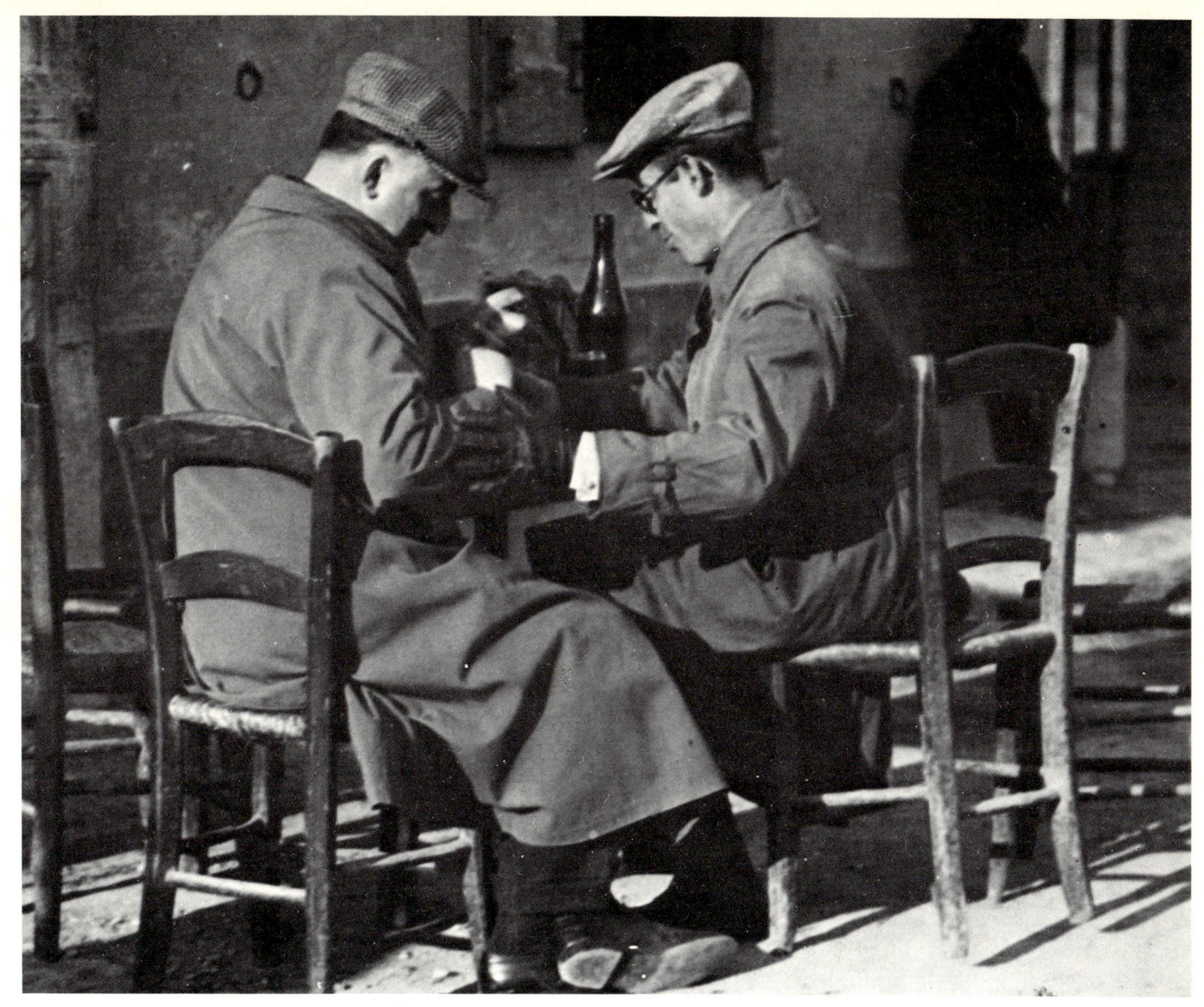

Modena 1931: Enzo Ferrari with Professor Poli of Pirelli, who together with the engineer Bottasso designed the first racing tires. The two men are shown at the Torrazzi tavern on the Navicello straight, scene of the record mile.

tined to be sold to the Ferrari clientele, started to appear in the early '50s and with them a whole series of cars which were to go down in the history of the automobile.

The bodywork of the Gran Turismo Ferraris was identified almost overnight with a brilliant designer, Giovan Battista Farina (later Pininfarina). The combination of Ferrari and Pininfarina was a happy encounter between two men who had devoted their lives to automobiles, although in different areas: one was in love primarily with engines, the other with line and style. It was a perfect case of symbiosis. The Ferrari-Pininfarina collaboration got under way in 1952 with the 2562 cc 212 Inter. The problem which faced the designer from Turin was far from easy: he had to mount a two-seater cabriolet on the 212 chassis. The result was an instant success. And it was followed up by the 212 Inter coupé (1953), the 342 America, and so on and so forth with a series of highly successful cars, culminating in the 365 GT4 BB and the 308 GT4. We should reserve a special word for the 250 Europa coupé 2 + 2 which, in its various versions, was welcomed by enthusiasts in a way which exceeded all expectations.

In the period in which the 2500 cc. Formula 1 remained in force (1954-1960), Ferrari did not win the satisfactory results which had been provided by the 4-cylinder 500. The return of the Mercedes, from the 1954 French Grand Prix (which was held at Rheims) on, posed major problems for the small Maranello factory. At that time, furthermore, Ferrari was involved in various types of competitions which obliged its technical division to perform some remarkable acrobatics in order to keep apace with the racing calendar. A helping hand was lent by Lancia which had decided to stop all its racing activites after the death of Alberto Ascari. This had occurred at Monza while he was test driving the

Giuseppe Campari at the wheel of an Alfa Romeo.

Ferrari 750 of his friend Castellotti (Ascari was still with Lancia and, in theory, could not have driven a Ferrari competitively at that time). This unexpected offer was accompanied by an altruistic gesture from Gianni Lancia who bequeathed to Ferrari all his racing equipment, including the 8-cylinder single seater D50s designed by Vittorio Jano. It was with a revised and up-dated Lancia D50 that Manuel Fangio, who drove for Ferrari for just one year (1956), won his fourth world championship title.

However, 1956 was a sad year for Ferrari, marked by the death of his son Dino, who was something of an anchor in his father's life.

He was to have followed in his father's footsteps as son and heir, but a cruel disease tore him from his parents at a very young age. Of Dino, Ferrari writes: "He was born into racing and with racing in his blood. He was filled with an overriding passion for this sport and he also drove the cars I was able to give him with skillful ease. This passion of his—I might add—caused me a lot of worries, not so much because of the risks he ran but rather because of the consequences which driving these cars could have for his frail health." Dino worked with his father both in the management of the factory and as a technician, having gained a diploma as an industrial expert in Modena, and subsequently earning an engineering diploma in Switzerland with a plan for a 1500 cc, 4-cylinder engine. He also attended the Faculty of Economics and Commerce at the University of Bologna. Dino had a great passion for mechanics and the 1500 cc, V-6 engine which he built in November 1956 certainly bore his stamp. Dino died of muscular dystrophy five months before that engine saw the light of day. Enzo Ferrari has sketched this noble memory of his much-loved son: "By bequeathing me his huge spiritual wealth, this young man has above all shown me that we remain children at all ages, until some fearful grief occurs, through which, as if all of a sudden, we learn what goodness, sacrifice, charity, and duty all are. This is the value of life, for a young man who leaves us."

In 1957 the Mille Miglia ended tragically with the death of De Portago and his teammate Nelson. The fact that nine spectators also died with the two drivers (the accident happened at Guidozzolo di Mantova) stirred up questions about the structure of the tires used. The press gave full coverage to this aspect of the tragedy. Ferrari went through a lengthy court trial, and, although he was fully cleared and acquitted, his morale was severaly jolted by the event. Accused of kindling and stimulating the spirit of adventure in many young people, he seriously considered retiring. But racing was his lifeblood, and he pursued this life and work all his life.

It is interesting, for the record, to reread the charge made against him as a result of that sad event. It ran: "Ferrari, Enzo, son of the late Alfredo, born in Modena on February 20, 1898, and resident in that place, accused of the offence laid out and punished by art. 589 p.p. and 590 par. I and II in relation to article 81 p.p. of the Penal Code in his capacity as proprietor of the Ferrari Company of Modena, which specializes in the construction of cars designed for sporting competitions both on the road and on the race track; the offence consisting in having used in the twenty-fourth Mille Miglia meeting on the cars from his Scuderia and in particular on the vehicle which bore racing number 531 driven by Alfonso Cabeza de Vaca Marchese De Portago, registration BO 81825, tires made by the Englebert company of Liège, Belgium, which, given their construction characteristics and their preparation (tread of 2.5 kg/sq.cm) were not suitable for the performances of the vehicles which, at full revolutions, developed maximum speeds on the track of about 280 kph (175 mph), these tires, conversely, permitting a speed of 220 kph (137 mph), and giving rise because of the overheating to consequent excessive inflation, the collapse of the central part of the tread and the subsequent explosion of the entire tire which caused the vehicle to skid, killing nine spectators and the two drivers."

Refutation of the charge was quite straightforward. It consisted mainly of drawing attention to the fact that the first three places in that class at the Mille Miglia went to three Ferraris with tires identical to those indicted. Ferrari himself was convinced that De Portago's tire had been "pinched" while skidding over the "cat's eyes" running along the center of the Volta Mantovana bend. The acquittal was handed out four and a half years after the accident.

The death of his son caused Ferrari to consider the timeliness of changing his company in such a way as to ensure that he had a successor. He entered into negotiations with Ford of America and was on the verge of signing an agreement, but at the very moment when he was faced by the lawyers flown over from Detroit and about to sign his name to each page of the agreement itself, he suddenly had second thoughts and cancelled the whole thing. He justified this attitude by admitting anxiety about losing all his say and autonomy, not least in the racing division which had always been dearest to him. With regard to this wish of his to secure a successor, he explains why he chose Fiat as follows: "Many people have wondered since the Fiat deal what would become of my factory. It's a logical enough question. If my son were still alive, there would be no cause for wondering. In life one makes many plans which are then overturned by fate, chance, circumstances, death, or a lack of courage. What we call fate or destiny, nevertheless, lies to a large extent in men's hands, when they have clear ideas and resolute propositions. I hope that I have managed to lay the foundations of a business concern which will be able to survive in the future, because if this were not so I would have to look with great regret on what happened to the great Bugatti of Milan, painter, automobile engineer in France, a man of eclectic genius, whose name is known and esteemed throughout the world, but who failed to find the continuity which he so richly deserved. The person who comes after me will have to take on a very simple inheritance: to keep alive that desire for progress which has been pursued in the past, even if it has involved the sacrifice of some of the noblest of human beings. There are those who wonder why I have never tried to turn my factory into a major industry. I don't know why. I have never thought in terms of being an industrialist; I have always thought I should be an engineer and a builder, because industry has requirements which I could not assimilate, in as much as they are opposed to my temperament as a promoter of research."

In fact, Ferrari defines himself as a "trouble-maker" in a year-round quest to stimulate others to do better.

Faithful to his principles and his own interests, in 1977 Ferrari resigned as chairman of the company created by him. The reason was that he no longer

Enzo Ferrari, in the background wearing suspenders, at the Modena Autodrome.
Nino Farina, wearing cap and goggles, has his back to the camera.

17

wanted to be involved with the production of Gran Turismo cars; he wanted to be able to devote all his time to the racing division, the only one which has ever really interested him.

In the sixty and more years in which he has been actively at work—first as a test-driver at CMN, then with Alfa Romeo as a driver and director of the Scuderia, and lastly as an industrial entrepreneur—Ferrari has frequently been a subject of interest to the press (profiles of him have been numerous). He has given countless interviews, although himself has always been very reticent, cautious, and reluctant to issue statements, to the point where he established the rules for recording any discussion. Invariably he has been called a genius, a superior man, a person with a deep knowledge of men, or, on the other side, a disagreeable man, a deceiver. His refusal to have Italian drivers on his team has been interpreted in various ways. In one interview, he apparently said that the reason for this refusal was caused by the attitude of the press to a fatal accident when the driver involved is Italian. He has denied saying this.

It is a fact that Ferrari's attitude is largely determined by the "moralizing" role which the press, and particularly the dailies, assumes when such sad things occur. The press forgets that anyone who accepts the role of racing driver knows full well that he is risking his life. It may be a choice which is open to discussion, but it is taken with a full awareness of the consequences. After the 1957 Mille Miglia and again after the 1961 Italian Grand Prix, Enzo Ferrari was once more the object of serious accusations. He was accused of having a very relative concept of the lives of other people, but the facts later showed that his cars had not the slightest thing to do with the unfolding of the two accidents which also involved several spectators.

The fact that he is never present at a race if one of his own cars is taking part, because "seeing it lose is like losing a son," has given vent to a whole series of insidious comments. The fact is that Ferrari sees his cars almost as real "creatures," in flesh and bone.

Even if corridor gossip, denouncements, and the intrigues of the racing world have tended to harp on the question, no driver—not a single one—has ever accused Ferrari of neglecting the aspect of safety. The vast wealth of equipment which goes to build his cars has, if anything, represented a handicap which has never bothered him.

People who have written about him, with objectivity, have always ended up by affirming that Ferrari will be a permanent fixture in the history of the automobile. Some of his attitudes are histrionic; he delights in keeping people on tenterhooks; he looks people in the eye, and then from tip to toe; he puts any interviewer in a subordinate role; he lets out far more than he feels inclined to; but he is fascinating.

The way he has lived his life, always to the same pattern, following a strict routine, has caused some people to accuse him of having no interests at all other than the automobile. This is the highest praise that he can be given, because what he has striven for he has achieved with zeal and with exemplary coherence. Arthur Rubinstein has been asked what the secret behind his extraordinary longevity has been. "It's easy," he replied, "because I love life." For Enzo Ferrari life means automobiles, and for this reason he too loves life. Rather than carry on as a driver, an activity from which—incidentally—he retired at an early age, he preferred to create, mold, discover and promote, and at the same time give as much elbow room as possible to his technicians. On occasions he has been ruthless with his colleagues and collaborators, crushing them with his authority. The prime reason for his leaving Alfa Romeo was the antipathy he felt for the Spanish technician Ricart (it is symptomatic that in his books, even in the reprinted editions, he stubbornly misspells the name and calls him Ricard), and this bears witness to his idiosyncratic behavior in ambiguous situations. Who was to run the racing division of Alfa Romeo? Ferrari or the newcomer? The problem, when posed in no uncertain terms to the then director of Alfa Romeo, Rimini, was not solved in a manner satisfactory to Ferrari, so he left. Years later, when one of his cars beat the Alfa Romeos at Silverstone, he sent a telegram to his former friends, almost asking forgiveness for having been so impetuous in the past, but in his heart of hearts that telegram may have had another purpose: it was intended to emphasize the fact that times had changed. Having been shown the door by the Alfa Romeo management, he had now had full revenge.

He doesn't like trains, or airplanes; for decades he has never been in an elevator; he rarely goes anywhere by car (at the most he'll drive to Milan or Florence); nothing in the world will keep him away from his own bed, not even for a night; he never goes more than fifty yards for a meal out; he reads a lot, and he watches television fairly often.

Anyone who has wanted to meet him, whether a driver, a politician or a monarch, has had to find his way to Modena. He boasts that he has not set foot in Rome for at least forty years. And yet he is always well-informed about everything. There is no race track in the world which he does not know like the back of his hand; and there is not a single automobile that has escaped his acquaintance. Every day he jots down comments, visitors' names, and the subject of conversations in a notebook. In this way he displays a formidable memory and a keen sense of observation. His sense of humor comes close to sarcasm, and his quips leave their mark. He is also tough, and when he can, he takes his revenge on anyone who does him ill; he does not forgive and forget. Those who have had the good fortune of knowing him can nevertheless say that they have met an unforgettable man.

Ferrari

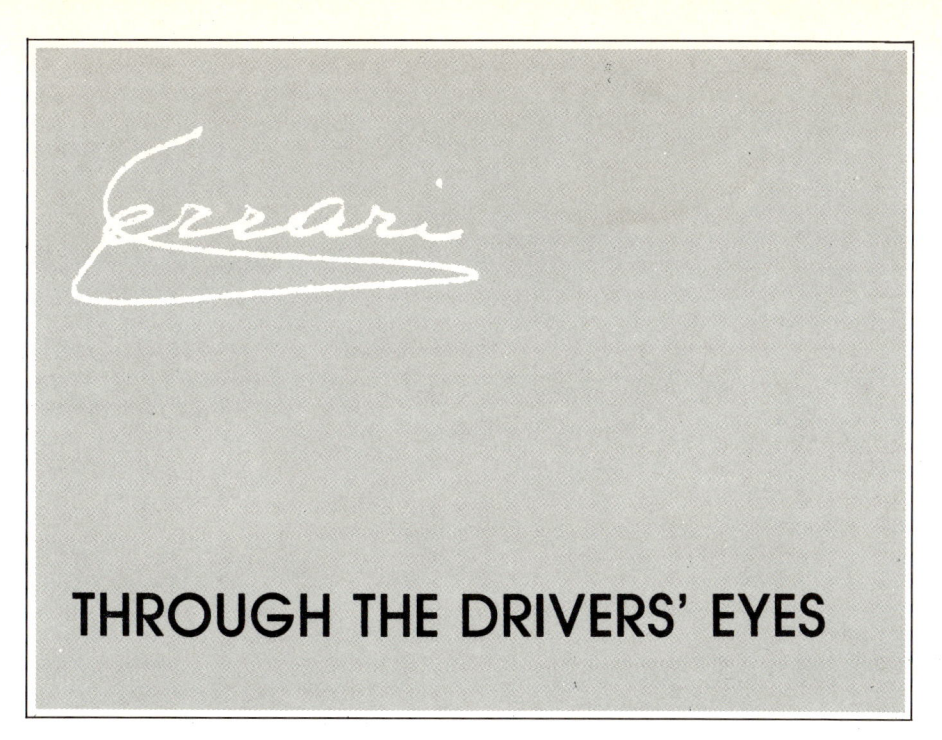

THROUGH THE DRIVERS' EYES

Phil Hill (left) with Peter Collins.

Passionate; subtly shrewd; at times daringly sincere; generous; and yet, on more than one occasion, ungrateful and quick-tempered; worshipped and hated—Enzo Ferrari has been the object of some harsh comments in his lifetime. Drivers have been the least kind of his critics, in particular, Olivier Gendebien and Philip (Phil) Hill.

Gendebien was a true "gentleman" when he joined up with Ferrari. He had already raced successfully, but at his own expense. He came from a well-to-do family and was a distinguished and extremely elegant man with an exceptional knowledge of vintage wines and a love of refined food. But he was taken off guard on the day that Ferrari summoned him for a "talk." Needless to say, the meeting took place in Modena. Ferrari does not travel out of his birthplace, or, rather, his neck-of-the woods, which includes the factory at Maranello and the Fiorano race track.

The first encounter was not one of the rosiest. Gendebien arrived for the appointment with split-second punctuality but was kept waiting for quite some time. When he was seriously considering leaving, he was finally shown in. He was to discover at a later date—and this is corroborated by Phil Hill as well—that the "waiting room" was part of Ferrari's strategy, used to intimidate and at the same time annoy those waiting to have words with him, even if they were expressly summoned by him.

It is hard to tell whether Ferrari considered the time which he gave to others very precious or whether this was a calculated pose. The story goes, in this respect, that Clemente Biondetti, the winner of four Mille Miglia races (two of which, in 1948 and 1949, were won in Ferraris), asked to see the "big boss" one day. He had just returned to his native Florence from Brescia following one of his successful wins with a car bearing the famous Ferrari horse. Ferrari refused to see him. Gossip had it that Ferrari was annoyed by the idea of having to thank the Tuscan driver.

But let us return to Olivier Gendebien. He was greatly surprised, after some rather icy opening remarks in the bare room with Amorotti present, to hear Ferrari offering him a contract which would bring him into the Ferrari fold

19

for a certain period of time. Ferrari was so sure that the Belgian driver would accept the offer that he did not discuss a single clause with him. He passed him an already-drawn-up contract and motioned to him to sign it. Gendebien admitted that he had never expected such an offer. The idea of joining a much-heralded team which numbered some real aces was beyond his wildest expectations.

Phil Hill had a no less off-hand encounter with Ferrari in 1955. The American driver has always been convinced that their later collaboration suffered considerably from the chilly atmosphere of that first encounter. When Hill went to Modena he already had a good career behind him. He had won several races held in California driving Ferraris and with a Ferrari he had come in second in the Carrera Panamericana. More than twenty years after going there, Phil Hill says that the time which he spent at Ferrari taught him, among other things, about the subtle and cunning way in which "the boss" kept people waiting. With Hill, Ferrari used the same tactic he had used with Gendebien. Having first put the interviewee in an awkward position, and after looking him up and down, Ferrari suddenly suggested that Hill should take part in the 24-hour Le Mans race with Umberto Maglioli. Phil Hill could not believe his own ears. Then Ferrari invited him into the workshop to show him the car he would be driving in the race.

Phil Hill is a retiring, shy man with interests outside motor racing (he is a keen listener to classical and operatic music), and he had to make more than a little effort to blend with the environment at Ferrari. It took him a while to find the best way of behaving there. He was encouraged to go flat-out and to give free rein to his own whims and attitudes, as long as he did not maltreat the car. Destruction of a car in a crash would have been a true disaster, aside from the personal injuries which the driver might have incurred. So, day by day, Hill learned that the best tactic was to treat everyone impersonally, even the mechanics, and to follow the main current, not swim against it. If he accepted the offer proposed by Enzo Ferrari to become a professional driver for his team, rather than for any other firm, it was because—as the American honestly admits—Ferrari was the top name in motor racing. And then, in the final analysis, no one asked him to be perfect, but Hill came to this realization much later in the day.

If it is true that with the passing of time things, facts and even major events take on another perspective, then the explanation given by Olivier Gendebien concerning the very serious accident in which he was involved in the 1956 Tourist Trophy is a weighty accusation levelled at Ferrari, because the reason for that accident could also explain the reason for Alberto Ascari's death in 1955.

For the 1956 Tourist Trophy Ferrari prepared three Monza-type cars, one of which had a serious under-steering problem. Gendebien recalls that this car responded so poorly to the steering controls that it was practically uncontrollable, no matter how much effort the driver made to correct the car's course. Gendebien was apparently assured by Ferrari that the car would be modified like the other two and made easy to steer, even in the riskiest of situations. But, according to the Belgian driver, the car he called the "coffin on wheels" fell to him in the Tourist Trophy, and during the trials he flew off the track. Gendebien came to in the hospital after a long period in a coma. It was Peter Collins who told him what had happened, because he had been following Gendebien at the time of the crash. At that particular moment, Gendebien was driving at about 180 kph (112 mph). Collins saw him enter the bend at the end of the straight; after veering slightly, the car carried on straight ahead crashing into an embankment and coming to rest on a flat area some ten feet below. The Ferrari ended up with its wheels in the air; the driver was flung forward some 40 meters (130 feet). Gendebien says that when Alberto Ascari died he was driving an identical car.

But Hawthorn has provided a different explanation for what happened to Ascari, which has nothing whatsoever to do with the mechanical defect claimed by Gendebien. In his book *Challenge me the Race*, Hawthorn states that he does not believe that Ascari was the victim of a collapse resulting from his spectacular dive into the sea four days before at Monte Carlo in the Monaco Grand Prix—he was driving a Lancia—or the victim of a delayed after-effect from that accident. Nor does he believe that, when Ascari entered the bend, which was to kill him and which is now named after him, he engaged third gear rather than fifth. For the English driver, who was later to lose his own life (in a road accident in his own country in 1959), the causes of Ascari's death must be looked for elsewhere. The tires fitted to the "Monza," he explains, should have been 6.50-16s; but at the time this size was not available because the manufacturer had run out of stock. As a result the car was fitted with 7.00-16 tires. Hawthorn test-drove the car at Monza with these tires and found them unsuitable, especially on the Vialone bend, where Ascari died, because of the unevenness of the track surface there. He came to the conclusion that the rims were too narrow for that type of tire, and he had them replaced. Hawthorn continues his explanation by mentioning that where Ascari's car overturned there were long, deep, wide tire marks, followed by ruts left in the surface by the rims. It is the English driver's view that Ascari moved into fifth gear precisely at the point where the asphalt was rough and it was then that his car started to skid. Because of this the tires were forced out of their rims, which then left their mark on the ground.

The oddest thing is that these two points of view about a front-page event with wide coverage in Italy (Ascari was a very popular personality) were completely ignored by the Italian press. It is true that the books which make mention of it have never been translated from the English and French (except for *Challenge me the Race*) but this does not exonerate the various media organizations in Italy from having failed to report sufficiently reliable opinions about the death of that great racing champion.

With great skill, and clearly speaking from the heart, Phil Hill has described the wrath and fury of Ferrari when one of his cars failed to finish a race because of mechanical troubles. The American has stated without hesitation that Ferrari always considered his cars to be the essential element in the races he has won. He has invariably given

Vincenzo Florio (right) with Oliver Gendebien (center) and Luigi Musso.

little credit for success to the driver, about ten percent according to Hill. The fact that things have not changed over the years, and that Ferrari has never been eager to create a hierarchy within his team is clearly demonstrated by the 1961 championship which ended with the tragic death of von Trips at Monza. A fierce rivalry existed between Hill and the German driver, and nothing was done by Ferrari to quench the flames. Hill believes that the death of von Trips was caused by the fact that right up until the last race of the championship, the Italian Grand Prix at Monza, it had not been established who, for that season at least, was to be the leading driver. The facts, as they developed, might lead one to think that the accident which claimed the life of the German driver was the result of the tense relations which existed between him and Phil Hill, over and above any specific blame attaching to Jim Clark, with whose Lotus von Trips collided.

Ferrari's reluctance to name a leading driver also caused the loss of the world championship in 1974. In that year Clay Regazzoni and Niki Lauda reached the end of the season with equal chances of winning, but at the last minute, the Swiss driver let the title slip through his fingers into the hands of Emerson Fittipaldi.

Phil Hill is taciturn, and apparently

21

absent-minded, but he is really a shrewd observer, and, as such, he has painted a perfect portrait of the fairly complex make-up of the team, of the absolute obedience of certain members to the "big boss," of the parasitic attitude of the mechanics, concerned with restricting their own actions to the narrow field of their own capabilities, and of the permanent state of blame hanging over the driver who was invariably held completely responsible for any poor performance by any car. No one has been able to grasp better than Phil Hill the greatness and the weakness of Enzo Ferrari: the influence he wielded and has continued to wield over the empire of which he is the hub, the dubious advisers by whom he is surrounded, the conspiratorial climate which has always reigned over Maranello, and to which he, above all, has fallen victim, a climate which has pushed him into hasty decisions, and then changes of mind dictated by regret. The case of Lauda is part of a series of situations created by certain elements of the press, sometimes friendly, sometimes hostile, which Ferrari has never really been able to ignore.

In his book *La mia vita a 300 all'ora* ("My Life at 300 mph"), written in collaboration with Marcello Giambertone, the five times world champion Manuel Fangio reveals that he found little satisfaction in the one year he spent with Ferrari in 1956; even though in this year he managed to win his fourth world championship title. To begin with, he says, he was pleased to be taken on by the Italian firm, and he calls their cars exceptional. They did not have the huge power of the Mercedes cars (in which he had raced for two years), but they had a rhythm, a musical quality and a nimbleness which turned them into "artistic tools." "I have always thought," the Argentinian writes, "that if Paganini had been a racing driver, rather than a genius with the violin, he would have driven Ferraris." Fangio won the first race of the 1956 championship with a great deal of luck. His car developed a problem with the feed system, and he had to make a pit stop. In the race once more, he hurled his car through the field and was suddenly lying behind Menditeguy, a compatriot who was at the wheel of a Maserati; Menditeguy went off the track, and the way ahead lay clear. Only Moss was between him and the tape. Then the Englishman also had to leave the course because of an oil leak. Now leading the field, Fangio went into a spin, but he was quickly helped back into the race, which gave rise to a protest from Nello Ugolini of Maserati who, in good faith, maintained that there were one or two spectators among the helping hands. Fangio denied this. In the end, the Argentinian did not win in his own car; he changed to Musso's car, and it is for this reason that the late Roman driver figures among the winners of the world championship, even though he did not, in fact, win. Before he returned to Europe, Fangio failed to classify in the Buenos Aires 1,000-kilometer event for sports cars, but he won the Mendoza Grand Prix and, together with Castellotti, the Sebring 12-hour race.

At this point Giambertone takes up the story. He starts by describing his perplexity over the treatment which was reserved for Juan Manuel Fangio. Having already won three world championship titles, Fangio had, in Giambertone's opinion, the right to be the "captain" of the Ferrari team. Giambertone acknowledges that every team pursues its own particular policy in favor of one driver over another, and does its utmost to give the favorite every assistance. For this reason Giambertone considered discussing the matter with Ferrari, "a man who mingles great technical competence with a subtle diplomacy worthy of a Metternich," with the hope that his words would not be interpreted as personal criticism. Giambertone decided to make this move not only to defend the interests of his colleague, but also because he had the impression that Ferrari preferred another driver, an impression which persisted throughout the 1956 season. Giambertone found it quite justifiable that for reasons of commercial politics Ferrari might attach the highest importance to an English driv-

Above: Nino Farina. Below: Maurice Trintignant with Prince Rainier of Monaco.

Froilan Gonzalez in a Formula 1 Ferrari of the 1950–51 period. This Argentinian raced for many years with Ferrari.

Enzo Ferrari with Juan Manuel Fangio. The relationship between these two men was difficult despite their mutual respect.

er (Collins), all the more so because, from this same viewpoint, the possible wins chalked up by Fangio would not have had any concrete outcome for the company, because Ferrari cars were not exported to Argentina. But the real reason for this different treatment, in Giambertone's view, was another one. "In my humble opinion," he writes, "Ferrari's aim in securing the world champion for himself, with a conventional contract, was to have him beaten by other drivers in the Scuderia." Giambertone does not criticize Ferrari's attitude: "The truth is that in his capacity as a subtle diplomat, Ferrari was trying to show that his cars were capable of beating anyone, including Manuel Fangio. I must confess, in all loyalty, that from a viewpoint of cold logic, expressed by an engineer, this tactic served his specific interests very well indeed." Giambertone steers a middle course between reasons of state and drivers' interests, but he does not conceal the fact that Fangio's situation had become very delicate in 1956, not least because, in view of his age, it was quite easy to look at the Argentinian as a man on the way down, or even a man whose career was over.

The races driven by Fangio for Ferrari in 1956, which are described one by one in his book, show that the world champion could find himself in many a strange situation. He drove the entire length of the Mille Miglia dripping wet because, in the rain which lashed the entire race that year, water found its way into the cabin in plentiful amounts through a hole made by a mechanic to provide better cooling for the brakes. Fangio thus found himself sitting in a pool of water for eleven hours. When asked to give an explanation for his bright idea, the mechanic defended himself by saying that he couldn't have known it was going to rain. In the following race, the Daily Express Trophy at Silverstone, things did not go any better; Fangio had to retire with a broken clutch. In the Monaco Grand Prix at Monte Carlo Fangio's single-seater car only completed forty laps because the suspension gave out, but he was changed to Collins's car and managed to come in second and to complete the fastest lap.

In the Nürburgring 1,000 kilometer race he drove with Castellotti and came in on the heels of Moss-Behra driving for Maserati. When the race was over, Fangio told Giambertone that he had been unable to drive the car flat out because of strange noises coming from the suspension. In the Belgian Grand Prix he had to pull off the track in the twenty-second lap because "something wasn't right with the differential." Once it had been dismantled, it was discovered that someone had forgotten to fill it up with oil. This was a bitter blow for Fangio, who was sure that he was the object of a plot. Via one of Ferrari's collaborators, Gardini, Giambertone informed the "big boss," who let it be known that he had given precise orders to the effect that the world champion should receive special treatment. He asked Giambertone and his protégé to stop imagining things that did not exist. But things did not improve, and in the French Grand Prix at Rheims Fangio had to stop because of a peculiar incident: his face was soaked with gasoline which was spurting from the tube of a pressure gauge. Fangio commented bitterly that at least his soaking at the Mille Miglia event had been with water, and not a shower of gasoline. It took a good minute to repair the leak, and Fangio had to be content with fourth place, despite climbing back up the field at a tremendous pace, and earning the fastest lap time.

The Argentinian's nerves now went to pieces. Professor Davide Alessi of the C. Besta Neurological Institute in Milan diagnosed a "reactive neurosis" characterized by "emotional anxiety" and malaise. Giambertone told Ferrari who proposed a second examination by a doctor who was, he said, a friend of Fangio's. In a frank exchange of words between Giambertone and "the boss," the former said things were in a bad way: the only way of restoring any confidence in Fangio was to let him have a really good mechanic, who would be with him in every race. This was done beginning with the British

Grand Prix at Silverstone; but, in the meantime, the world champion had dropped out of the French Grand Prix at Rouen because of his mental state. At Silverstone, however, he once again tasted the joy of a win, and, when he went to the German Grand Prix at the Nürburgring, he managed to beat Lang's lap record (set in a Mercedes) which had stood the test of time for seventeen years. The championship reached its last lap, the Italian Grand Prix, which, in that year, was also the European Grand Prix. The stakes were very high. Fangio decided to race the first few laps at a moderate speed because he was worried about early wear and tear on his tires, a problem which assailed Castellotti from the very first lap. But his tactic did not produce favorable results. On the nineteenth lap, he had to make a pit stop because of steering trouble—and the same trouble also held up Musso and von Trips. The fault was attributed to metal fatigue. For Fangio, who was now without a car, it was the last straw. Giambertone tried to persuade the then racing manager of Ferrari, Eraldo Sculati, to let Fangio continue in one of the other Ferraris that was still in the race. According to Giambertone an argument ensued, at the end of which Sculati left the pits and took refuge in the press-box. Giambertone took over the reins, and the first thing he did was to flag down Collins by showing him a wheel, which meant a tire change. When the Englishman stopped on the next lap, Giambertone asked him if he would be prepared to hand his car over to Fangio. Without a moment's hesitation Collins agreed. Giambertone is the first to admit that this was a very noble gesture. Once more at the wheel, after nineteen laps in the pits, Fangio sped through the field and managed to finish in second place, thus winning the minimum number of points necessary to win his fourth world championship.

Giambertone concludes the chapter dealing with the 1956 season by recounting that at the customary end-of-year awards ceremony Ferrari gave gold medals to all his drivers except Fangio, who was in Argentina. When Giambertone asked Ferrari for the Argentinian's medal, he received no reply. The same attitude was displayed by Romolo Tavoni, who had taken over as racing manager at Ferrari in 1957: complete silence.

If one retraces the history of motor racing, the incidents such as those described by Giambertone and experienced by Fangio number in the hundreds. The famous Alfred Neubauer, who for years was the racing manager at Mercedes, deserves the nickname of "iron sergeant" because of the strict and determined way in which he managed the Mercedes team. He would not tolerate being contradicted, his judgements were irrevocable, and yet there was an Italian driver, Luigi Fagioli who was bold enough to mount an open rebellion on more than one occasion. In one race he even parked his car beside the track as a sign of his manifest disapproval of Neubauer.

Colin Chapman enjoyed the reputation of being a "tough guy." The dismissal of a top-quality though possibly too-flexible driver such as John Miles was a brutal act. With Emerson Fittipaldi things did not always go smoothly either, when it came down to human relationships. The late Jochen Rindt was one person who was brave enough to tell Colin Chapman to his face that his method of designing the single-seater Lotus was an outrage to the safety and security of his drivers. Graham Hill was no less outspoken.

Teddy Mayer is another of the "tough guys" in Formula 1 racing, and he showed this quality on several occasions. With a few exceptions, there has always been an essentially mixed climate of diffidence and incomprehension between engineers and drivers. Among the exceptions is the case of Chapman and Jim Clark, whose relationship seems to have been, and probably was, perfect, as was the relationship between Ken Tyrell and Jackie Stewart.

Frank Williams brought a great deal of glory to a few drivers, but he also sacrificed a great many, including Arturo Merzario, to whom a brilliant future was offered by Ferrari, but who ended in a state of semi-activity in Formula 1; the unwitting victim of other peoples' ill intentions.

One driver who has expressed a positive opinion of Enzo Ferrari is Stirling Moss, possibly because he was never directly under Ferrari's thumb. The two men had a long friendship by correspondence, in that on several occasions they exchanged statements of esteem and admiration, but these never culminated in anything concrete. The formula for a relationship between Ferrari and the Englishman was worked out up to a certain point. The Italian was to have made available to Rob Walker's group one or more cars with which Moss was to race under the colors of the English team, but this plan never actually materialized because of the serious accident on Easter Monday, 1962, which put an end to the British driver's dazzling career. It would have been an extremely interesting experiment. Enzo Ferrari's decision to let his own cars be managed outside his own Scuderia shows the esteem in which he held Moss. In fact, Moss was supposed to have driven a Formula 2 Ferrari, very early in his career—in September, 1951, at Bari. Moss was twenty-two years old and had earned a solid reputation for himself with Cooper and HWM, but this collaboration never took place, because at the last moment Ferrari decided to use Taruffi. This greatly annoyed the British driver, who swore that he would break off relations with Ferrari. But things turned out differently, and Moss often agreed to drive cars bearing the famous rampant horse (GT and sports models), although they belonged to English teams and were not entered by Ferrari.

According to Moss, the esteem which Enzo Ferrari showed for him on more than one occasion derived from the fact he liked the Englishman's style of racing, which may have reminded him of Tazio Nuvolari's. Moss had a lot of admiration for Juan Manuel Fangio and thought him to be the best driver of his day. He confessed that he could offer nothing to rival the Argentinian, be it racing tactics, the patience with which he lay down the field when his car was giving problems, or his respect for the car itself. For Moss a race was always and only a do-or-die event: victory, or retire. If he had not thought in this way, he would never have set his incredible record at the Mille Miglia meeting in 1955. Years after being in the thick of the fiery climate of motor racing, Moss accords Enzo Ferrari the stature of a genius in his field, with all the pros and cons which such a word implies. Besides judging the Italian engineer's cars as a result of having driven them, he assesses their qualities on the basis of having seen them race. For him Ferrari cars are always the best built and the most reliable, even though this reliability has been achieved at the expense of weight. In saying this he echoes an observation expressed by many others with regard to Ferraris, i.e. their greater weight, but Ferrari himself has always boasted of this feature. Moss has also expressed an opinion which is certainly no secret to anyone: Ferrari has always had more confidence in cars then in drivers. If you do not accept this philosophy, an atmosphere of mutual distrust builds up between engineer and driver, which helps neither in his job. Moss is of the opinion that Ferrari has always considered a driver as an important part of the marriage between man and car rather than as a human individual per se; but he denies that, as other drivers have stated, Ferrari does not have respect for the drivers in his team at any level. It seems probable that the many instances of misunderstanding, mistrust, and coolness that have sprung up at a certain point between Ferrari and his drivers were caused by a change in the relationship between the two parties concerned. Ferrari has always demanded the maximum, at every moment and on every occasion. Rogues and opportunists have never gotten anywhere with him. Whenever a driver has tried to wriggle out of criticism, in whatever way, it has marked the end of the conversation.

Being lucky enough to drive the best racing cars in the world, Stirling Moss has been quoted as saying, involves a commitment to give the maximum of oneself. If results are not forthcoming, this indicates that all is not well with the driver. Moss is categorical about this and has quoted the example of the 1974 world championship and, in particular, the American Grand Prix of that year in which, in his view, the Ferrari drivers did not altogether do their duty and thus allowed Emerson Fittipaldi to win the championship.

Moss has also underlined a failing of Ferrari as a team, which is the fact that they never establish a hierarchy

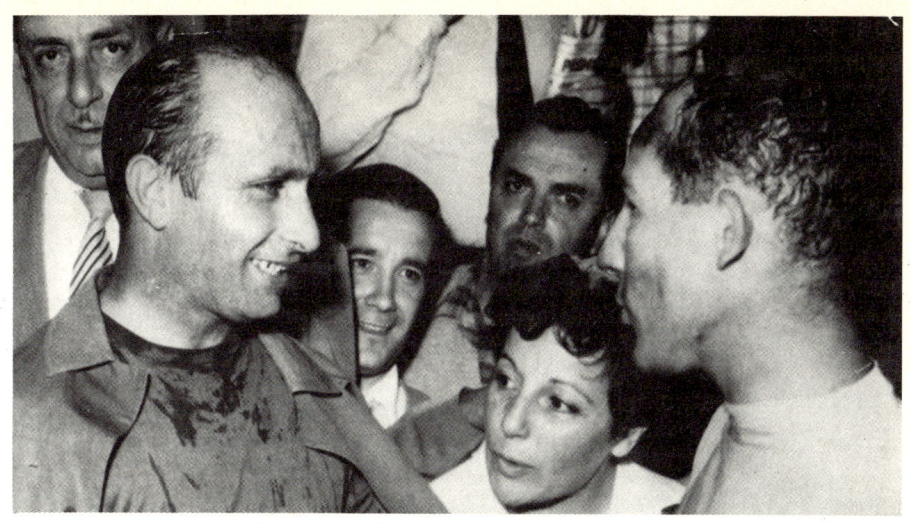

Juan Manuel Fangio (left) with Stirling Moss. In 1955 they were both members of the Mercedes team.

among their drivers, and instead leave each one to fend for himself. This has often proved all the more damaging for the team by the way in which it has taken place, and the fact that it has been noticed by other drivers.

Stirling Moss is considered one of the most controversial, conceited, and determined figures in the world of motor racing; so his tribute to Ferrari is perhaps an unexpected eulogy. As such, it is all the more welcome to the ears of the grand old man of Maranello. People may say that the reason for this very high esteem shown by the English driver for Ferrari derives from the fact that there has never been any actual association between the two men. Stirling Moss has never had a tie of this sort with anyone except Mercedes in 1955, and he certainly did not find it easy to get along with the harsh discipline imposed by Neubauer.

One of the aspects of Ferrari's behavior which comes in for the most criticism from drivers is that he never lets them forget the accidents in which they have been involved. He is so sure of the high quality of his cars that he never doubts their reliability and their response to the demands made on them. For all that, he has created what he calls his "museum of errors," a room with a display of parts of cars which have broken down during such and such a race. But this apparent participation in the failure of a car, is, it is said, a subtle way of reshuffling the cards. The driver is always at fault.

This is the basic charge which Phil Hill has placed at the top of his list of criticisms of his former boss. He regrets this attitude, but, at the same time, he is moved by Ferrari's attachment to his cars. So, having spoken in highly controversial terms, without mincing his words, Phil Hill ends up by being intrigued by Ferrari's personality; and he compares him to the great conductors of his time or, in the industrial sector, to Henry Ford or Ettore Bugatti. He recognizes in him such a forceful personality that it leaves its mark on almost everything it becomes involved with. "In this violent world," Phil Hill writes, "I cannot imagine a man such he being able to exist in years to come." It is significant that such a warm eulogy for Ferrari comes from a man who, at a certain stage in his life, hated him, but who, years later, recognized his human qualities.

Another very positive verdict comes from Giancarlo Baghetti. It is true that twenty years have passed since he was actively involved with Ferrari. Baghetti joined the firm, or rather started to drive for it, in 1961, having been named the most promising driver by the FISA (Federazione Italiana Scuderie Automobilistiche). This organization had taken the praiseworthy step of drawing attention to one or more talented young drivers each year. Enzo Ferrari seconded their view and gave Baghetti a car which, in this particular case, was managed by the Sant'Ambroeus Scuderia. The Milanese driver made his debut at Syracuse with a car fitted with a 65° 6-cylinder engine, and he won convincingly. He scored another win at the Grand Prix at Naples and was included, unofficially, in the Ferrari Formula 1 team. Baghetti was fully up to the situation, even in the first world championship race in which he took part, the French Grand Prix at Rheims, which he won. In the next race, the British Grand Prix, he left the track because of the rain.

Baghetti sees a great quality in Enzo Ferrari: the ability to let the members of his team express their capabilities the best they can. He weighs up the qualities and failings, the worth of a man and his limitations; and he knows how to extract from everyone much more than they thought they were able to give. But contact is tricky (or was) because a dialogue with Ferrari was never direct; in Baghetti's day, it took place via intermediaries, who were not always without prejudice and not always rational in their opinions. According to Baghetti, Ferrari did his thinking essentially with someone else's head and adjusted his views on the basis of impressions and sensations which were reported back to him. It is symptomatic, he says, that many of the drivers who drove for him left quarrelling. He too left, not quite slamming the door, but almost, despite the great affection "the boss" had for him. Having joined the Ferrari team officially in 1962, Baghetti moved to ATS early in 1963, but this was one of his leanest years.

His future was probably affected negatively by the great fuss the press made over him after his sensational success in the 1961 French Grand Prix. Enzo Ferrari has never appreciated it (and Baghetti shares this view) when the newspapers place a driver on a higher rung than a car. The fact that he had won three races running backed up Ferrari's thesis that even a beginner could have the luxury of beating more celebrated opponents. It was the superiority of the car that made this possible. But when it seemed to him that the sides of the equation had been switched round, he no longer wanted to play the game. Is it right to criticize him for this? Baghetti thinks not. In fact he calls Ferrari the "greatest" figure in the world of car engines.

Niki Lauda's view of Enzo Ferrari is not very unlike that of others who have had dealings with him. The Austrian's words are also extremely frank. In fact, you cannot call Lauda anything but candid. If there is a difference between his views and what Phil Hill and Olivier Gendebien wrote in their day, it is that Lauda made his views known when he was at the height of his involvement with Ferrari. This was not so for the other two.

In his book *Protokoll*, written in collaboration with Herbert Voelker (Verlag Orac, Vienna, 1977. Italian edition: *I miei anni con Ferrari*, Editioriale Olimpia, 1979), Lauda recounts, perhaps a little brutally, the years he spent with the Italian firm and quickly draws a portrait of Ferrari, the man, as he saw him. Among other things, he writes: "Ferrari—the Scuderia, that is—is unique in the world and it also has unique problems. It starts with the myth of the eighty-year-old Commendatore who, for Italians, is so sacred that people bow when he passes. When I would greet him with the words 'ciao Enzo' those present would never cease to be amazed, because no one else could get away with anything less resounding than 'Presidente,' or 'Commendatore,' or possibly 'Ingegnere.' The people around him have a great deal of respect for this national monument of a patriarch and this fear is a major cause of misunderstandings and mistaken decisions. People prefer to ingratiate themselves by telling him things he wants to hear, and these do not always tally with the truth."

Lauda then says that he has always considered Ferrari only as head of his Scuderia. He treated him with respect but frankness. If he wanted to have words with him, he would knock at the door and go in, whereas his closer employees would have to go through nothing less than a ritual to catch his ear. "But I must admit that once you are in the office you feel fairly uneasy: it's an austere dark-blue room, with a large picture of his dead son, usually with candles burning beneath it, and the elderly 'presidente' sitting at his desk. If you went in depressed, you came out even more so, stifled by the solemn grandeur. But when you talk normally with him, everything carries on normally: the old man is not only a personality, he is a man with a quality of good-naturedness, I would even say benevolence." In another passage, Lauda describes an attitude among those who worked at Ferrari, which has been backed up by others. "In all my years at Ferrari I never had any problems with face-to-face exchanges —never. The problems always started and only started when the consultants were going in and out of that door. To survive as a driver at Ferrari, you need some political weight within the core of people surrounding the boss."

Lauda is almost violent when describing his resignation from Ferrari. "The Italian press exacerbated Ferrari's feelings against me. The result of this was that the old man became more and more furious in his remarks, so a simple exit from the scene, such as I had imagined, became impossible. When I went to Maranello to take part in the Watkins Glen trials, I bumped into the Commendatore quite by chance. Shouting, he asked me if I still had the courage to shake his hand. 'Of course,' I said, 'but of course.' And I gave him my hand. He started shouting again, telling me I was nothing more than an impudent rascal and that I was also trying to stir up trouble between him and the people working for him. He was so angry that he was shouting nonsense, and that made me start shouting too. In the end he saw me off his property. Except for reasons of work, I could never have set foot there again.

"I didn't like seeing him surrounded by his people showing all his powerless rage: he was just too old; he could no longer connect things coherently; he did not understand the situation; and he suffered needlessly. Why did all those emotions pour forth from him? Why should he have burned all the bridges instead of accepting the end of our working relationship as such, in accordance with the normal rules of the business world?"

"A week later," Lauda writes in another passage in his book, "Ferrari said in an interview: 'Lauda is worse than Judas. He's sold out to the competition for thirty salamis.' This was not true at all. What is more, he must have been the first to know the price. But in this respect I don't want to criticize the man who, by many, is considered the

Niki Lauda before the accident in the 1976 German Grand Prix in which he was badly injured. Since then he has always worn headgear to hide the lasting signs of that day.

greatest figure in the history of the automobile. Ferrari the man, his cars, his team, and his employees had all played a leading part in those years of my racing career; they had had an effect which was at times suffocating, at others uplifting. There are no tales to tell: we're quits. I think that both parties have benefitted from the other, and there's nothing to be gained from emotional outbursts after the event."

Two years after writing his book, Nika Lauda unexpectedly bade farewell to the racing world. He took this decisive step with all the forthrightness and spontaneity peculiar to him, with no regrets (at least for the time being) after having driven in 113 races.

In an interview on October 4, 1979, Fulvio Astori of the *Corriere della Sera* asked Lauda, among other things: "You finished with a win at Imola [with a Brabham-Alfa Romeo, for whom Lauda drove after leaving Ferrari]. You dedicated that win to Ferrari. This was interpreted in various ways: was that dedication ironical, sincere, or made out of revenge?" Lauda replied: "I am sorry not everyone understood me. The race was on the Dino Ferrari circuit and I know what Enzo Ferrari's son meant to him. The Ferraris had been beaten, and having raced and won for Enzo Ferrari for four years I wanted to dedicate this win to him to tell him in some way or other that if his cars had been beaten by mine, one of them had also won: Niki Lauda."

Astori then asked Lauda: "Will people be fond of Lauda?" Lauda replied: "I have been employed by many people; some have liked me, and I have preferred some to others: Enzo Ferrari, for example. He's very human in one sense and also crazy in another, in the way that he could sometimes make a few strange decisions; but he always had class, backed up by his huge personality. I prefer people with true, authentic, dominant personalities to insignificant people who follow the current and never leave their mark on it. People with character are people, above all, and always will be." There could be no more fitting way for Niki Lauda to wind up his debate with Enzo Ferrari.

Jacky Ickx, one of the most controversial, but also one of the most intelligent drivers also has a decidedly favorable opinion of the Ferrari and of Enzo Ferrari. "The relentlessness, the perseverance, and the determination with which Enzo Ferrari has pursued his goals are simply mind-boggling," says the Belgian driver. "My dealings with him," he says, "were excellent. Whenever I am in Italy, for one reason or another, I go see him, and, although I usually do not announce my visit in advance, he doesn't hesitate to make time for me."

How important was the period spent at Ferrari for Jacky Ickx? "Enormously important," he answers. "The last year I was with Ferrari coincided with the agreement with Fiat. This made people a bit nervous and tense. In a word, things did not go as everyone might have wanted, but, all in all, during my time with Ferrari I can say in all sincerity that I enjoyed the very best in Formula 1. The structure of the Ferrari and its power are both beyond discussion." Ickx, who has said goodbye to racing except for possibly taking part in the 24-hour race at Le Mans, also denies that Enzo Ferrari considers the contribution of the car more decisive than that of the driver. In fact he calls Ferrari a "sentimentalist."

Jacky Ickx.

TALKING ABOUT DRIVERS

Enzo Ferrari admonishing Carletto Pintacuda at the Imola checkpoint in the 1935 Mille Miglia. Together with Della Stufa, Pintacuda won the race that year in a B-type Alfa Romeo P3.

Enzo Ferrari with Achille Varzi during the 1934 Parma–Poggio di Berceto trials. The car is a single-seater, B-type Alfa Romeo P3.

Because he used to be a driver himself, and because he has seen so many drivers at work, first as manager of the racing division of Alfa Romeo, then as head of the Scuderia named after him, Enzo Ferrari has always delivered very concise and precise verdicts about drivers who have featured on the motor-racing stage in the past fifty years. One of his views of Juan Manuel Fangio can be read in the introduction to the book *Tutto Fangio* ("All About Fangio") written by Severo Boschi in 1961, when the five times world champion had given up racing (Calderini, Bologna).

Ferrari starts by saying that he had only seen Fangio in trials, and once in a race. He had not spoken to him more than five or six times at that time.

"In the spring of 1949," Ferrari writes, "I saw him at the track at Modena, test driving a single-seater, and I was struck by his style which, among other things, consisted in coming out of bends, even if at high speed, plum in the middle of the track, rather than scattering the bales of straw, which is what almost all the other drivers did.

"In that period he came to me, together with Guzzi, who was employed with the Argentinian Automobile Club, and someone else whose name I forget. We had quite a long chat, I ended up predicting that within a year he would be a possible world champion. There was, as it turned out, some foundation to my forecast, even though I was a year off."

At this point Ferrari takes a slight jab at the Argentinian and his way of behaving on certain occasions, a manner somewhere between shyness and a disinclination to engage in a dialogue. In fact, Ferrari writes: "I never had a tête-à-tête with Fangio because he was always with other people, whom he called friends and colleagues, and he displayed a distinct preference for being spoken for by them."

Later we find another opinion of Fangio's qualities as a driver: "In June, when he was racing in the Formula 2 Grand Prix at Monza, and won it in a Ferrari, which I had given to the Argentinian Team, I had clear proof of his clever technical abilities. From the start, he was ahead of the official Ferrari cars driven by Ascari, Villoresi, Bonetto, and Cortese, and he built up quite a lead. In the latter stages of the race, when he slowed his pace and was being tailed by the others, the late Bignami, who had been Nuvolari's mechanic and Varzi's at a later date, saw his champion in trouble, took a wheel, and was about to signal with the mallet for Fangio to stop on the pretext of refuelling. Although I virtually never go to races, I intervened and stopped him making that absurd gesture, which, in his view, would have saved Fangio the bitter defeat of being overtaken. I had sniffed out the real reason for Fangio slowing up momentarily— the oil temperature was far too high, and he was afraid of losing his connecting rods at the very end of the race. The way Fangio stared at the instrument panel when he passed through the pits was enough to make me come to that conclusion and tell Bignami not to interfere. He told me later that the temperature had soared to 130° (265°); and as a result everything was as clear as day, even the mutterings of my drivers who had seen how the new car being used by the Argentinian Team was going possibly even better than theirs.

"What more can I say?" Ferrari asks. "Fangio was a great driver with intelligence and a fighting spirit. He always demanded from his cars everything they could give, but no more. He fought hard and not only for first place but also for placings lower down the field, so long as he crossed the finishing line. He never signed a marriage contract with any organization. He was well aware of his own abilities and by establishing them beforehand he took advantage of every possibility to drive the best cars, at all times. He managed to do this by putting his justifiable natural egoism before the sort of affection which formed a bond between other drivers and the life of a particular make of car, for better or for worse.

"The real impossibility of having a close conversation with him, of holding his fleeting glances still for a second (something I never once managed to do), his constant faint squinting smile, his small voice that sounded like aluminum, all these things make it impossible for me to make any judgement about this man who is still an unknown quantity as far as I am concerned."

In the chapter about drivers in his book written in 1974, Ferrari expresses an opinion of Fangio which more or less tallies with the one in the preface to Boschi's book. He adds a few more glowing words about the Argentinian driver: "His stature as a sportsman was beyond discussion. He definitely had a higher vision of racing and a sense of balance, a sportsman's intelligence and an insistence on safety when he raced, which were all truly exceptional."

The occasion seems right for Ferrari to annotate the book which the world champion and Marcello Giambertone wrote in the intervening period: "When he retired from the race track, having won the world championship five times, he wrote a book of memoirs in which another Fangio emerged. It is true that for half the book he used someone else's pen to say certain things and to level certain naive but no less rash accusations. That was his style. But I did not rise to the bait. There were people who used Fangio, having once helped him, and the row that would have been caused by any interjection from me would have made the book a sensation, which was obviously the object of the exercise. So I kept quiet. But now I'll have my say."
Point for point Ferrari rebuts all the accusations that appear in the book *La mia vita a 300 all'ora*. In so doing he clearly put the Argentinian in something of a spot, not least by saying that he suffered from a persecution mania. He reminds him that without the sacrifice made by Musso, in the first instance, and the two sacrifices made by Collins, he would not have won the 1956 world championship. More recently, in the publication *Année Automobile 1977-78*, Ferrari once more takes up the topic of drivers and sums up the opinions already expressed about Fangio. He makes a distinction between the driver and the man by saying that "his stature as a fighter was absolutely beyond discussion. I think it would be hard to find an ace driver who shows such subtle continuity in his successful career," but he also repeats how he finds Fangio, the man, an enigma.

Ferrari rightly says that it is impossible to say who has been the best driver in an absolute sense. He has been asked the question countless times, and he has invariably been unable to answer it. He insists that it is impossible to draw up a list, because drivers have to be classified in the context of the period when they were racing, taking into account the conditions of the race tracks and the specific features of the cars they drove. He groups drivers more rationally in three clearly distinct generations: from 1920 to 1930, from 1930 to 1939, and the post-war generation. In the first group he includes Antonio Ascari, father of Alberto, Giuseppe Campari, Felice Nazzaro, Pietro Bordino, Giulio Masetti, Gastone Brilli-Peri, Nando Minoia, Louis Wagner, Carlo Salamano, Mario U. Borzacchini, and Enrico Giaccone. This generation of drivers had three major handicaps when compared with the present one: the greater physical effort and stamina which driving required because of the condition of the roads in those days, and the general condition of the race tracks, the dubious road-holding ability of the cars they drove, and the greater distance of the races, which sometimes covered 800 km (500 miles). The Targa Florio, which to begin with was raced over dusty dirt roads (this was before the days of asphalt), was also longer then than it was later on.

Ferrari skillfully encapsulates the human qualities of Antonio Ascari. As a driver he says that he was extremely daring and off-the-cuff, a dashing Garibaldi-like figure, always at the limit. Giuseppe Campari was out of the same mold, and here again Ferrari draws a many-sided portrait. Both these drivers died at the wheel: the former at Montlhéry in 1925 during the French Grand Prix, the latter at Monza in 1933 after a collision with Borzacchini, who also lost his life. Ferrari does not dwell on Borzacchini or on the others he places in the first group of drivers, but the fact that he does list them is already, by implication, an acknow-

Enzo Ferrari with his mechanic Nino in a CMN in the 1919 Targa Florio. It was that year that Ferrari had his strange experience in the Sicilian race.

Campari and Ramponi in a 6-cylinder Alfa Romeo 1500 on the Raticosa Pass in the 1928 Mille Miglia, which they won.

ledgement of their stature. It might be said that Borzacchini, Brilli-Peri, and Carlo Salamano, in his way, raced more with their hearts than their heads, unlike all the others mentioned by Ferrari. Pietro Bordino was as "polished" at the wheel as were Nazzaro, Masetti, and Wagner. But those were days when the brave and fighting driver delighted the public much more than the driver whose stature was measured in terms of style, tactics, and his respect for his car.

In the second generation of drivers, the two classic names attached to this different method of racing were Tazio Nuvolari and Achille Varzi, the one a bundle of nerves capable of braving what others would not dare, the other a steely, polished, elegant driver, both on the track and in his personal life. In their day Italy was divided between Nuvolari and Varzi fans, but the former were definitely in the majority, because the method of driving used by the man from Mantua appealed more to the crowds. Nuvolari was a difficult, cantankerous, and argumentative person. In their relationship, which was a long one interrupted on several occasions by rowdy break-ups, Ferrari has revealed that Nuvolari never called him by his Christian name, only by his surname, which is often the custom in the provinces. A characteristic aspect of Nuvolari's way of thinking is illustrated by an episode described by Ferrari. In 1932 the Mantuan ace was about to leave for the Targa Florio, by train, and his boss gave him the return ticket. "People say you're a good organizer," Nuvolari remarked, "but I can see you're not. You should only give me a one-way ticket, because when you set off for a race you must be aware of the chances of making the return journey in a wooden box."

While on the subject of that particular race, Ferrari recounts another amusing incident. He offered Nuvolari a mechanic called Paride Mambelli, who was already an experienced man as a result of his friendship with Luigi Arcangeli. Tazio looked askance at him and asked him if he was afraid, warning him that whenever he took a bend too fast he would yell so that Mambelli could protect himself as best he could by wedging himself between the seat and the dashboard. When they returned from Palermo glowing with Nuvolari's sensational win, Ferrari asked Mambelli how things had gone. Mambelli replied: "Nuvolari started yelling at the first bend and did not stop yelling until the last one. So I spent the whole race from start to finish in a huddle." Ferrari has another tasty tale to tell about Nuvolari too. The driver was training on the Targa Florio circuit with Campari as a passenger. They hurtled off the road because of the recently laid tar and gravel. Campari was able to throw himself out of the car, but not so Nuvolari. Despite his size, Campari flung himself down the slope in search of his companion. The silence that hung over the place made him fear the worst. Then he came across Nuvolari staring into a bush with a finger on his lips, signaling Campari to be quiet. Nuvolari had discovered a nest full of warblers and, being a fine hunter, did not want Campari to disturb the show.

Ferrari's highest praise of the moral fiber of the greatest of drivers from Mantua, who in the flesh was minute and skinny, is his affirmation that Nuvolari did not suffer from an inferiority complex. Furthermore he gives a very clear idea of Nuvolari's style—his secret—by describing the emotions he felt in 1931, at the trials on the "Three Provinces" Circuit, when he asked his companion (Ferrari was also driving there with a more powerful car than the Mantuan's) to take him with him. It should be added that Nuvolari did not know that circuit. "At the first bend," Ferrari writes, "I had the clear sensation that Tazio had taken it badly and that we would end up in the ditch; I felt myself stiffen as I waited for the crunch. Instead, we found ourselves on the next straight with the car in a perfect position. I looked at him," Ferrari goes on. "His rugged face was calm, just as it always was, and certainly not the face of someone who had just escaped a hair-raising spin. I had the same sensation at the second bend. By the fourth or fifth bend I began to understand; in the meantime, I had noticed that through the entire bend Tazio did not lift his foot from the accelerator, and that, in fact, it was flat on the floor. As bend followed bend, I discovered his secret. Nuvolari entered the bend somewhat earlier than my driver's instinct would have told me to. But he went into the bend in an unusual way: with one movement he aimed the nose of the car at the inside edge, just where the curve itself started. His foot was flat down, and he had obviously changed down to the right gear before going through this fearsome rigmarole. In this way he put the car into a four-wheel drift, making the most of the thrust of the centrifugal force and keeping it on the road with the traction of the driving wheels. Throughout the bend the car shaved the inside edge, and when the bend turned into the straight the car was in the normal position for accelerating down it, with no need for any corrections." Ferrari honestly admits that he soon became used to this exercise, because he saw Nuvolari do it countless times. "But each time I seemed to be climbing into a roller coaster and finding myself coming through the downhill run with that sort of dazed feeling that we all know." Ferrari completes his X-ray examination of Nuvolari by emphasizing that when suspension became independent and tires were pumped up to average pressures, even Nuvolari was unable to skid with such acrobatic skill. But at that time he still applied one of his tactics, after revising and correcting it. He always aimed toward the inside of the bend, letting the car go into a drift but correcting it with small but precise movements of the wheel—his foot, by the way, was no longer flat on the floor.

Tazio Nuvolari's last feat was at the Mille Miglia in 1948. Driving a Ferrari, and with a huge lead over the car lying second, he had to stop at Villa Ospizion, near Reggio Emilia. The end was in sight, but the pivot pin in one of the springs had broken, and he was forced to retire. He was fifty-six. Ferrari went to pick him up and comfort him, and Nuvolari remarked: "Ferrari, at our age, days like these are rare. We must try to enjoy them to the full, if we can." Five years later, in August 1953, Nuvolari died.

It has been mentioned that Achille Varzi was the opposite of Nuvolari, both in terms of his background and of his style and manner. He was a perfectionist. Because he was calculating and unswerving when it was necessary to KO an opponent, Ferrari calls him "ruthless." Here again, an incident observed by Ferrari tells all. He went to Monte Carlo for the 1931 Grand Prix and found his colleague Luigi Bazzi in a state of consternation. Varzi had made the mechanics replace a dozen or so bearings and was still not satisfied. Bazzi took him off under some pretext, and when he came back the driver was finally happy about the bearings. Bazzi had simply slipped a newspaper folded into four beneath the two bearings which were worrying Varzi. That half centimeter more (0.2″) was what he had been after. Varzi's life, which was somewhat chaotic, greatly affected his performance as a driver, but, when he died in trials on the Bremgarten circuit at Geneva, driving an Alfa Romeo 158 in 1948, he had learned how to master his car and left the track as the result of a sudden downpour in a way few could have done. While his car slewed sideways and was dying on the slope encircling the track, it overturned. Varzi was taken by surprise, possibly because he did not envisage that last development; and he did not even bother to tuck himself inside the cockpit. His head was crushed by the car. His fans were stunned. A true artist at the wheel thus took his leave, a craftsman, the silent star of a thousand battles, a man who, even off the track, attracted much comment, above all because of his unsociable nature. With his class as a driver he had turned automobile racing from an explosion of brute force into an exercise in flexibility, which he wielded wearing his characteristic white gloves.

Particularly in the years when he was running the Scuderia, Ferrari had dozens of drivers at his beck and call. He recalls some more fully than others—perhaps these were the more affectionate towards him, or he appreciated them more because they kindled more hopes than the others. For example, he talks at length about a young Algerian, Guy Moll, whose career was meteoric. He joined the Ferrari team in 1934 and died that same year at Pescara. It is not easy to retrace the career of his driver, born to a Spanish mother and a French father. Ferrari readily equates him with Nuvolari on the basis of certain singularities and strange mental similarities but, above all, because of his aggressive approach, his casual ease at the wheel, and his daring. Ferrari draws a full-length portrait of Moll, starting from his win at Monte Carlo, when he beat Varzi in the last lap. Ferrari says he started to esteem him first because of the coolness he showed in a spin during the Montenero Grand Prix. While he was pirouetting with his car, Moll gestured to Ferrari that he had understood the boss's signal made just a split-second before he went into his terrifying spin.

Obviously enough, Enzo Ferrari talks more warmly and fully about the details of drivers whom he was able to get to know personally. Thus, while he dwells at length on Carlo Felice Trossi, who was also the chairman of Scuderia Ferrari, he says little or nothing about Bernd Rosemeyer, who was a very great driver indeed. Ferrari attributes Trossi with unsuspected talents and also calls him a great driver. He was from an aristocratic family, gifted and easy-going. Death crept up on him not on a race track but in the form of a terrible disease, which attacked his brain and which he bravely treated to the very last with mocking detachment.

Ferrari reveals that between Nuvolari and Varzi there were also other fine drivers such as Fagioli, Farina, Brivio, Pintacuda, and the already mentioned Trossi. He has highlighted Fagioli's fiery character and his innate lack of discipline, which, being well off, he could afford. One of most significant victories, which is also referred to by Ferrari, was his win at the Italian Grand Prix in 1933, after a fierce duel with Nuvolari.

The highest praise that could be given to this warm-hearted and extroverted driver is that he was summoned to join the official Mercedes team in 1950, when he was already fifty-two years old, and Alfa Romeo did not exist to include him in their team for the first world championship. Fagioli was extremely useful to the Milanese firm, coming in second on many occasions. His lust for driving betrayed him at Monte Carlo where, driving a GT car, he had an accident in the tunnel, from which he emerged in very bad shape. He died a few days later, when it was actually thought he might recover. When recalling the driver from the Marches, Ferrari refers only to his win

Tazio Nuvolari at Masaryk Circuit III (Brno, September 4, 1932).

Nino Farina, the driver who invented a style by driving with arms extended and straight.

in the 1933 Italian Grand Prix, overlooking those obtained with Mercedes (Italian and Spanish Grand Prix in 1934; at Monaco, in the Acerbo Cup, at the Avus and the Peña Rhin in 1935).

For Ferrari, Giuseppe ("Nino") Farina was "a very great driver," and he shows a close acquaintance with this man's virtues and inconceivable lapses when he says that "he bordered on the improbable" and that, for him, "it was always necessary to be worried, especially at the start of a race or one or two laps from the finish. At the start he was like a thoroughbred; nearing the finish he could do the craziest things, but he risked his own skin without being foolish or doing things which would put others in danger."

Tonino Brivio, another polished driver who was forecast as Varzi's natural heir, receives little comment from Ferrari. He says simply of this driver that if marriage is the tomb of love, for him it was the tomb of racing, because once he had gone to the altar he said farewell to the sport for which he had such a great passion.

Carletto Pintacuda was a driver greatly admired by the crowd, but Ferrari sees him as a top-quality road racer (in fact he won the Mille Miglia in 1935 and 1937) and an inferior driver on the track. Nevertheless, because of his style at the wheel, Pintacuda was a drawing card, and the spectators would only really become excited when it was announced that he was about to pass them on the endless roads of the race at Brescia.

Giovanni Bracco, a bon vivant and an extrovert, who was happier in the café than at church, is remembered by Ferrari particularly for his memorable Mille Miglia in 1952, which he won, defeating the Mercedes entries. The way this driver from Biella handled the winding roads of Futa and Raticosa no longer belongs just to the annals of motor racing, but to legend. Bracco found the energy to drive the Florence-Bologna leg in a record time, risking disaster more times than one cares to mention, by "refuelling" with some fine wine or cognac at the checkpoint in Florence. But Bracco was also a powerful "climber," and he set numerous records in uphill races.

Franco Cortese deserves a special place in the history of Ferrari, because

33

it was he who christened the first car to bear this name (at the Piacenza circuit in 1947); but "the boss" got rid of him with little ceremony, saying that "he would not have become an ace, although he had basic talents as far as style and technical skill were concerned." In fact Cortese was, to use a slang expression, a "clean" driver, who never abused his cars and who drove with great elegance.

With a brief but demolishing portrait of Villoresi, Enzo Ferrari starts his review of the post-war drivers; and, as we shall see, this review is made in many cases with supreme objectivity. Ferrari is always ready to dot his i's and cross his t's when it comes to establishing the responsibility for a fatal accident. He throws light on Villoresi's cunning, his fund of mischief, and his readiness to exploit the weak spots of his colleagues. He finishes his portrait by saying that he only, and unfortunately, got to know Villoresi as man when he was interviewed by a newspaper which went back over his life as a driver. Villoresi was clearly not kind about Ferrari in that interview.

When he comes to Taruffi, Ferrari takes the credit for having enabled him to pick up the first and last wins of his career. Taruffi started with motorcycles, and quickly drew attention to himself. Ferrari offered him four wheels for the Bolsena race in 1931, and the Roman won. He also won the 1957 Mille Miglia, his last race, because he had to keep his promise to his wife Isabella that he would give up racing if he managed to come home first in it. But this win is overshadowed by an incident about which Ferrari speaks openly. "At the Bologna checkpoint," Ferrari writes, "Taruffi was quite tired, mentally as well as physically, and among other things, he blamed a minor fault in his car." Ferrari persuaded him to carry on. For Taruffi the only dangerous foe was the German, von Trips. Ferrari begged von Trips not to "be cruel" to the Roman and to let him go ahead. "This most noble of young men obeyed the order." Years later, Ferrari recounts, Taruffi said that "he had had a fierce battle with von Trips who wanted to overtake him at any price." Ferrari concludes with an enigmatic sentence: "By that time von Trips had died at Monza in

Piero Taruffi in the Ferrari 500 in the 1952 Swiss Grand Prix, which he won.

the accident with Clark." How exactly does Piero Taruffi interpret this controversial incident? In his book *Bandiera a scacchi* ("Checkered Flag") written five years later, he recounts that he reached the Bologna checkpoint with his car, in effect, in a mess: "On the last pass in the Appennines, between Florence and Bologna, I started to hear a noise in the transmission, every time I accelerated in the low gears. 'Here we go!' I said to myself, and I was filled with a feeling of dismay that what had happened on previous occasions was about to be repeated, before I had even had a chance of completing the course. It was raining when I refuelled at Bologna. The next leg included the Via Emilia straights, and parts of them were quite slippery. A few days before, while testing the car in the wet, I had experimented in fourth gear at 200 kph (125 mph), trying to use all the engine's power, and found that the rear wheels started to skid a lot. To get above that speed it was important to use the accelerator delicately and move the wheel even more delicately. If I had suddenly slowed down I might well have lost control of the car. I thought it was dangerous to carry on under those conditions; and what if things had been even worse half way down the straight and the wheels had suddenly seized up? I remembered the accident at the Nürburgring in 1933."

"I intended to stop" Taruffi continues, "when Ferrari himself told me that it was not raining 30 km (20 miles) out of Bologna. When he told me that Collins also had transmission trouble, I put the

Piero Taruffi with his wife, Isabella, after his victory in the 1954 Targa Florio at the wheel of a Lancia.

34

Monza 1961: the bend known as the "parabolica" shortly after the accident which claimed the lives of Wolfgang von Trips and fifteen spectators.

car into gear and set off again. At that moment the loudspeaker at the checkpoint announced the arrival of von Trips at Livergnano, a village some 15 km (10 miles) from Bologna. I tried to change gear as little as possible, and accelerated carefully, which was not hard, because there are few bends between Bologna and Brescia. I also kept my speed down: 220-230 kph (135-140 mph) maximum, and I could reach this speed only using half the power of the engine. Less than 100 km (60 miles) from the finish I started to glimpse a red car in the rear-view mirror, and after a while it caught up with me: it was von Trips. I made a swift calculation: there was about half an hour of the race left and in that position I still had a lead of three minutes—in other words ten percent. If von Trips kept up an average speed that was 20-25 kph (12-15 mph) higher than mine, he would overtake me; and this was something that he could easily do because no team orders had been handed out. I was sure that von Trips did not know about my problem, so I had to keep him from sensing that I was in trouble. On the other hand, he would soon understand if I did not accelerate and carried on at that slow speed. I accelerated up to 240-250 kph (150-155 mph) signalling to him to slow down and he condescendingly remained behind for a few kilometers. But in the end he asked me to move over, and past he went. We were coming into a village, Piadena, about 30 km (20 miles) past Cremona. I remember it very well." At this point Taruffi describes a double S-bend, in Piadena itself, which he had had a chance to look at in detail one morning at dawn while training. He had noticed that the width of the road could be widened by using a small square on the left which was usually used by carts coming to the local market. The race was decided at this moment.

Taruffi describes the crucial moment in this way: "As we approached Piadena, von Trips, who had driven flat out to get away from me, was about 200 meters (220 yards) ahead. With the village in sight, at about 100 meters (110 yards) from the level crossing, I picked up and saw from his red brake lights that he had started to brake. I felt I could overtake him. I did not take my foot from the position I had kept it in up to then, i.e., for three-quarters of the race, and I aimed for the left-hand side as I entered the square which had been completely emptied for the race. With the road being almost twice as wide, because with that arrangement it had grown from the normal 7 meters (23') to at least 12 meters (39'), I was able to increase the radius of the curve I was making quite considerably. Seen from that angle, and looking at the way the road carried on through the archway of the house there, the bend seemed to have straightened out. I decelerated 150 meters (500') from the corner of the house, and accelerated again 50 meters (160') before reaching it, getting ready to take the corner as close as possible. From then on, I kept my foot flat on the floor, remembering that the two following bends were quicker. As I came out of the last one, and entered the straight, von Trips' car was a few meters away and I was able to overtake it quite easily. In just a few bends, and without warning, I had wiped out the lead that the German driver had over me, but, more importantly, I had shown him that I was more than a match for him, at least in that race. I signalled to him to take it easy and in a very comradely fashion he obeyed. Without knowing it I had sealed my victory on those bends in Piadena.

"We reached the finish line together but with the three minute lead I had from the start, I won," Taruffi writes, before describing the cheering crowd and his joyful embrace with his wife Isabella.

The Frenchmen Wimille, Trintignant and Chiron are dealt with hastily. Ferrari says rightly that Wimille was one of the greatest aces to have come out of France, and that "Trintignant and Behra are also in this class." The results chalked up by Wimille make him a far superior driver to the other two. If anything he can be compared to Chiron, to whom Italian automobile racing owes a great deal and who, with his verve and his very profitable driving style, can boast a career that few others can. One reason for this may be that this driver from Monaco, who died recently, was lucky enough to finish his long career virtually unscathed.

Talking of Alberto Ascari, Ferrari underlines his complex character, his seriousness and his singular love for his family and in particular for his children, who received from him more smacks than hugs so that they would not love him too much and thus not suffer too much were he to die in a crash during a race. This surprising spiritual attitude of the greatest driver, in an absolute sense, that Italy has had in the postwar period leaves one undeniably perplexed, but Ferrari, who knew him well, may be right. Far more arguable is the cause of Ascari's death referred to in Ferrari's first book, *Le mie gioie terribili* ("My Terrible Joys"). In this book Ferrari talks of a possible after-effect of the accident involving Ascari four days earlier at Monte Carlo, when he ended up in the water with the Lancia D50. The long marks left on the asphalt by the tires of the Ferrari 750 Monza he was driving that day, were caused, according to Ferrari, by the desperate attempt, in braking, to avoid a workman who was crossing the track at that very spot. Ferrari also hints that the workman later confessed his guilt to a priest. Unfortunately there were no witnesses, so any of the different arguments may be valid. It is a fact that Gendebien and Hawthorn express different theories about that crash, as we mention in another part of this book.

It is the character, the special qualities, and the warmheartedness, rather than the class of Eugenio Castellotti which are perfectly caught by Ferrari; but the cause of his death is, once again, slightly embroidered. At that time Eugenio was emotionally involved with one of the best-known stars of the comic theater in Italy. "He died," Ferrari says, "in a banal accident while training at the Modena track, at a particularly bad moment in his emotional life, when a certain bewilderment was preying on his mind."

When it comes to the death of Luigi Musso, Ferrari weaves a long story based on the rivalry which then existed between the Roman driver and Mike Hawthorn, although they were both on the same team. The equal chances of both winning the title accentuated this rivalry at Rheims. It is Ferrari's view that, at the Muizon bend, Musso kept his foot flat on the accelerator instead of lifting it slightly, and this was unwise. Another reason for Musso's rash move was that he was desperately in need of money, and the prize offered to the winner of the Rheims race was ten times the amount offered in other races.

Hawthorn was a disconcerting driver, because he was erratic. But when he was in form few could match him, and, in fact, he scored two victories (the French Grand Prix in 1953 and the Spanish Grand Prix in 1954) in which he beat all the top drivers of the day. Another sensational win was in the 1955 Tourist Trophy, driving the only Ferrari. At the tape, he was ahead of both the Lancias and the Jaguars.

Turning to Collins, for whom he had great esteem and admiration, Ferrari recalls the episode at Monza which, in his version, was very different from the description given by Fangio and Giambertone in *La mia vita a 300 all'ora*. Because the motor racing season had been arranged so that Peter Collins also had a chance of winning the world championship, Ferrari summoned the Englishman and asked him

Enzo Ferrari with Alberto Ascari.

Luigi Musso joined Ferrari in 1956 and raced both Formula 1 and sports cars. In 1958, at Rheims, during the French Grand Prix he went off the track and died not long afterwards in the hospital.

what his intentions were, without asking him explicitly to stand down in favor of Fangio. Collins replied as follows: "I never thought a young twenty-five year old like me could have such a huge responsibility. Fangio must be the world champion again this year, because he deserves it, and I'll always be ready to give him my car whenever it might help him out." Ferrari saw great class in Collins, together with a perfect knowledge of mechanics. In other words, he had all the ingredients for becoming a top driver, but it was his bad luck, according to Ferrari, that he met an American actress, Louise, who "took away his dream," just as Banquo took away Macbeth's dream. Certainly, Louise was very beautiful and, above all, disturbingly feminine.

With the death of Luigi Musso in 1957, followed by that of Peter Collins in 1958, and the retirement of Mike Hawthorn at the end of the 1958 season, Ferrari lost three brilliant drivers. Fate had it that Hawthorn was also soon to die (in January, 1959) in a road accident in England.

Ferrari is grateful to Froilan Gonzales—nicknamed "el cabezon" ("the mule") because of his stubbornness—above all for the win that the Argentinian scored in the British Grand Prix in 1951, when Alfa Romeo was beaten for the very first time. As Ferrari himself reveals, Gonzales could be irritatingly passive at times. He was the exact opposite of Alberto Ascari. He was passive when he was in the lead and

36

Enzo Ferrari with Peter Collins at Monza in 1956.

full of beans when he was lying down the field. Ascari enjoyed being in first place and rarely finished a race if he was not.

The qualities that most struck Enzo Ferrari about Wolfgang von Trips were his noble heart, the slight air of melancholy that hung over his aristocratic features, and his ability, as a driver, to drive at speeds which were always very high.

Ferrari has few memories of the three Americans who drove for him (Phil Hill, Dan Gurney, and Ritchie Ginther). He calls Hill a driver who was much happier on straights than on curves, "not in the top class, but safe and competent especially on fast circuits." The fact that Ferrari was not all that fond of Hill is shown by the fact that he does not mention any of the wins chalked up by the Californian at Le Mans (three, all with Gendebien co-driving, in 1958, 1961, and 1962). He is grateful to Ginther for his valuable contribution to Ferrari as a test driver. Of the three, he clearly had most time for Dan Gurney, who had a loyal look about him and the physique of nothing less than a marine.

Ferrari also considered Mairesse an excellent test driver. His extraordinary enthusiasm soon laid bare any defects in the cars entrusted to his care, and in a much shorter time than in the case of drivers who were better technicians than he.

Although Gendebien is the author of a book in which he criticizes Ferrari severely, Ferrari forgives him because he accepts his nobility and the elegant and shrewd impetuosity which Gendebien brought to his driving. He also recognizes other talents in him: a smooth quality at the wheel, consistency, good character, and intelligence. Here again, however, Ferrari fails to refer to Gendebien's four wins at Le Mans, one with his fellow countryman, Paul Frère. Ferrari did not much like the Belgian's talkativeness when he won, nor did he much like his book "in which he was mean in his acknowledgements, except toward himself."

Where Ricardo Rodriguez is concerned, Ferrari reproaches him above all for his scorn of danger and his impatience to reach the tape, two characteristics which were to claim his life. He has few words for his brother, Pedro. Pedro was eager to be taken on full time by Ferrari; in other words he wanted to drive Formula 1 cars as well as sports models. Ferrari more or less refused him the Formula 1 cars and was accused of being short-sighted as a result.

Ferrari also has little to say about Giancarlo Baghetti and accuses the press of having acclaimed him as a reborn Varzi. Of course, his verdict of the man is colored by the choice the driver made at a certain juncture, when he left Ferrari of his own accord at the end of 1962.

Ferrari rightly considers Maglioli above all a road racer of great courage, but the driver from Biella has remained convinced that his potential with Formula 1 cars was never adequately explored, even though on the rare occasions when he took part in trials, his performances with the single-seaters were not the most dazzling. Ferrari also considers road racer Nino Vaccarella "an excellent sports car driver"; whereas in his remarks on Abate, he underlines "certain spirited moments" with GT cars.

Ferrari puts Scarfiotti and Parkes in the same bag. In fact the two men were great friends, and their styles were somewhat similar. He says that both of them had a huge desire to race and

Enzo Ferrari with Eugenio Castellotti and Delia Scala.

37

would have done so with any car. The Monza incident (Italian Grand Prix, 1966) was an example, according to Ferrari, of Parkes' altruism and of the genuine affection in which he held his friend. But this deep bond of brotherhood cracked at Le Mans the following year when Scarfiotti refused to carry out the plan worked out by Ferrari for beating Ford. It was the indecision of the driver from the Marches which made it possible for the American car to win, or at least helped it to win.

Scarfiotti's huge desire to race Formula cars lead to his divorce from Ferrari, but he repented, according to the boss of Maranello, and, although this is not generally known, there was already an agreement for him to return to the fold, under the old flag, as a driver of sports cars. But fate decreed otherwise. Scarfiotti died at an early age in an accident during the uphill trials at Rossfeld, driving a Porsche.

Ferrari then turns to the Scarfiotti-Bandini rivalry, and in particular the financial well-being of the former as compared with the poverty suffered by the latter. He does not judge Bandini's qualities as a driver. He prefers to recall his humble origins and the great sadness that overcame him when he lost his father. The young Bandini had a huge urge to succeed, a devouring passion for racing cars and a sacred love of the land. Ferrari dwells at length on the accident which claimed the life of the young driver. While watching the race on television, he sensed that the flames bursting from one of the cars in the race came from the car driven by Bandini. It was a sad presentiment. The TV commentator for the race that day was, by chance, the author of this book, but Ferrari simply calls him the "telecaster." A few years later, in the last book, chronologically speaking, written by Ferrari, *Il Flobert*, he corrects his unintentional omission with the words: "I have a debt to pay to Casucci. In my memoirs, when I described Bandini's accident at Monte Carlo, a 'telecaster' is mentioned but not named. I know this accident must have distressed him, and I can sense that his distress goes much deeper than not having his name mentioned. At Monte Carlo it was in fact he, as an Italian and a sportsman, who shared with me that tragic day of intense emotions." May I be allowed to speak in the first person for moment, simply to say that that accident and the way in which I experienced it, without having any news of Bandini's true condition (after about half an hour I was handed an official communiqué which I have kept and which read: "*La voiture no. 18, la Ferrari de Bandini, a heurté à la chicane. Le pilote est indemne*" ["Car no. 18, Bandini's Ferrari, has hit the retaining wall. The driver is unhurt"] convinced me that being a television racing commentator was a job which no longer appealed to me, especially from the human viewpoint. Unfortunately, I foolishly let a few more years pass before hanging up the microphone. Nevertheless Ferrari's acknowledgement gave me a lot of pleasure, because he understood perfectly what a tragic day that was for me."

The verdict that Ferrari delivers about Surtees is positive all the way. This is worth stressing, because it is not easy for Ferrari to dwell on a driver when his relations with him are abruptly ended, as was the case with this Englishman on the eve of the Le Mans 24-hour race in 1966. For Ferrari, Surtees had the great talents of all drivers who have previously raced on motorcycles and, in addition, a particular passion for mechanics and a tireless urge to improve both himself and the cars that it fell to him to drive. If the sudden break just referred to had not happened, Ferrari confirms that Surtees would easily have become world champion in 1966 as well.

Ferrari has little to say about the contributions of Gunther Klass, Jean Guichet, Paul Hawkins, John Sutcliffe, Jonathan Williams, and Derek Bell. But he draws a perfect picture of Chris Amon in whom Ferrari recognizes great talents both at the wheel (he compares him to Felice Nazzaro) and as a test driver; but he adds, quite rightly, that Amon always lacked that dash of courage which could have made him one of the greats.

Ferrari acknowledges the courage and professionalism of Mario Andretti. Were it not for the fact that Mario has serious commitments in his adopted country in the form of contracts which tie him down almost all the year, Ferrari would have taken him on as an official driver in the Indianapolis 500, after Ascari's performance there in 1952. Ferrari says it would have been possible to have an "all Italian" victory, but Andretti feels such a weak bond with his native land that he writes in his book: "The happiest day of my life was when I was given American citizenship."

Ferrari writes only a few lines about Peter Schetty, saying that "he had started off very well, but his secret passion, deep down, was always to become an industrialist."

He paints an accurate portrait of the Belgian, Jacky Ickx: "For four years we went after a title, and during those years we were accused of disagreements, which went beyond journalistic acrobatics. Some of his attitudes earned him the nickname "Pierino il terribile" from some of my colleagues, but I still have memories of a boy who grew up in a hurry, and the lasting impression of his fine and daring driving in the rain."

There are few lines about the other Italians who were members of his team. He recognizes great will-power and flexibility in Tino Brambilla, but accuses Nanni Galli of no more than a "formal" desire to race with Ferrari. He sees Andrea de Adamich as a very wily man and refers to Merzario's mistake in having wanted to "marry some of the press." He says firmly that he would have had much more to say about Ignazio Giunti, had it not been for the disaster at Buenos Aires.

He reveals a soft spot for Clay Regazzoni, "an excellent professional whom I respect, as I know others do as well. It was he who advised me about Lauda, and because that name was already firmly rooted in my mind, I didn't have to have second thoughts."

In 1974 Ferrari's opinion of the Austrian was positive through and through. "He is a serious young man, punctilious about preparing his cars, in a natural, instinctive way. On the track he shows a lot of determination and a deep concern for safety. I would compare him with a Collins, in terms of style and conduct. He has everything it takes to become one of the top drivers." Three years later, following the break between Lauda and Ferrari, the latter adds: "With us, in a four-year period, he won the world title twice

Andrea de Adamich in the 1968 South African Grand Prix. He was one of the few Italians to be included in the official Ferrari team.

Niki Lauda, above, in the 312 T2 with which he won his second world title.

and missed doing so a third time by just one point, having dominated the season up until that terrible accident at the Nürburgring. That is the only Lauda I wish to remember."
McLaren gets little attention ("he found in the Can-Am his gold mine of success"), as does Dennis Hulme ("a long and honest routine"). About Mitter, Ferrari says: "I did not know him well, but I respected him as a hill climber." Luciano Bianchi was "a good lad, whose modesty was disproportionate with his qualities." Jochen Rindt "was a true acrobat at the start of his career," and Siffert was "almost a revelation"; but of Mike Hailwood he says: "he never managed to repeat the feats he achieved in motorcycling when it came to automobile racing." Cévert "reached high points where he was in a class of his own." Emerson Fittipaldi and Peter Revson "were both under consideration by Ferrari, but no agreements were reached for various reasons, and they both had different

Giancarlo Baghetti. The Milanese driver can boast of a feat as yet unmatched: he won a world championship race (the 1961 French Grand Prix) in his debut in championship competition.

fates." Stewart "was a genuine champion, a man who never gave in to his opponents; he knew what he wanted, and he still does; on his balance sheet he always dealt in a scrupulous way with risks as well. I admire him, even though he had no time for cars with covered wheels, and even though the crowd found him unimaginative and lacking spontaneity. He is certainly one of the best drivers of all time."
Ferrari also devotes some space to Stirling Moss, the man he has always and repeatedly likened to Nuvolari. Moss also had what Ferrari calls Nuvolari's "accident sense," in as much as none of the times he left the track ended in tragedy. In 1962, in the course of a long visit which the British driver paid to Ferrari, the foundations were laid for a program of collaboration between the two. This could never materialize, however, because of the accident in which Moss was injured at Goodwood, which put an end to his dazzling career as a driver.

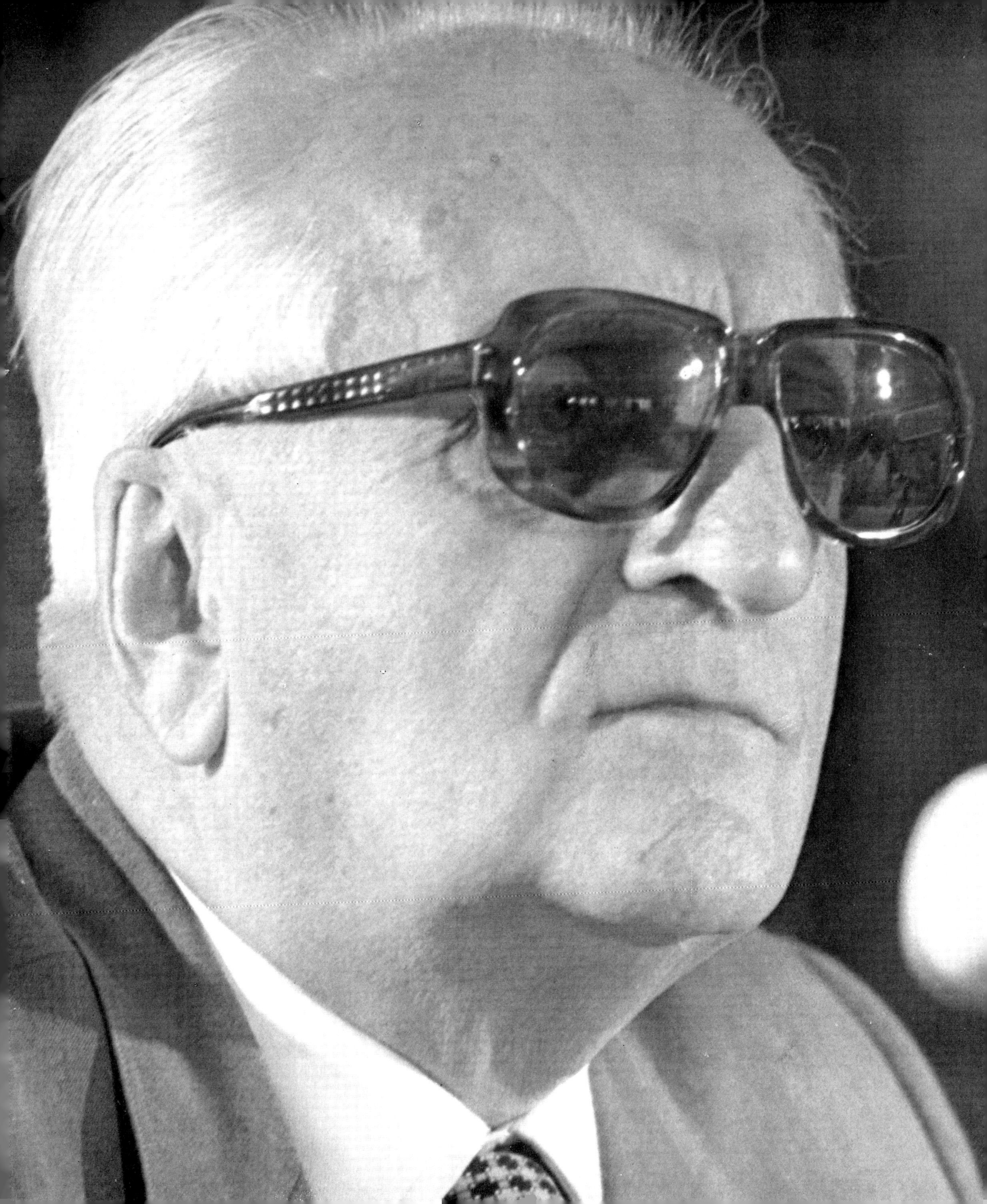

THAT'S THE WAY I AM

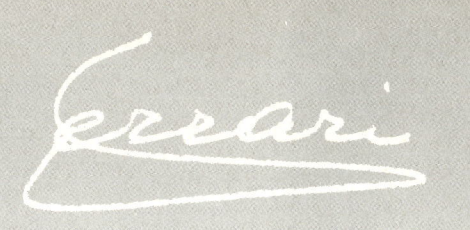

Q. - All the racing Ferraris have a reputation for being exceptionally well built. You have never made any compromises in this respect. What runs through your mind, then, after an accident that is clearly caused by the "physical" failure of a car built by one of your rivals?
A. - *In many cases, "physical" failures of a car are claimed to have caused an accident, but this verdict is later retracted after in-depth inspections have been made. However, I find myself constantly doubting if it is a good idea to interpret the racing formula at the extreme limits of the minimum weight allowed rather than offset the weight handicap of a heavier but generally better "protected" car by using a more powerful engine. Even though I am convinced that accidents are never caused by just one thing, but by a combination of things, I have always encouraged my technicians to adopt the latter solution.*

Q. - The introduction of sponsors to the world of motor racing has completely changed the relationship between builders and drivers. At one time, it was the former who decided on the choice of the latter. Now it's the other way round, more or less. Do you think drivers deserve the large sums of money that they earn nowadays? Has the disappearance of the "gentlemen driver" harmed motor racing as a sport, or was he just a symbolic figure who is now obsolete?
A. - *The introduction to the world of motor racing of so-called sponsors who advertise consumer products, which have nothing whatsoever to do with the progress and development of the automobile, has in effect harmed the relationship between builders and drivers in the vast majority of cases. Ferrari has not experienced this change, because we have only allowed the advertisements of outside technical collaborators to appear on our cars. Sponsors have a decisive influence on builders by suggesting or dictating the choice of the driver who will give them the best publicity.*
As far as the money which drivers earn, I think that, if you

weigh up the risks involved, the amount of money which each driver manages to earn is deserved; but it is obvious that figures have now been reached which far outstrip the earnings in any other sporting profession, even where there are more risks involved than in motor racing. Finally, as far as gentlemen drivers are concerned, I would say that there have been quite a few gentlemen, true gentlemen, throughout the history of motor racing; but their gentlemanliness has been limited to the beginning of their sporting careers, when it was necessary to get hold of a car and manage it directly. These initial sacrifices were offset as soon as a driver's first successes started to indicate his real potential. Even nowadays, there are still embryonic gentlemen who spend considerable sums of money to buy their way into the limelight, especially in Formula 1. I would conclude by saying that there is nothing different about the sums of money invested by gentlemen today, if you take into account the value of the lira in the 1920s, when the bank accounts of Masetti, Niccolini, Brilli-Peri, Maggi, Mazzotti, Trossi, and a score of others helped to launch their careers as gentlemen drivers.

Q. - You have travelled more or less the whole length and breadth of the history of motor racing. In what field do you think the most significant progress has been made? Engines, tires, construction, or technology?
A. - *In my opinion, the most significant progress has been the metallurgical revolution, which has enabled substantial developments to take place. As far as tires are concerned, the days when they were considered a mere accessory are now dead and buried. Since 1919, I have followed the development of racing tires, and I think I can safely say that today, to a very large extent, the final results obtained depend on the behavior of the tires. But we must not forget that engines have reached a specific output of 175 hp per liter of cubic capacity, and, finally, we must take into account how much aviation has contributed, and still contributes, to the automobile.*

Q. - You said once that you started off beyond the top of the mountain. So you can do and say what you please. Can you give a definitive answer to the question, Is racing useful or not to the progress of the automobile in general?
A. - *The automobile was born out of racing; it has advanced with racing; and it continues on its upward path of improvement by drawing from the fund of results offered by racing. Any laboratory research or computer analysis, any new discovery of any type whatsoever that has to do with the automobile will find its real endorsement nowhere else than in the characteristics that emerge from the practical experiment carried out on the track. It is precisely racing that forces the driver to make*

maneuvers, and bring about stresses and uses which cannot be programmed or calculated on a computer, because they are irrational and caused solely by the requirements he finds himself having to meet in the course of a race. These situations and circumstances, which cannot be theorized about, occur on ordinary roads and with ordinary cars.

Q. - There have been major and minor racing car engineers: Chevrolet, Bugatti, the Dusenberg brothers, the Maseratis, the Orsis. Do you think you have outstripped them all? What do Ferraris have which their cars do not?
A. - *Thank you for the compliment. I have never thought that I have outstripped them, either collectively or individually. Ferraris have their own tradition, which got off to a timid start in 1929 with the Scuderia and has become more refined with the years in our interpretation of the many different formulas. We have always been resolutely determined to develop our products in the way most consistent with the circumstances prevailing, in tune with the modest resources at our disposal and instilling them with our great love of motor sport.*

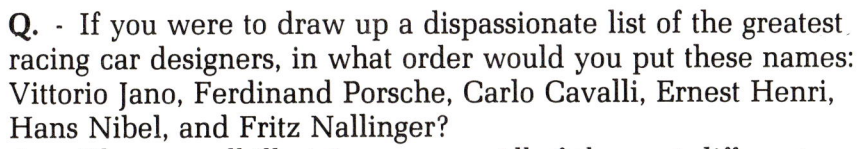

Q. - If you were to draw up a dispassionate list of the greatest racing car designers, in what order would you put these names: Vittorio Jano, Ferdinand Porsche, Carlo Cavalli, Ernest Henri, Hans Nibel, and Fritz Nallinger?
A. - *They are all illustrious names. All of them, at different times, have added a tangible contribution to the history of the automobile. My preference would probably tend towards Jano and Porsche, whom I have known personally, but at the same time I might well be biased.*

Q. - You maintain, rightly, that it is not possible to say who has been the greatest driver, in an absolute sense, because every driver has to be seen in the context of his time. But there is a "greatness" which goes beyond time and space. In what order would you list these names: Pietro Bordino, Felice Nazzaro, Achille Varzi, Tazio Nuvolari, Rudolf Caracciola, Bernd Rosemeyer, Alberto Ascari, Jim Clark, and Jackie Stewart?
A. - *Once again I'll repeat that an "all-time" listing is not feasible because each driver has to be judged in the context of the times and on the basis of the conditions in which he operated. If we really want to establish a "greatness" beyond time and space, a greatness comparable to the brightness of a star driver, I would have to say that Nuvolari was the brightest star. In saying that, I do not intend any detriment to any of the drivers mentioned by you, or to any of the others whom I have known from experience to be equally valiant and competent.*

Q. - Of the single seater Formula 1 cars, the 375 gave you the greatest satisfaction by beating the Alfa Romeos in 1951. Which car do you consider to be the most successful in an absolute sense?
A. - *I can't lay my finger on the most successful car in an absolute sense, because as soon as the latest product lets out its first infant sounds, I always feel the dissatisfaction of the engineer. It has to be that way. It's only to be expected that the most successful car is the one I think about with the most stubborn persistence, but it has still to be built.*

Q. - And what about the GT cars? According to the English magazine *Autocar*, the Daytona is still a car that has not been surpassed. What do you think?
A. - *There's no doubt that because of its abundant range of features which tallied with the period in which it was marketed the Daytona has left its mark. But there are other excellent sisters of the Daytona, both before and after it.*

Q. - Your phrase "wrapped up in petrol" hits the nail right on the head in describing the most serious danger run by drivers in modern single-seater racing cars. If you were given free rein, what would you do to improve the safety aspect of racing?
A. - *You could write a whole volume of suggestions to improve the safety of racing, but who's going to read it? A theoretical answer can only lay down the main initial requirements: first and foremost, it is necessary to make sure that the formula which has to be interpreted by the engineers does not contain within it the seeds of an accident; then there's the design of the circuits and the protective measures adopted in them; and finally, there's the vital discipline of the various competitors and drivers and of a body of professional sporting organizers, who must bring real ability to their important and responsible jobs.*

Q. - Why haven't you set up a Ferrari museum? Have you got a horror of what you've done?
A. - *That's a good point, why haven't I set up a Ferrari museum? The answer is extremely simple: I haven't been able to. I've often been forced to sell my racing cars to settle bills with colleagues and suppliers. As for what I think about what I've done, I have no desire to evaluate it, but I'm not horrified by it.*

Q. - You've threatened to quit several times, but has there been a time when you've really wanted to? If so, when?

A. - *Twice I've been on the point of quitting: when they tried to bring me to court for a technical fault which I did not commit and when I was morally lynched after the death of an Italian driver.*

Q. - In your book Flobert you provide some proof of your perspicacity and powers of observation in what you say about motoring correspondents. Is that the whole truth? There are people who say that the first version, which was later considerably modified, was much more ruthless. Is that so?
A. - *In Flobert I told the whole truth as it applied at that time. Those who say I wrote a first version and then softened it show that they don't know me by thinking that I might go beyond certain limits in the instinctive expression of my views.*

Q. - You are sometimes affectionately called "that hooligan of '98'" or the "Drake." You are notorious as a man of wit and thoughts. How would you define yourself if you had to come up with a nickname?
A. - *I have often called myself the living expression of the fantasy of journalists. I'll let them choose a nickname for me.*

Q. - You have clearly demonstrated your intolerance of governments and the authorities in general by declaring your ostracism of the city of Rome, where you haven't set foot for forty years. What do you reproach them for? If the President invited you to Rome, what would you do?
A. - *I am not intolerant of the government or of the authorities in general. If I haven't been to Rome for forty years, it's because I have always thought that a country ought to be governed by a strict respect for the laws of economics rather than by various multi-colored political ideologies. If the President sent me an invitation I would justify myself by saying that my age no longer permits me the enviable activity which he pursues.*

Q. - Goethe said: "Do you want to know more? Then travel, my friend." No one has been as rooted to the spot as you, and yet few other people know the racing world as well as you do. What is the secret behind this?
A. - *I've never been rooted to the spot. In 1922 I was in Paris; in 1923 in London; in 1924 I worked in Switzerland; and so on and so forth until 1956, when I stopped moving about. But it didn't stop me from knowing many people and obtaining all the*

information that filters down through the racing world and that has to be sifted with great care. So I have no secrets, only a keen desire to learn, and this is what keeps me up-to-date with so many different situations.

Q. - You have always been considered a very good driver, one who "understands" cars. Which of these three cars seems to you to have introduced something really new at the time it appeared: Model T Ford, Volkswagen Beetle, or Mini?
A. - *I have called the Model T Ford one of man's first conquests of freedom. The Volkswagen Beetle was an instrument of labor and war. The Mini is an exemplary conception of a very small front-wheel-drive car. With it, Issigonis showed how this type of car was bound to be more like a match-box in shape than a traditional automobile.*

Q. - In your excellent autobiography of 1974, you conclude by saying: "I have never repented. I've often had regrets, but repented, never. Because I would do the same things all over again, although in a completely different way." How would you do them? Where do you think you made mistakes?
A. - *I repeat, I think I've made mistakes all the way through, not least because of my lack of culture and formal education. So for this reason, if I were allowed to live it all again, I would bring my actions into harmony with these two elements. But I am still convinced that our actions throughout our lives are almost always dictated by emotions rather than by reason.*

Q. - When you were at the height of fitness what did you love most: women or cars?
A. - *I have always considered a woman to be the best prize a man can desire after his work. I have never put women before cars, but I have always considered them to be precious and capable of helping with decisions connected with one's work. I think we must love them dearly, even if sometimes we must give up trying to understand them. That goes for whatever age we are.*

Q. - How would you like to be remembered: as a great Italian, an idealist, or an extraordinarily coherent man?
A. - *None of them. If anything, only as a sportsman, but so much has been said about me that I would rather be quickly forgotten.*

THE BIRTH OF FERRARI

The history of Ferrari, the automobile factory, can be traced back to the formation of Scuderia Ferrari in 1929. "The idea came into being," Ferrari writes, "over supper in Bologna one evening." The aim of the Scuderia was to provide assistance to Alfa's clients who had grown considerably in number since the Milanese factory had become heavily involved in racing activities. What is more, at a certain point, Alfa toyed with the idea of reducing this involvement, so that some of the energy deployed in the racing division could be used for ordinary production. This, incidentally, was the same reason which made Mercedes stop its racing activities on more than one occasion.

With his organization Enzo Ferrari virtually replaced Alfa Romeo in the racing field and also took over the job of solving certain technical problems, although he mainly used men and equipment supplied to him by Alfa. In this way, he gained an autonomy which enabled him to take on the best drivers available on the market directly.

The importance that became attached to the Scuderia as time passed is demonstrated by the large number of competitions and races in which it took part from its fourth year of activity (1932) onwards. The total reached thirty-nine, in fact, some of which were in the top league. These included the Grand Prix events of Tripoli, Alexandria, Berlin, Nîmes, France, the Marne, Belgium, Nice, Italy, Masaryk (Hungary), and Spain, as well as the Mille Miglia, the Targa Florio, the Ciano Cup, the Acerbo Cup, the Stelvio Cup and the Spa 24-hour race. In all, the Scuderia's drivers, in that year, were placed first on twenty-six occasions, second on thirteen, and won twelve category championships. There was also a motorcycling division which took part in twelve competitions and which numbered among its ranks illustrious names such as that of Giordano Aldrighetti, who won eight races in that year.

The Scuderia did more than merely assist clients in the form and scope which its activities assumed. It had its own offices on via Trento in Modena and in Trieste (they still exist although the original architecture has changed), and it had its own trucks for transporting cars. Scuderia mechanics started to roam the world, taking a great deal of equipment with them, spending sleepless nights at the various tracks, and dismantling and reassembling the cars every time they returned home. It was exactly as it is today with the sole difference that today technical progress has made it possible to replace an engine or a gearbox in an infinitely shorter time. In addition, trips abroad are now, obviously, made by air rather than by sea. This is perhaps the only aspect of progress which the mechanics do not welcome, since the sea voyages allowed them a well-earned rest.

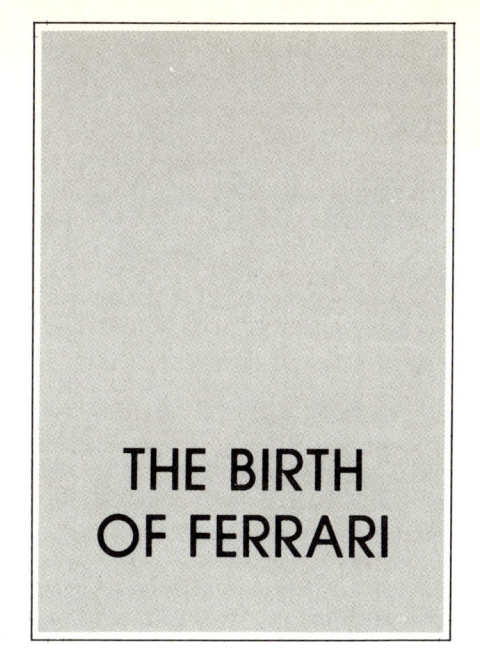

It is not hard to guess that Enzo Ferrari's spirit of initiative, the fact that he considered himself a "trouble maker," and his qualities of leadership all created a certain rivalry between Milan and Modena. It was true that Alfa Romeo had entrusted Enzo Ferrari with the management of their racing cars, but he had taken his duties too literally. When the Germans came back on the scene in force in 1934, he was forced to match their superiority as best he could. There was only one way of doing this: squeeze the most out of the engines, and improve the road-holding of the cars. The crowded racing calendar was a good excuse for putting into practice solutions which could not, on every occasion, be agreed upon first with Alfa. It was a question of acting quickly, or not at all.

It was thus inevitable that some of the most important cars bearing the Alfa Romeo mark were born, in effect, at Modena. This was the case with the 1935 Bimotore and the 158 of 1937, for which Ferrari took all the credit for himself. The official historian of the Milanese firm, Luigi Fusi, says that they were, on the contrary, built "with the technical personnel dispatched expressly for that purpose by Alfa Romeo." This does not mean that Ferrari did not represent a valuable incentive without which, in all probability, Alfa Romeo would have lost contact with the race track.

The Scuderia stopped being Alfa Romeo's *longa manus* in 1937. In 1938 Enzo Ferrari was appointed the latter's racing manager, a job which he gave up almost immediately because of differences of opinion between him and the then managing director of Alfa. With the proceeds from the closure of the Scuderia, which was a corporation, and with his own savings, Enzo Ferrari founded, in Modena, the firm Auto Avio Costruzioni which was involved in various sectors (4-cylinder engines for training aircraft, machine tools, and grinding machines) including automobiles. The first car produced by the new company was the 815, but it could not be called a Ferrari for reasons already described (a clause signed with Alfa Romeo that prohibited Ferrari from using his own name for four years in the automotive field). In fact the 815 was only a Ferrari up to a certain point, because it incorporated mechanical parts made by Fiat.

As is well known, the 815 had its moment of glory in 1940 when it took part in the Mille Miglia, which that year was held over a road circuit (Brescia-Cremona-Brescia). Of the two cars entered, one was in the hands of Alberto Ascari and the other in the hands of the "gentleman" from Modena, Lotario Rangoni. Both were forced to retire from the race.

In 1943 Ferrari's company moved to Maranello, to a plot of land owned by Enzo Ferrari. The war did not leave the works unscathed, and they were bombed and partly destroyed in November, 1944 and February, 1945. When the war came to an end, Ferrari gave up manufacturing machine tools

Bologna 1932: The Scuderia Ferrari stand. In that year Enzo Ferrari retired for good from racing and took on the Alfa Romeo agency for Emilia, Romagna, and the Marches.

and devoted himself heart and soul to automobiles. He could now do this without risk. The contract binding him to Alfa Romeo had expired.

It is hard to say whether at this point Ferrari was already thinking in terms of becoming a builder of GT cars. He became involved in this sector as a result of circumstances, in the wake of the successes which his racing cars were achieving, and because of the interest that they were arousing in racing circles in general. But Ferrari reveals that from the construction of the first 1500 onwards, he had set up "an ambitious program." When he was with Alfa Romeo, that firm aimed to produce a car a day. He thought he would do the same. In fact he has considerably exceeded that rate of production, not least because of the assistance from Fiat which became formally associated with Ferrari on June 21, 1969.

In 1955, the small factory at Maranello started to reach the levels which had been set with the production of 306 cars. In 1961, the total increased to 441 cars, and thereafter it rose steadily, apart from the years 1969 and 1973 and the period following the oil crisis.

Ferrari writes of Maranello in 1974: "The factory has become an impressive place. It has 1,000 employees, and that is just at Maranello. If we add the offices in Modena and the Carrozzeria Scaglietti (Scaglietti body-building works), in which Ferrari has had a majority share-holding since 1970, the total rises to 1,450. In 1973, 1,800 cars were produced, and this would have risen to 3,000 in 1974, had it not been for the energy crisis."

Oil crisis apart, would Maranello have assumed the proportions of a medium-sized car factory? Enzo Ferrari has always rejected the idea. Maranello is a small country town and it has been partly converted—thanks to Ferrari— to industrial activities; but its best-known inhabitant has never wanted his factory to turn into an industry. He has not wanted to let this happen for the simple reason that he has never felt himself made of the stuff of an entrepreneur. "Industry involves requirements which I could never meet because they are antithetical to my temperament as someone who is keen on promoting research."

Two trucks belonging to Scuderia Ferrari (a Ceirano and a Lancia) used for transporting race cars. The cars were loaded onto the trucks and transported more or less as they are today (photo at left).

Tazio Nuvolari playing ping-pong. This photo was taken at a restaurant in Sidi-Bou-Saïd on the eve of the 1933 Tunisian Grand Prix.

The cover of the only edition of the Scuderia Ferrari magazine, dating back to 1933: in the foreground a single-seater Alfa Romeo with the rampant horse in the background.

Enzo Ferrari with Piero Taruffi before the start of the Coppa del Mare in 1932. It was Ferrari who believed in Taruffi as a car driver. The Roman driver had started his racing career on two wheels.

He has justified his definition of himself as a "trouble maker" by his constant desire to introduce something new into his cars, every day. And this way of going about things is undoubtedly diametrically opposed to any industrial concept, where mass production is the name of the game. Conversely, he maintains that this attitude is beneficial to a small factory which is concerned mainly with racing. All the innovations that come out of Sunday racing can be translated to ordinary production models in a short period of time. What is more, "in a small factory there is a more marked team spirit."

As an industrialist, Enzo Ferrari's first crisis struck him after the death of his son Dino. Who would carry on his work now that his son and heir had gone? Ford of America showed a great deal of interest and concern in the fate of Ferrari and said it was ready to sign an agreement which would, to all appearances, leave Enzo Ferrari with a great deal of autonomy and control as far as the racing sector was concerned, and almost no say where the production of GT cars was concerned. But nothing came of it, despite the fact that was the sort of arrangement that appealed to Ferrari, because it would allow him to devote himself almost entirely to racing cars. This is how things unfolded according to the detailed description included by Enzo Ferrari in his 1974 book:

"On April 10, 1963 I received a telephone call from the number one at Ford in Italy, asking me for an appointment. We met two days later in my office at Modena. The conversation soon became lively. The Ford representative, whom I had already met a couple of years earlier, asked me if I was interested in discussing a plan of collaboration with his company. He said that the expansion of Ford sales in Italy and the European development program had given him the idea of approaching me. In substance, it would have involved producing a prototype which would then be manufactured in fairly large numbers for the European market. I soon realized that this proposition also introduced another one, which was considerably more meaty, and which was, in fact, the real purpose of his visit: the final proposal was to draw up an industrial agree-

Vittorio Jano with Achille Varzi: one of the greatest racing car designers with one of the greatest drivers of all time.

ment. I said I was interested, simply because I had never felt myself to be an industrialist, but an engineer. The production growth of my company would only interest me if others handled the administration of it. I wanted just one thing: to be able to devote myself to prototypes and racing cars, but under conditions of absolute independence, and with a store of technical equipment and finance which I did not have. I reminded the man opposite me that in 1962 I had spent on the racing division the sum of about 450,000,000 lire, (over $750,000 or £260,000); this was virtual madness for such a small firm as mine. Then there was a visit to Maranello, and we parted on the understanding that he would return with his specialists in the various fields.

"From April 12 to May 15 there was a constant stream of technicians, designers, stylists, marketing people, publicity people, lawyers, and planners at Modena and Maranello. Not a sector, not a nook, of my firm escaped being

November 1944. The Ferrari works after the first bombardment. A second one hit the factory in February 1945.

explored, examined, and evaluated from every angle. And finally the day came when things were to be finalized.

"In the meantime the press had got wind that something was going on, and ears pricked up. Indiscreet remarks started to fly, and inferences started to circulate. Before anything had been decided, newspapers, and not all of them Italian, were running headlines such as, "Ford buys Ferrari." I kept quiet, of course; but I felt calm, given the premises under which the negotiations had been conducted from the outset. The Ferrari, as a racing car, would have been made more powerful, and it would continue to race throughout the world, backed up by technical and financial assistance which I had never known before; but this new life would not change the car's color, the red of Italy. For its part, the town of Maranello would see this small factory enlarged on an unprecedented scale, and that would certainly help the inhabitants.

"But I felt some kind of scruple, I would even say a deep sense of being Italian, and I wanted to call in some industrialists in the automobile industry, either directly or via intermediaries. I had three oddly different replies. Here they are:

" 'It is with a feeling of humiliation that we cannot do everything that a great firm like Ferrari requires and deserves, but we cannot put oursleves in competition with a colossus like Ford.'

" 'The technical and racing wealth of Ferrari is undoubtedly of great importance, but in our view racing cars do not serve a purpose in the construction of good touring cars.'

" 'An agreement with Ferrari would be an ideal combination, but the first thing we must ask ourselves is which of the two of us should give way to the newcomer.'

"I was thus convinced that what I was doing would not arouse any surprise or criticism within the automobile industry. The decisive meeting with the emissaries from Detroit took place at Maranello on May 15. Three of the senior officials of that huge organization flew in from the States, and we signed a very short memo written by me by hand, whereby two new companies would be formed: Ferrari-Ford and Ford-Ferrari, the former with the purpose of building prototypes and racing cars to compete in all the major races in the world. I would have been the chairman of Ferrari-Ford, with full powers; I would retain ninety percent of the shareholding, with ten percent going to Ford. Ford-Ferrari, on the other hand, would make GT automobiles for the Italian and European markets. I would have been the vice-president of this company with ten percent of the shares; Ford would hold the other ninety percent. My activities in the Ford-Ferrari company would be limited to the technical supervision of production.

The entrance to the works on the road to Abetone.

"So we come to the afternoon of May 20, which was to overturn the situation which looked so hopeful. All the numerous typewritten documents, compiled by an army of lawyers who did not speak Italian, lay across the table. Every sentence had to be translated, discussed, and agreed to. Before signing, the Americans called Detroit for approval. At a certain point, we came to the rider entitled GS. It had to do with the racing management division, and it had been kept to the last, which was strange. I had already, on several occasions, conceded to various modifications and variants to the memo signed and sealed five days before. But now I realized that the contents of the document at which I was now looking—the GS—meant that I would have become the chairman of Ferrari, so far so good, with ninety percent of the shares, but that my activities would in no way be independent, but rather dependent on the approval of the Board.

"My surprise, or rather my anger, exploded. The basic condition of all the neogotiations had always been, from the outset, from the first discussion on April 10, that I would remain absolutely free and independent in my sector: free to set up economically viable programs, and free to choose my equipment and my personnel.

"The reply I was given really upset me: 'But Mister Ferrari, you're selling your company, and you still want to have a free say?'

"I replied that if this was largely true for the whole industrial sector, it certainly was not for the racing and experimental divisions, where the bureaucratically proper industrial rules and regulations of a large organization could obviously not be in harmony with the spirit which it required. In the end, I addressed a question to the person in the American delegation who seemed most interested: Up to what limit can you enter a commitment without previous authorization from Detroit? He replied: up to $10,000. My anger turned to dejection. I was obviously not a suitable person for that grandiose and marvellous industrial machine, where everything moved on predetermined tracks. And among other things, I asked myself why I had not borne in mind that episode in 1938 when I handed everything over to become Alfa's racing manager. It is in fact true that even if people claim to have a good memory, they are just so many scatter-brained stubborn mules.

"So the Ford-Ferrari agreement went

Fiorano: the garage-cum-workshop on the left, and the premises housing the offices, the conference room, and the guest rooms.

52

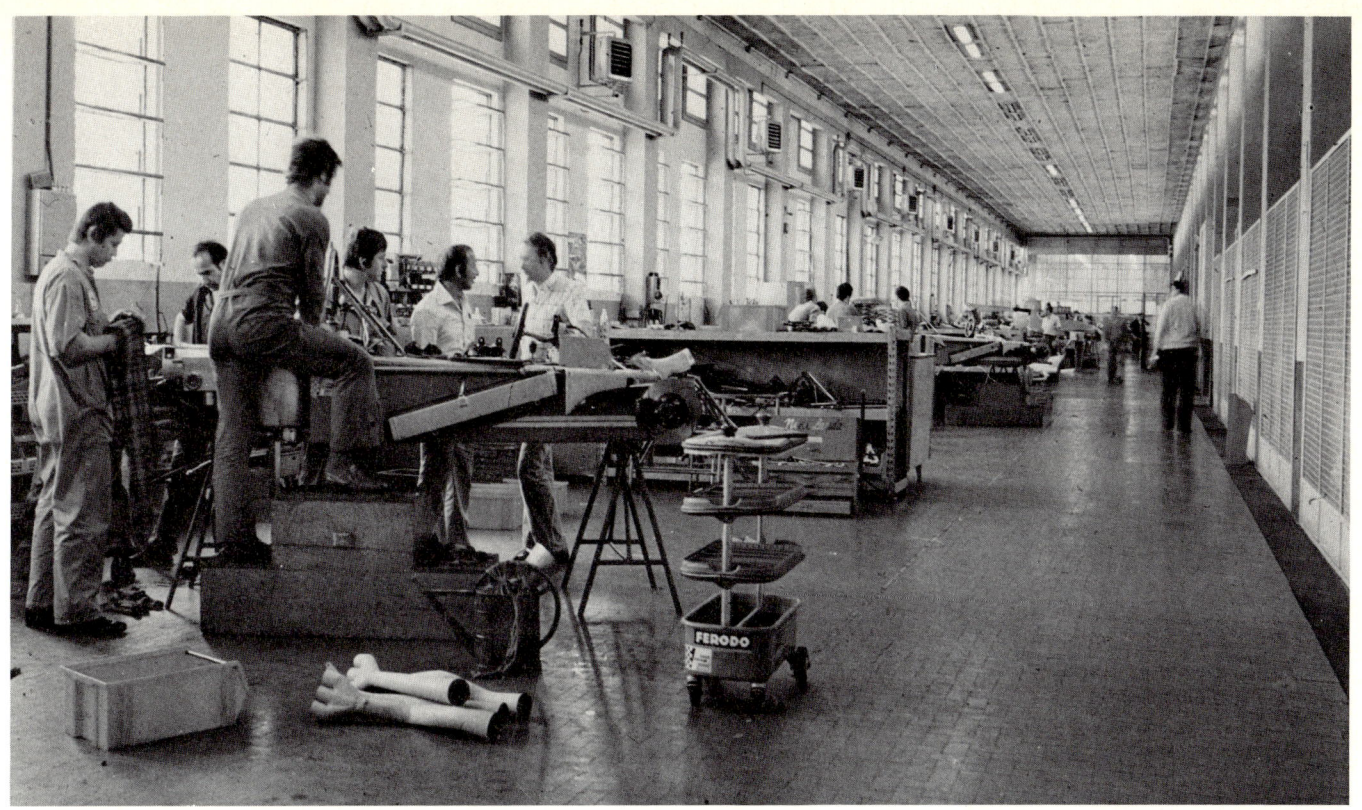

The Ferrari racing division. Altogether about hundred people are employed here. Below: the GT assembly line. Only a few cars come off the line each day as with other luxury makes.

Fiorano: a view of the track. Some of the curves are modeled directly on those of famous race tracks. Below: with the help of ten television monitors, it is possible to keep a constant eye on cars being test driven.

up in smoke in five short minutes. As you can imagine this incident earned me another cluster of enemies."

The speculations made at that time about the reasons for the abortive negotiations between Ferrari and Ford were so many and varied that the version recounted by Ferrari becomes something of an historical document. Ferrari, the firm, would have emerged greatly enlarged from the accord, but not Enzo Ferrari. The agreement with Fiat was signed with an absolute respect for his personality and his wishes. There had been something of a dress rehearsal in the proposition advanced by the Turin firm to Ferrari in 1965 to work on a 1600 cc. engine which Fiat would mass-produce and Ferrari would have used in a Formula 2 single-seater car. Enzo Ferrari considered Fiat's interest in Ferrari's affairs to be "the final act in a story that had been maturing amidst a great deal of internal and external speculation" and, further, "the right future for the company to which I gave birth."

The Ferrari-Fiat marriage has not brought about any substantial changes for the Ferrari firm except for an increase in the production of GT cars. Enzo Ferrari has continued to reign supreme in the racing division to which he has given his all, after stepping down from the chairmanship of the company. He has been unwaveringly consistent throughout his long life. He has travelled a long road and by taking short steps. From test driver to driver, driver to manager, manager to industrialist, via the phase which he enjoyed most, when he was a small-time engineer. The racing car is what has really interested him since his childhood. Paradoxically it could be said that he has accepted either passively or with resignation the development of the industrial branch of his firm by transferring to the touring car division all the experience amassed with single-seater and sports models, including the rear engine design. This decanting of ideas has always been a constant feature at Ferrari.

FORMULA 1

The 125 was the first F1 single-seater to be built by Ferrari; it was designed by Gioachino Colombo. A 12-cylinder engine was chosen, because both Ferrari and Colombo were convinced that this was the engine best suited to a modern racing car. The 12-cylinder engine has been the hallmark of Ferrari cars in the thirty-plus years of the firm's racing involvement; although other solutions have been tried: the straight 4- and 6-cylinder engine, the 65° and 120° V-6, and the V-8. There was also the "boxer" version of the 12-cylinder engine, i.e., with the cylinders set flat and opposed.

The 125 had a 60° 12-cylinder engine with 55 mm bore and 52.5 mm stroke; total cylinder capacity: 1467.77 cc. It was supported on 7 mountings. The crankcase and engine-block were made of magnesium alloy. Timing system: single overhead camshaft per cylinder bank, chain-driven. Carburation: single Weber 40 DO3C and single-stage Roots supercharger. Twin-magneto ignition, 1 spark plug per cylinder. Maximum power output: 225 hp at 7,000 rpm. Single dry-disk clutch; 5-speed constant-mesh gearbox. Tubular frame with oval-sectioned members. Fuel-tank capacity: 120 liters. Front suspension by unequal length wishbones, transverse leaf spring and Houdaille vane-type hydraulic shock absorbers. Drum brakes of light alloy. Rear suspension: swing axles and hydraulic Houdaille shock absorbers. Wheelbase: 2.16 m (7′ 1″); front track: 1.25 m (4′ 1″); rear track: 1.20 m (3′ 11″). Weight: 700 kg (1,543.2 lb).

In 1949, the 125 was fitted with twin overhead camshafts and a twin-stage Roots supercharger; the compression ratio was increased to 7:1, the power output to 290 hp at 7,500 rpm, and the weight to 730 kg (1,650 lb). In 1950, the power was increased to 290 hp at 7,500 rpm. There was now a 4-speed gearbox, and the De Dion axle was used for the rear suspension. The wheelbase was extended to 2.32 m (7′ 7″) and the weight reduced to 700 kg (1,543.2 lb).

The most illustrious F1 car in Ferrari's formative period, and the first car to beat the Alfa Romeos, the 375 had two, no less illustrious forebears, the 275 and the 340, both with induction engines.

The 275 was built in 1950, again with a 12-cylinder engine (72 mm bore, 68 mm stroke, giving a cylinder capacity of 3322.34 cc in all), 7 mountings; and the crankcase, cylinder block and head all in aluminum alloy. Timing system: single camshaft, 2 valves per cylinder. Carburation: 3 Weber 38 DCF carburetors. 2 magnetos. Compression ratio, 10:1. Power output: 280 hp at 7,000 rpm. Front suspension by unequal wishbones, hydraulic Houdaille shock absorbers; rear suspension with swing axles and De Dion axle. Fuel tank capacity: 160 liters.

The 340 was identical to the 275 except for the engine which had a total cylinder capacity of 4101.66 cc (80 mm bore and 68 mm stroke) with a compression ratio of 11:1 and power output of 325 hp at 7,000 rpm. Fuel tank capacity: 180 liters.

The 375 came into being in the winter of 1950-51 with a cylinder capacity at the upper limit permitted (4493.73 cc.), 3 Weber 40 DCF carburetors, a compression ratio of 11:1, and a power output of 350 hp at 7,000 rpm. In 1951, a version was built with duel ignition, 2 valves per cylinder, a compression ratio of 12:1, and a power output of 380 hp at 7,500 rpm. In 1952 this latest single-seater was fitted out as a Free Formula version: the power output was raised to 390 hp at 7,500 rpm; the tubular frame had smaller tubes; the wheelbase was lengthened to 2.42 m (7′ 11″) (from 2.32 m [7′ 7″] in the 275, 340, and 375); and the weight was reduced to 780 kg (1,755 lb). The 375 won three world championship races in 1951, the first in the history of Ferrari: the British Grand Prix, driven by Froilan Gonzales, the German Grand Prix, and the Italian Grand Prix, both won by Alberto Ascari.

125 F1 - 1949

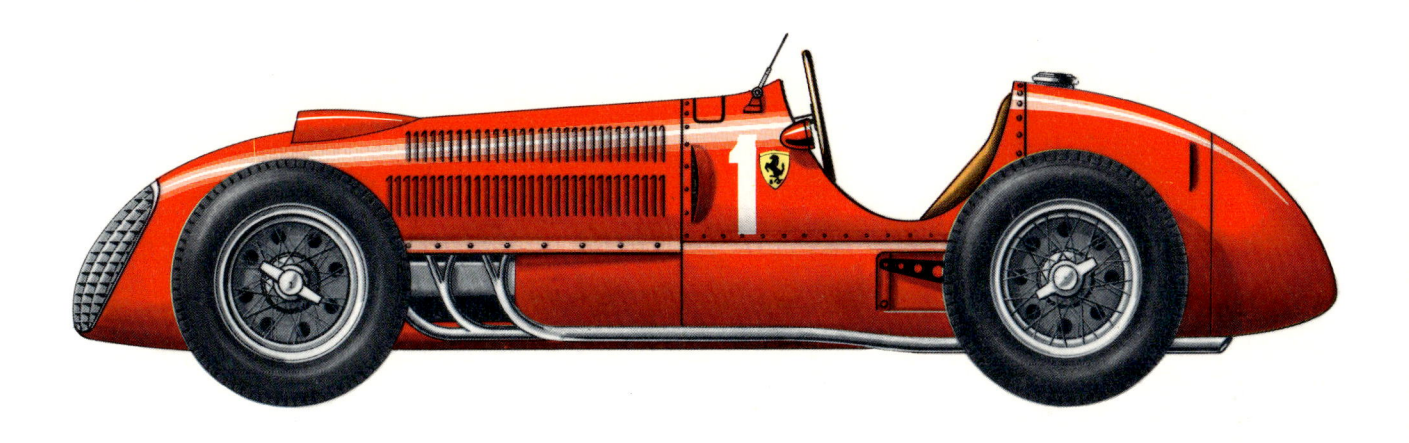

375 F1 - 1951

500 F2 - 1952

Placings of Alberto Ascari's 500 F2 in 1952

RACE	DATE	RESULT
Swiss GP	May 18	did not race
Belgian GP	June 22	1st
French GP	July 6	1st
British GP	July 19	1st
German GP	August 3	1st
Dutch GP	August 17	1st
Italian GP	September 7	1st

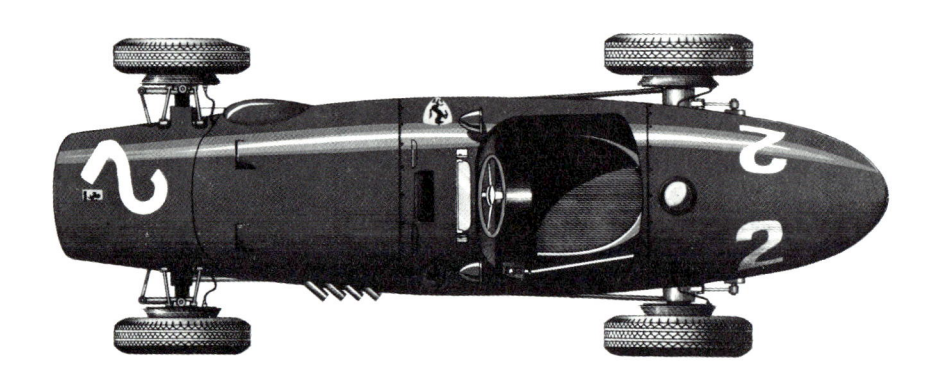

500 F2 - 1952-1953

This is perhaps the most famous (and it was certainly the most victorious) of the single-seater Ferraris, enabling Alberto Ascari to win two world titles (1952 and 1953). It was built in 1951. The engine was designed by Aurelio Lampredi in a single day. The significant novelty of this car was the straight 4-cylinder engine. Hitherto Ferrari had only built 12-cylinder engines. It had a 90 mm bore and a 78 mm stroke, giving a total cylinder capacity of 1984.85 cc; a compression ratio of 13:1; 5 mountings; crankcase and engine-block of aluminum alloy with removable cylinder liners; 2 Weber 50 DCO carburetors; 2 magnetos; 2 valves per cylinder, a power output of 185 hp at 7,500 rpm; dry multi-disk clutch; and 4-speed constant-mesh gearbox. Its frame was tubular with oval members. Front suspension was by wishbones and with Houdaille shock absorbers. Wheelbase: 2.16 m (7' 1''); front track: 1.27 m (4' 2''), rear track 1.25 m (4' 1''). Weight: 560 kg 1,260 lb. Fuel tank capacity: 150 liters.

The unprecedented reliability of this car is illustrated by its performances during the first year of its life. It took part in all the world championship races (seven of them) and won them all. Alberto Ascari, was the driver in all but the Swiss Grand Prix, which the Milanese driver did not enter because he was unsuccessfully competing at Indianapolis. But the Swiss race was won by Piero Taruffi, also driving a Ferrari 500.

The Formula 1 class should really have come to

TECHNICAL DATA

Engine: Ferrari straight 4-cylinder, front
Cylinder capacity: 1985 cc
Bore × stroke: 90 × 78
Power output: 185 hp at 7,500 rpm
Carburation: carburetors
Gearbox: Ferrari 4-speed + reverse
Frame: tubular
Wheelbase: 219.8 cm (86.5'')
Front track: 130.8 cm (51.5'')
Rear track: 124.5 cm (50'')
Weight: 600 kg (1,322.75 lb)

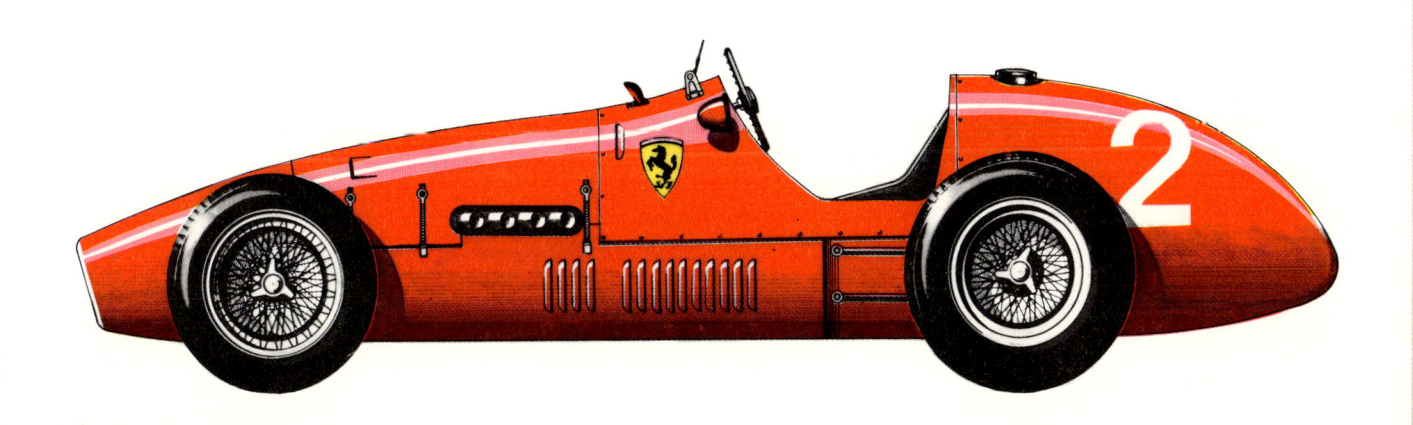

500 F2 - 1952-1953

an end at the end of 1953; but Alfa Romeo's withdrawal from racing and the suspicion, borne out by the facts, that the number of Formula 1 cars participating in the championship was too small to provide a real spectacle, persuaded the International Sporting Committee, under pressure from the race organizers, to promote the Formula 2 class to the rank of the largest formula. This decision enabled Ferrari to consolidate its position as a car builder on the excellent foundations laid by the 375.

Early in 1952 the number of Weber 45 DOE carburetors was increased to 4; the compression ratio was 12:1, the power output remained unchanged, and the weight was increased to 564 kg (1,270 lb). At the end of 1952, the compression ratio was increased again to 12.8:1 and the weight rose to 580 kg (1,305 lb). In its final stage in late 1953, with the adoption of Weber 50 DCOA carburetors, the power output of the 500 F2 touched 190 hp, and the weight was 615 (1,385 lb).

There were eight championship races in all and Ferrari won seven of them. The Italian GP eluded them, however, and was won by the cunning and skillful Juan Manual Fangio in an exciting climax in which, at the south curve, Ascari found his path blocked by the English driver Fairman.

Ascari dominated the racing scene that year, as he had done the year before, and won five races in all, earning his second world title. One win went to Nino Farina at the Nürburgring, a particularly difficult circuit, which he nevertheless found congenial; and another went to Mike Hawthorn after a race-long epic duel with Fangio in the French Grand Prix.

The 500 paved the way for the 625, because the latter was also a 4-cylinder model, but, as was to happen several times as the championship proceeded, Ferrari's fortunes waned, marking the start of an unsettling period.

The 500 phenomenon could not, in effect, be repeated. As time passed racing single-seaters became much more sophisticated, the advent of the rear engine transformed them from top to

Placings of Alberto Ascari's 500 F2 in 1953

RACE	DATE	RESULT
Argentinian GP	January 18	1st
Dutch GP	June 7	1st
Belgian GP	June 21	1st
French GP	July 5	4th
British GP	July 18	1st
German GP	August 2	8th
Swiss GP	August 23	1st
Italian GP	September 13	retired: accident

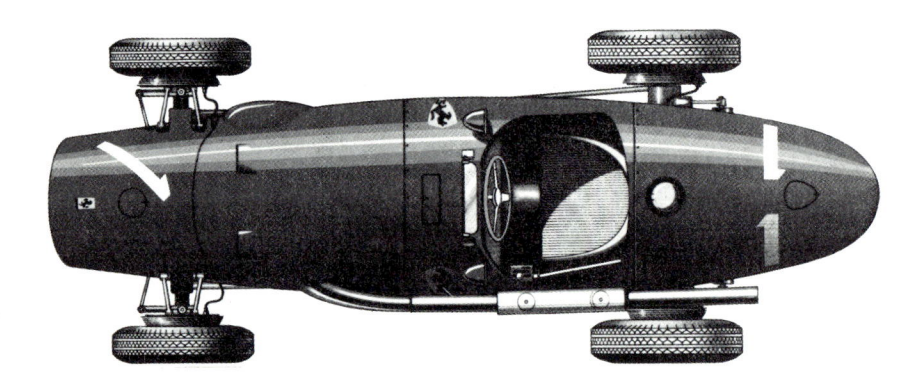

500 F2 - 1953

toe, the new wide tires tended to equalize their performances, and, on the whole, the races became less spectacular. The recurrent theme for all the engineers was the choice of tires, with the combination of one type rather than another. The handling of the cars was greatly affected, giving rise to both over- and under-steering. This is why the Ferrari 500 is one of the last examples of a genuine racing car, a sort of "country cousin," a good all-round car, and very good to drive.

TECHNICAL DATA

Engine: Ferrari straight 4-cylinder, front
Cylinder capacity: 1985 cc.
Bore × stroke: 90 × 78
Power output: 190 hp at 7,500 rpm
Carburation: carburetors
Gearbox: Ferrari 4-speed + reverse
Frame: tubular
Wheelbase: 219.8 cm (86.5")
Front track: 130.8 cm (51.5")
Rear track: 124.5 cm (50")
Weight: 600 kg (1,322.75 lb)

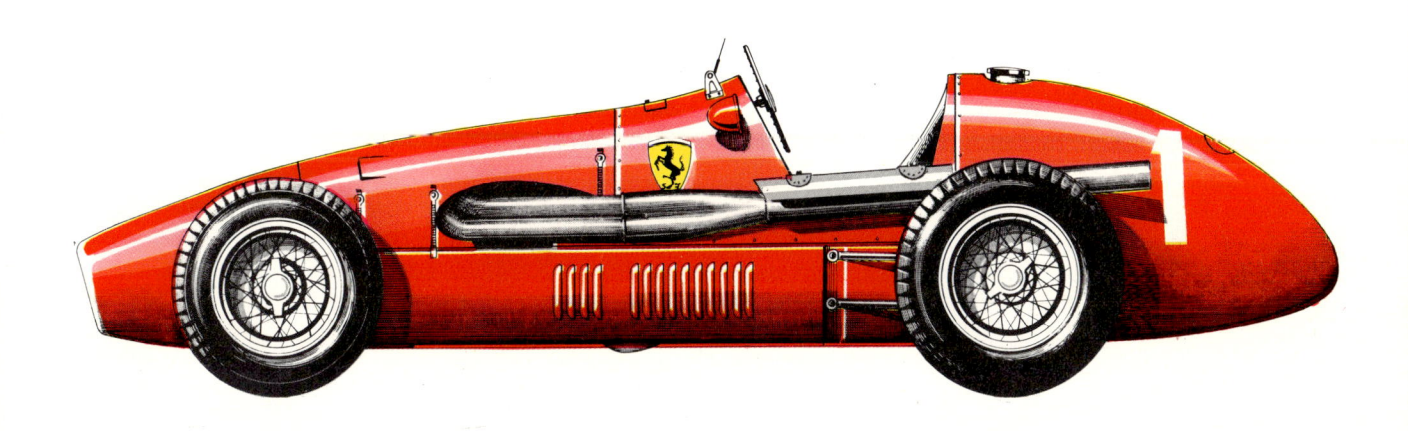

The 625 was developed from the 500 and prepared for the 1954-1960 Formula 1. This admitted engines up to 2500 cc non-supercharged or 750 cc supercharged. In 1958, it became obligatory to use commercial fuel, which put an end to fuel mixtures. No weight limits were imposed.

The 1951-1955 625 was driven by a straight 4-cylinder 2498 cc engine (94 mm bore, 90 mm stroke) on 5 mountings. It had crankcase and cylinder block of aluminum alloy, removable head and cylinder liners, twin overhead camshafts, 2 valves per cylinder. Carburation: 2 Weber 50 DCO carburetors. Power output: 210 hp at 7,000 rpm. Dry multi-disk clutch, constant-mesh 4-speed gearbox. Tubular frame with oval members. Fuel tank capacity: 150 liters. Front suspension by wishbones, transverse leaf springs, hydraulic Houdaille shock absorbers, anti-roll bar; rear suspension with De Dion axle, transverse leaf spring and hydraulic Houdaille shock absorbers. Wheelbase: 2.16 m (7' 1''); front track: 1.27 m (4' 2''); rear track: 1.25 m (4'). Weight: 600 kg (1,322.7 lb).

In 1954, the engine was fitted with two Weber 50 DCOA carburetors and the power output increased to 230 hp at 7,800 rpm. During the season the power output of the engines was increased once more to 245 hp at 7,500 rpm, and the compression ratio rose to 12.8:1.

Overall the 625 was no match for the Maserati 250, and even less for the Mercedes W 196, which raced in 1954 and 1955 and won virtually all the GP events, hands down. The 625 scored just two victories: the win by Froilan Gonzales in the 1954 British Grand Prix when the Mercedes entries had serious trouble with their bodywork, and the other by Trintignant in the Monaco GP in 1955 on a day when the Mercedes were dogged by such bad luck that two were forced to retire (Fangio and Simon), and the third, driven by Moss, crawled home in ninth position.

This car, numbered 533 and also 555, was a complete anomaly in the history of Ferrari, representing as it did an attempt to introduce a different structure by placing two lateral fuel tanks at the height of the driver's seat. Hence the unusual shape of the car, and its name. The Squalo ("Shark") came into being in 1953 as a Formula 2 model. In 1954, it was fitted with an engine which, though having the same cylinder capacity as the 625, had different characteristics: 100 mm bore, 79.5 mm stroke, giving a total cylinder capacity of 2479.6 cc; power output: 240 hp at 7,500 rpm. For the first time a specific power output in excess of 100 hp/liter was achieved with this engine. The Supersqualo made its debut in 1955. The engine data remained the same; the power output was raised to 270 hp at 7,500 rpm with a compression ratio of 14:1, which was very high for those days. Later on, this car was fitted with a 5-speed gearbox, and, in 1956, it was fitted with the V-8 engine of the former Lancia D50. The weight was 630 kg (1,420 lb).

The Squalo and the Supersqualo were not very lucky cars. They scored only one win when Mike Hawthorn won the 1954 Spanish Grand Prix. They were considered unstable by the drivers, who often felt happier at the wheel of the now aging 625. With the 500 F2, the 625, the Squalo, and the Supersqualo, which were also Formula 2 models to begin with, Ferrari came to the end of its experiments with 4-cylinder engines in Formula 1. Except for the 500, these had been fairly unconvincing engines, and had borne little fruit.

In fact the two-year period of the 500 was followed by a period of uncertainty in the top technical circles at Ferrari, a fact made even more evident by the superiority of the Mercedes W 196. The Italian firm was no match with its inadequate cars, which were usually prepared in too much of a hurry.

625 F1 - 1954

553 F2 Squalo - 1953

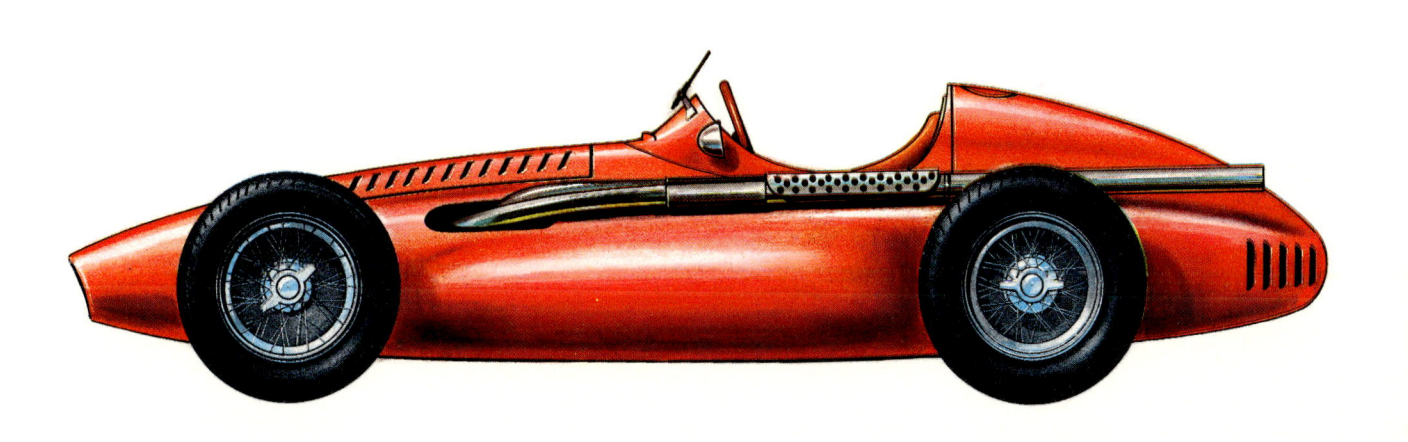

Lancia Ferrari D50 - 1956

The D50s were given to Ferrari by Gianni Lancia after the death of Alberto Ascari at Monza on May 26, 1955. It was all the more timely a "gift" because Ferrari was going through a very delicate period with the 625, the Squalo, and the Supersqualo. Designed by the refined technician Jano, the D50 was a very sound car.

It was powered by a 90° V-8 engine on 5 mountings (73.6 mm bore; 73.1 mm stroke giving a total cylinder capacity of 2488 cc). Timing system: twin overhead camshafts, 2 valves per cylinder. Carburation: 4 Solex 40 PII carburetors. Power output: 250 hp at 8,100 rpm; compression ratio 11.9:1; specific power output 100.5 hp /liter. Dry multi-disk clutch, 5-speed gearbox mounted transversally in the rear part; tubular frame. Front suspension by wishbones, transverse leaf-springs and telescopic dampers; rear suspension with drive-shafts and De Dion axle. Wheelbase 2.28 m (7' 6''), front and rear tracks 1.27 m (4' 2''). Weight: 620 kg (1395 lb); weight; power ratio: 2.48 kg (5.58 lb) hp.

When Ferrari inherited it, the D50 did not

Placings of Juan Manuel Fangio's D50 in 1956

RACE	DATE	RESULT
Argentinian GP	January 22	1st
Monaco GP	May 13	2nd
Belgian GP	June 3	retired: transmission
French GP	July 1	4th
British GP	July 14	1st
German GP	August 5	1st
Italian GP	September 2	2nd

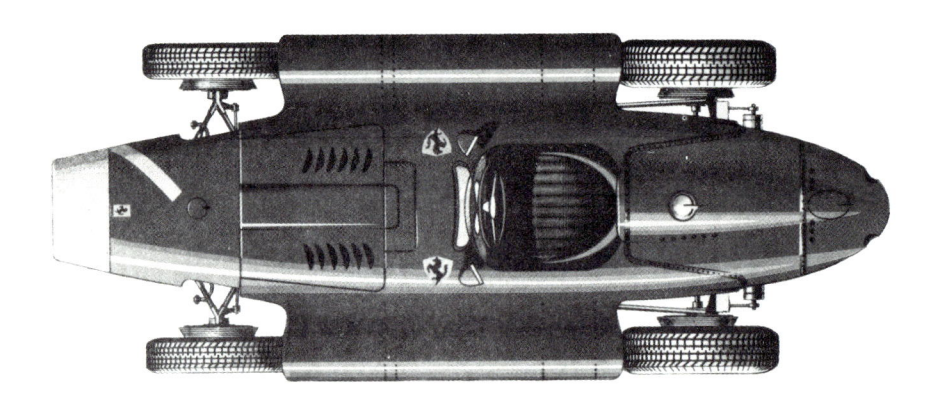

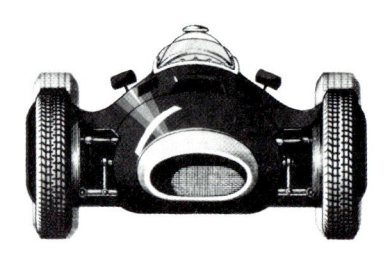

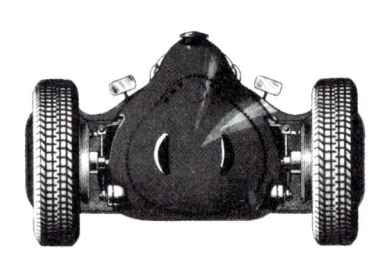

Lancia Ferrari D50 - 1956

undergo any modifications except for the replacement of the Pirelli tires with Engleberts; but in 1956, the power output of the engine was raised to 260 hp at 8,000 rpm (104.5 hp/liter). The frame was altered at the front, and a fuel tank was fitted in the rear section of the car (the two lateral ones stayed put). The total capacity of the three tanks thus reached 190 liters. Modifications were also made to the suspension. The weight increased to 640 kg (1,440 lb), giving a weight: power ratio of 2.4 kg (5.4 lb)/hp). In 1956, a new 8-cylinder model was built with a bore of 76 mm and a stroke of 68.5 mm, giving a total cylinder capacity of 2487 cc, a power output of 265 hp at 8,000 rpm (specific power: 106.5 hp/liter). The weight rose slightly (645 kg [1,450 lb]) as did the weight: power ratio (2.43 kg [5.46 lb]/hp).

During 1956, this single-seater bore the markings: Ferrari-Lancia 801 F1. The engine was again modified (80mm bore, 62mm stroke, total cylinder capacity 2498.8 cc.), the power output increased to a maximum of 275 hp at 8,200 rpm (specific power: 110.2 hp/liter). Fitted with 4 Weber 40 DCS carburetors on an experimental basis, the power output reached 280 hp at 8,500 rpm (specific power: 112.2 hp/liter). When the lateral fuel tanks were done away with, the capacity of the rear one was increased to 185 liters. Small modifications were also made to the frame, and the front track was increased to 1.32 m (4' 4"); the weight totalled 650 kg (1,462 lb) and the weight: power ratio rose to 2.32 kg (5.22 lb)/hp.

TECHNICAL DATA

Engine: Lancia 90° V-8, front.
Cylinder capacity: 2485 cc.
Bore × stroke: 76 × 68.5
Power output: 270 hp at 8,000 rpm.
Carburation: carburetors
Gearbox: Ferrari 4-speed + reverse
Frame: tubular
Wheelbase: 228.7 cm (7' 6")
Front track: 127 cm (4' 2")
Rear track: 127 cm (4' 2")
Weight: 625 kg (1,406 lb)

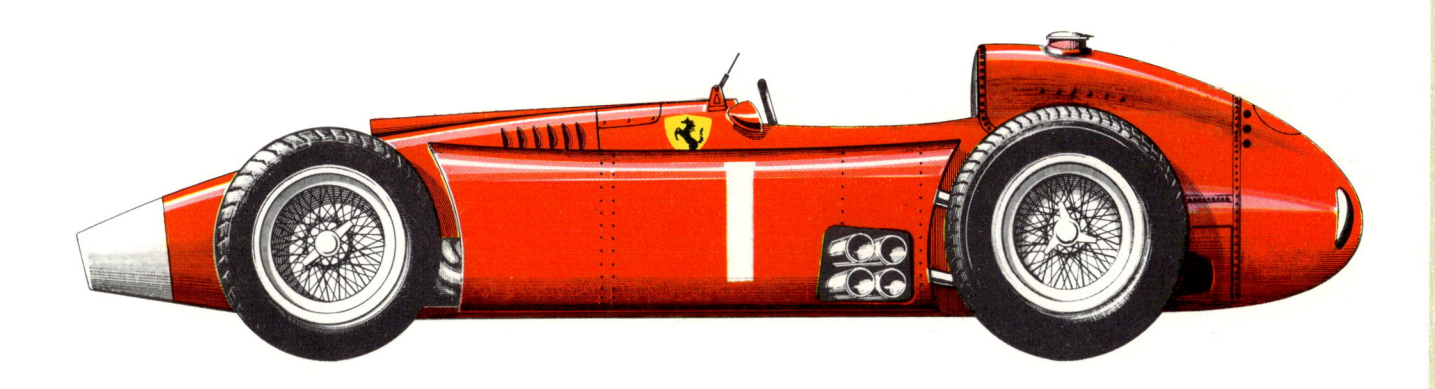

246 F1 - 1958

The 246 marked another decisive turning-point for Ferrari, technically speaking: the 8-cylinder engine was dropped for a V-6, which was called the Dino, in memory of Alfredo ("Alfredino") Ferrari, Enzo's only son. The 246 came into being as a Formula 2 model and was called the 156 F2. Its main feature was the 65° V-engine (73 mm bore, 58.8 mm stroke, giving a total cylinder capacity of 1476.60 cc). Timing system: twin overhead camshafts; power output: 150 hp at 8,000 rpm; compression ratio: 9.2:1. Dry multi-disk clutch; 4-speed gearbox mounted transversely in the rear section; tubular frame. Front suspension by wishbones, coil springs, and hydraulic telescopic Houdaille shock absorbers; rear suspension with driveshafts, De Dion axle, transverse leaf spring and hydraulic Houdaille shock absorbers. Wheelbase: 2.16 m (7' 1"), front track: 1.27 m (4' 2"), rear track: 1.24 m (4' 1"); weight: 512 kg (1,150 lb). In 1957, the Formula 2 became Formula 1.

Placings of Mike Hawthorn's 246 in 1958

RACE	DATE	RESULT
Argentinian GP	January 19	3rd
Monaco GP	May 18	retired: fuel pump
Dutch GP	May 25	5th
Belgian GP	June 15	2nd
French GP	July 6	1st
British GP	July 19	2nd
German GP	August 3	retired: clutch
Portuguese GP	August 24	2nd
Italian GP	September 7	2nd
Moroccan GP	October 19	2nd

246 F1 - 1958

Everything remained the same except, obviously, the engine which was increased by degrees to the maximum cylinder capacity permitted (2500 cc). 1957 saw a 1860 cc. version (76.6 mm bore, × 64.5 mm stroke) with a power output of 215 hp at 8,500 rpm. In 1958, the cylinder capacity was increased again to 2417.33 cc (bore increased to 85 mm, and stroke to 71 mm) and the power output to 250 hp at 8,000 rpm. The other stages of the development of this car can be summarized as follows:

1958 - Engine with the following new features: 86 mm bore, 81 mm stroke, giving a total cylinder capacity of 2474.54 cc; power output: 290 hp at 7,500 rpm; compression ratio: 9.8:1. This engine and the car in which it was mounted took on the marking 256. The 256 also had Dunlop disc brakes.

1959 - 60° V-engine, 86.4 mm bore, 71 mm stroke, with a total cylinder capacity of 2497.62 cc; power output: 245 hp at 7,600 rpm; compression ratio: 11:1. This engine was also called the 256.

1960 - The engine was positioned slightly transversely in relation to the car's axis. The tubular frame was a development of the F2 frame. Lateral fuel tanks and a rear tank with a total capacity of 150 liters. Rear track: 1.30 meters (4' 3'').

1960 - New 65° version: 85 mm bore, 71 mm stroke, giving a total cylinder capacity of 2417.33 cc, a power output of 280 hp at 8,500 rpm, and a compression ratio of 9.1:1. The 246 and 256 Ferraris won two Grand Prix races in 1958 (Hawthorn in France and Collins in Great Britain), two in 1959 (Brooks in France and Germany), and one in 1960 (Phil Hill in Italy). Hawthorn became world champion in 1958.

TECHNICAL DATA

Engine: Ferrari 65° V-6, front.
Cylinder capacity: 2417 cc
Bore × stroke: 85 × 71
Power output: 280 hp at 8,500 rpm
Carburation: carburetors
Gearbox: Ferrari 5-speed + reverse
Frame: tubular
Wheelbase: 235 cm (7' 8.5'')
Front tracks: 123.9 cm (4' 0.7'')
Rear Track: 123.9 cm (4' 0.7'')
Weight: 540 kg (1,215 lb)

156 F1 - 1961

Another radical change took place with the introduction of the new Formula 1 (1961-1965) which admitted engines with a maximum cylinder capacity of 1500 cc and a minimum of 1300 cc with no supercharger in either case. The minimum weight, including oil and water but not fuel was 450 kg (1,010 lb). Automatic starter motor: built in.

Following the trend established by English firms, the 156 was rear engined, but the first experiment with this arrangement was made with a 246 F1, which made its debut, on an experimental basis, in the Monaco GP in 1960. So, in strict chronological order, the first rear-engined Ferrari was a 246.

The 156 came into being directly with the engine situated at the rear, but a Formula 2 model had first been built to this design in the same year as the rear-engined 246. The engine was a 65° V-6: 73 mm bore, 58.8 mm stroke, giving a total cylinder capacity of 1476.60 cc; power output: 185 hp at 9,200 rpm; compression ratio: 9.8:1; weight: 490 kg (1,100 lb).

The 156 F1 had exactly the same characteristics once the cylinder capacity of the F2 had been brought into alignment with that of the new F1. But, at the same time, Ferrari built an engine with different characteristics, which was later preferred. It had a bore of 73 mm and a stroke of 58.8 mm, giving a total cylinder capacity of 1476.60 cc, i.e., identical to the 65° model but with a 120° angle. The power output was 190 hp at 9,500 rpm, and the compression ratio was 9.8:1. In 1962, the 120° model was fitted with a 6-speed gearbox. The power output increased to 200 hp at 10,000 rpm. Wheelbase: 2.35 meters (7' 8.5''); weight: 490 kg (1,100 lb). At the same time, the tubular frame became multi-tubular, with small tubing sections. Shortly after that, during 1962, the wheelbase was reduced to 2.32 meters (7' 7''), the front track changed to 1.34 m (4' 5''),

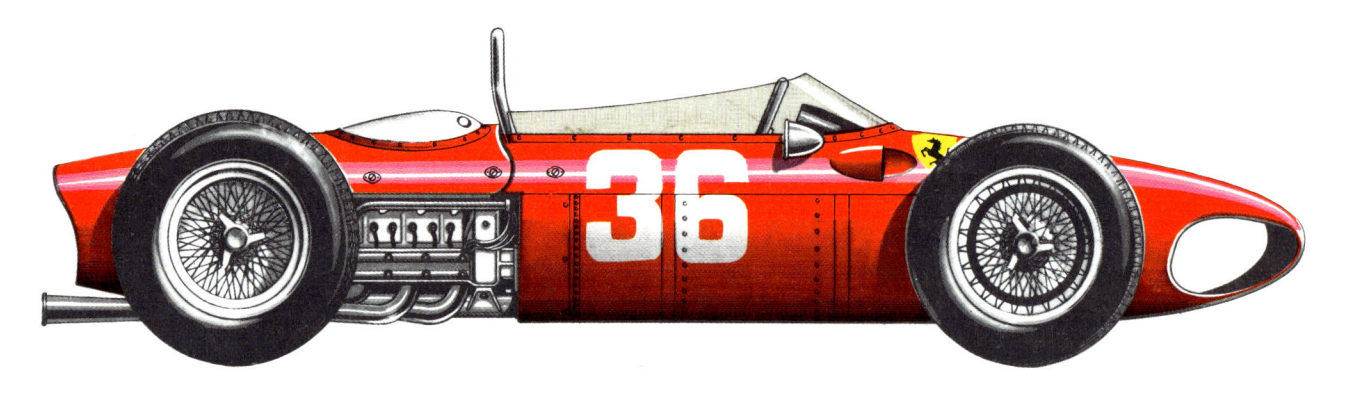

TECHNICAL DATA

Engine: Ferrari 120° V-6, rear
Cylinder capacity: 1476 cc.
Bore × stroke: 73 × 58.8
Power output: 190 hp at 9,500 rpm
Carburation: carburetors
Gearbox: Ferrari 5-speed + reverse
Frame: tubular
Wheelbase: 231.2 cm (7' 7'')
Front track: 120 cm (3' 11'')
Rear track: 120 cm (3' 11'')
Weight: 435 kg (980 lb)

156 F1 - 1961

and the rear track to 1.32 m (4′ 4″). The weight was reduced to 460 kg (1,035 lb).

In 1963 the carburation was by Bosch direct injection (power output: 200 hp at 10,200 rpm). The frame was modified once again, and the weight rose to 465 kg (1,045 lb). The most significant innovation in 1963 was the adoption of a semi-monocoque frame. The weight dropped back to 460 kg (1,035 lb), and the gearbox was once more fitted with 5 speeds.

In the two 65° and 120° versions the 165 won seven races in all (in 1961, von Trips in Holland and Great Britain, Phil Hill in Belgium and Italy, Baghetti in France; Surtees in Germany in 1963; and Bandini in Austria in 1964).

Placings of Phil Hill's 156 in 1961

RACE	DATE	RESULT
Monaco GP	May 14	3rd
Dutch GP	May 22	2nd
Belgian GP	June 18	1st
French GP	July 2	9th
British GP	July 15	2nd
German GP	August 6	3rd
Italian GP	September 10	1st
American GP	October 8	did not race

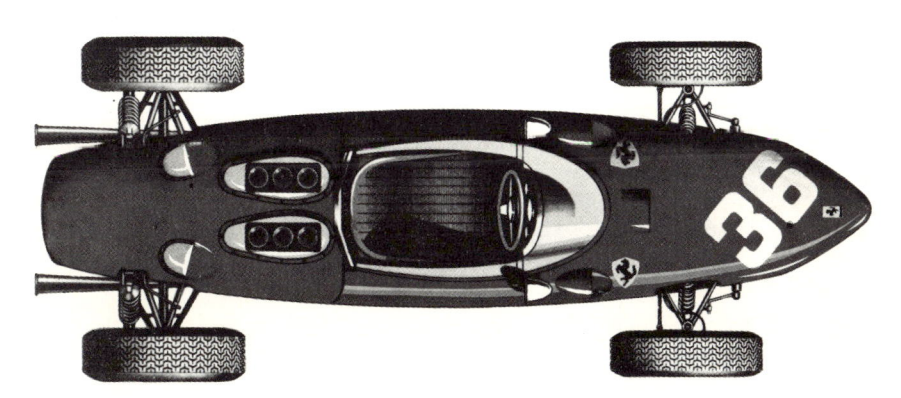

158 F1 - 1964

The 156 had a very successful debut, and dominated the 1961 season, but its supremacy was undoubtedly helped by the fact that the English firms did not have a sound engine during that first year when the new formula came into effect. They did in the following year, and things changed markedly. Ferrari thought that the right moment had come to build a new car, and for the first time in its racing career it used a V-8 engine.

It was ready in late 1963. The engine had a bore of 64 mm, and a stroke of 57.8 mm, giving a total cylinder capacity of 1487.54 cc. It was fitted on 5 mountings. The crankcase, and cylinder block were of aluminum alloy. Timing system: two overhead camshafts for each bank of cylinders; compression ratio: 9.8:1; power output: 190 hp at 10,700 rpm; dry multi-disk clutch. The frame was of monocoque construction and the capacity of the fuel tanks was 125 liters. The front suspension was by wishbones and coil springs; the rear was the same, but with coil spring shock

Placings of John Surtees' 158 in 1964

RACE	DATE	RESULT
Monaco GP	May 10	retired: gearbox
Dutch GP	May 24	2nd
Belgian GP	June 14	retired: engine
French GP	June 28	retired: engine
British GP	July 11	3rd
German GP	August 2	1st
Austrian GP	August 23	retired: suspension
Italian GP	September 6	1st
American GP	October 4	2nd
Mexican GP	October 25	2nd

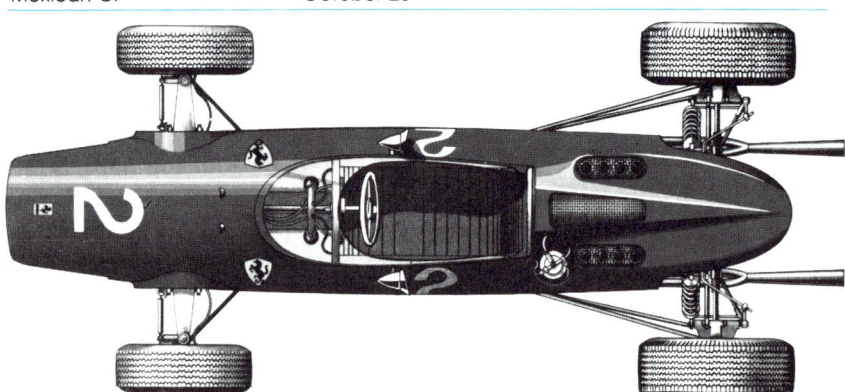

158 F1 - 1964

absorbers. The brakes were of the Dunlop disc type. Wheelbase: 2.38 meters (7′ 10″), front track: 1.35 meters (4′ 5″); rear track: 1.34 meters (4′ 4.5″). Weight 468 kg (1,055 lb). The engine was modified at a later date (67 mm bore, 52.8 mm stroke, with a total cylinder capacity of 1489.33 cc); compression ratio 9.8:1; power output: 210 hp at 11,000 rpm. The front and rear tracks were also modified (1.35 m [4′ 5″]). The 8-cylinder model had a short-lived career and won two Grand Prix events (German and Italian in 1964, both driven by John Surtees, who was the world champion that year).

In 1964 and 1965 Ferrari fielded the 512 F1, which was to become the parent of the 312. The engine had a bore of 56 mm and a stroke of 50.4 mm, giving a total cylinder capacity of 1489.63 cc. It had 7 mountings. Carburation: indirect Lucas injection; 1 spark plug per cylinder; compression ratio 9.8:1; power output 200 hp at 12,000 rpm. Wheelbase: 2.40 meters (7′ 10.5″); weight: 475 kg (1,070 lb).

In 1965, which was the last year of the 1500–1300 formula, the 512 was fitted with 2 spark plugs per cylinder. The power output increased to 225 hp at 11,500 rpm. It went almost unnoticed, but its "boxer" engine was to become one of the strong points of the 312, ten years later.

TECHNICAL DATA

Engine: Ferrari 90° V-8, rear
Cylinder capacity: 1489 cc
Bore × stroke: 67 × 52.8
Power output: 210 hp at 11,000 rpm
Carburation: injection
Gearbox: Ferrari 6-speed + reverse
Frame: monocoque
Wheelbase: 238.7 cm (7′ 10″)
Front track: 135 cm (4′ 5″)
Rear Track: 135 cm (4′ 5″)
Weight: 460 kg (1,035 lb)

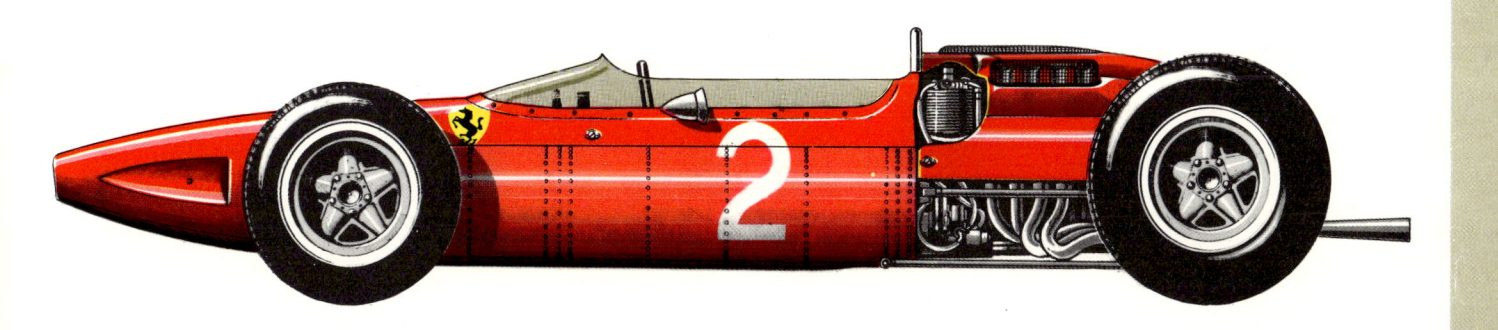

The new Formula 1 came into force in 1966: maximum cylinder capacity 3000 cc, non-supercharged, 1,500 cc supercharged; minimum weight 500 kg (1,125 lb)—in 1969, 530 kg (1,192.5 lb) and in 1973, 575 kg (1,295 lb)—capacity of each fuel tank 80 liters, giving a total capacity of 250 liters, adoption of safety structures designed to protect the driver. Ferrari met the challenge by harking back to its "old flame" the 60° V-12 engine (77 mm bore, 53.5 mm stroke, giving a total cylinder capacity of 2989.56 cc). Power output: 360 hp at 10,000 rpm, compression ratio 11:2, dry multi-disk clutch, 5-speed gearbox, monocoque frame. Fuel tank capacity: 150 liters. Suspension by wishbones, rear coil springs, coil spring shock absorbers, Girling disc brakes. Wheelbase: 2.40 meters (7' 10.5''); front track: 1.45 (4' 9''); rear track: 1.43 (4' 8''). Weight: 595 kg (1,338 lb).
This car should have been the best candidate in the first year of the new Formula 1, given that once again the English were without a competitive engine, but the 312 only won one race, and turned out to be too heavy.
During the Italian Grand Prix, which Lodovico Scarfiotti turned into the only Formula 1 win of his life, the 312's 12 cylinders had already undergone a major modification with the adoption of a third valve (two inlet and one exhaust). The compression ratio was also reduced to 10.5:1 and the power output rose to 375 hp at 10,000 rpm.
Its unsatisfactory performance in the championship was undoubtedly aggravated by the fact that John Surtees left Ferrari. His place was filled by compatriot Mike Parkes, who was not a Formula 1 driver and was only promoted to that sector out of force of circumstance. Scarfiotti was, in turn, used in Formula 1 from the German GP on. Two weeks later, he won the Italian Grand Prix, not least because of the altruistic behavior of Parkes.

Ferrari embarked on the new season with the same car used in the 1966 Italian Grand Prix, except for an increase in the compression ratio (to 11:1) and in the power output (to 385 hp at 10,000 rpm). The fuel tank capacity was reduced to 140 liters. The front track and the rear were modified (to 1.55 m [5' 1''] and 1.53 m [5' 0''] respectively). The weight was dropped to 550 kg (1,237 lb).
During 1967 the Ferrari underwent another major change: 48 valves, i.e., 4 per cylinder; compression ratio 11.8:1; 390 hp at 10,500 rpm; weight 530 kg (1,192 lb). But the season bore little fruit. 1967 was one of the few years when Ferrari won no races at all. The appearance of the 8-cylinder Ford-Cosworth put the English engineers back at the top of the league, but the person most harmed by the arrival of this engine was Jack Brabham, who had given added proof of his thriftiness and perspicacity in his choice of an apparently worthless engine, the Australian 8-cylinder Repco, taken from the Oldsmobile engine block. A Brabham won the world championship for the second time in 1967 (Brabham had also won it in 1966). But things went badly for him in 1968; and in 1970 Jack Brabham was also forced to resort to the 8-cylinder Ford-Cosworth engine.
Beginning in 1969 Ferrari found new faith in the 60° V-12 engine with 48 valves; the power output was raised first to 412 hp at 10,500 rpm and subsequently to 436 hp at 11,000 rpm. All it could achieve, however, was one win in the hands of Jacky Ickx in the 1968 French Grand Prix in a rain-lashed race which certainly helped the Belgian driver to victory. Shortly before the start, it was decided to alter the tread of his car's tires by hand. And as a result, Ickx was the only man, that day, to race with wet-weather tires.

312 F1 - 1966

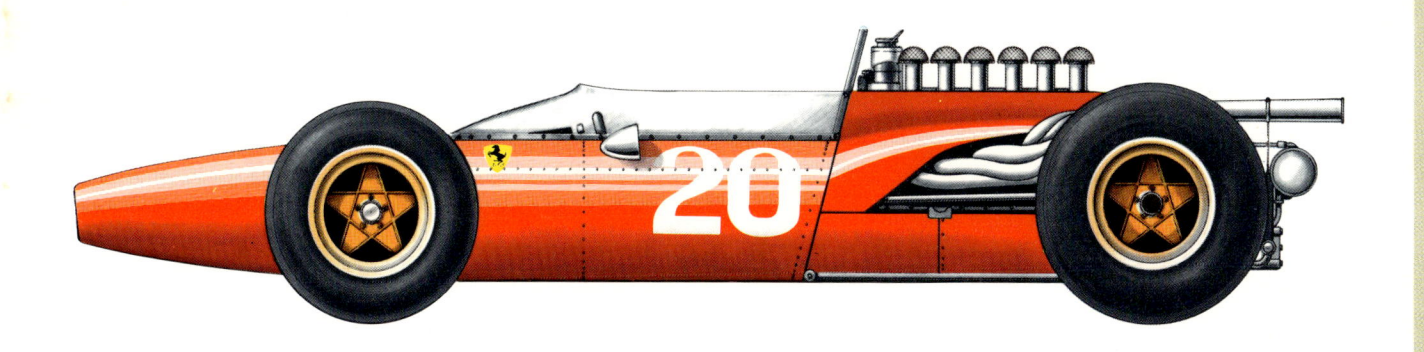

312 F1 - 1967

73

The Flat-12 was built in 1969 and made its debut in the 1970 South African Grand Prix, driven by Jacky Ickx. In that maiden version, it had a bore of 78.5 mm and a stroke of 51.5 mm, giving a total cylinder capacity of 2,991.01 cc. There were 4 mountings; the crankcase and cylinder-block were of aluminum alloy, with cast iron cylinder liners. Timing system: twin overhead camshafts, 2 inlet and 2 exhaust valves; carburation: Lucas injection; transistorized Marelli ignition; compression ratio 11.8:1; power output 455 hp at 11,500 rpm; dry multi-disk clutch, 5-speed gearbox; monocoque frame, fuel tank capacity 200 liters. Front suspension by wishbones, with coil spring shock absorbers; rear suspension by swing-axles, wishbones, and coil spring shock absorbers; Girling disc brakes; wheelbase: 2.38 meters (7' 10''); front track: 1.56 m (5' 1''), rear track: 1.57 m (5' 2''); weight: 534 kg (1,200 lb).

The 12-cylinder "boxer"-type engine was not new to the Ferrari works, having been used without much success in a Formula 1 1500, the 512, and with much more positive results in a 2000 cc sports car, the 212 E.

The choice of the Flat 12 proved to be a happy one from the 1970 season onwards. Four Grand Prix races were won in that season, three by Jacky Ickx (the Austrian, Canadian and Mexican) and one by Regazzoni (the Italian GP). Such was the superiority of the 312 B at the close of the season that the English firms actually considered that the days of their 8-cylinder Ford-Cosworth were now numbered.

Ickx was in the running for the world championship title, but this went posthumously to Jochen Rindt. After a dazzling start to the season, Rindt died in trials for the Italian Grand Prix at Monza in a crash which may have been caused by suspension failure.

In 1971 the 312 B had its power output increased to 470 hp by considerably raising the rpm to 12,500; this made the Ferrari Flat-12 one of the fastest-revving engines going. The frame of the car was also modified, in particular the rear suspension. The Girling disc brakes were replaced by Lockheed brakes. Weight: 540 kg (1,215 lb). The power : weight ratio thus became one of the lowest in the whole range of Ferrari cars (1.15 kg [2.58 lb] / hp). But the 312 B2 did not live up to the expectations of the previous year and won only two races, the South African Grand Prix driven by Mario Andretti and the Dutch Grand Prix driven by Jacky Ickx. In fact, the former drove the 312 B and not the new B2 in South Africa.

Given the much better over-all results obtained by the B, when compared with the B2, it was thought that the B had been replaced in too much of a hurry, in as much as it had not played all its cards. The B2 plunged designers and engineers into a state of despair.

A significant debilitating factor was that the racing team was starting to fall to pieces, because Ickx was becoming more and more lax and disinclined to collaborate in the preparation of the car—always a vital task.

Andretti only raced in four of the eleven championship races (South Africa, Spain, Germany and Canada). The Italo-American was still undecided whether to aim for the world title or deal with his many commitments in the United States. He tried to do both, but to little effect. It was the fact that Mario Andretti was often unavailable that induced Ferrari to use Regazzoni, who had made his Formula 1 debut with a Ferrari in the 1970 Dutch Grand Prix. Regazzoni was to have taken turns in Formula 1 with Ignazio Giunti, but the Roman driver lost his life on January 10, 1971, in Buenos Aires.

312 B - 1970

312 B2 - 1971

75

In 1972 Ferrari once again used the 312 B2, although with much retouching. The engine underwent major modifications which accentuated its "super-square" features: the bore was raised to 80 mm, and the stroke reduced to 49.6 mm, giving a total cylinder capacity which was slightly larger than that of the previous engine (2991.80 as opposed to 2991.01 cc). The fuel tank capacity rose to 220 liters. The front suspension was altered by moving the spring coil shock absorbers outside the body. 13-inch wheels were also used back and front.

1972 was also a lean year. The B2 only won one race, driven by Jacky Ickx in the German Grand Prix, on a circuit which particularly suits the Belgian driver. At the end of the season he had collected a fairly modest 27 points as compared with Emerson Fittipaldi's 61, Jackie Stewart's 45, and Dennis Hulme's 39.

In addition to coming in first in Germany, Ickx came in second at Monaco and in Spain, third in Argentina, and fifth in the United States. Once again, Andretti only took part in a few races (Argentina, South Africa, Spain, Italy, and the United States), thus reconfirming that he was unavailable as a full-time driver for Ferrari. From the "historical" point of view, 1972 was an important year, because it marked the beginning of the massive activity of sponsors who had nothing to do with motor racing. Lotus, which was financed by a cigarette manufacturer, gave up its own colors and took on those of John Player; it also took on the latter's name, thus erasing its own far more glorious one. It is hard to say whether the interference of sponsors, or "backers," has been beneficial or otherwise. There is no doubt that running a team of racing cars, or even one car, was costing colossal sums of money back in 1972, and the Grand Prix organizers were no longer in a position to secure such sums.

The 1973 B 3 was another unlucky car. That year, once again, Ferrari failed to win a single race, despite the ritual modifications made to the latest single-seater, whose power output was raised to 485 hp at 12,500 rpm. The car's outline was refashioned by moving the lateral radiator to a point in front of the rear wheels (later on, a single forward-placed radiator was fitted). The fuel tank capacity was reduced to 175 liters, the front track to 1.62 meters (5′ 4″) and the rear track to 1.60 meters (5′ 3″). The weight rose to 578 kg (1,300 lb), giving an increased power : weight ratio—compared with the B2—of 1.19 kg (2.67 lb) / hp. Towards the end of the season, the B3 underwent further modifications, with the radiators being repositioned once again (water and oil were located together behind the front wheels).

This was the last year which Jacky Ickx spent with Ferrari. The Belgian was on the verge of leaving Maranello and did not even complete the season. Both parties peacefully rescinded the contract after the Italian Grand Prix. The atmosphere of demobilization which reigned at Ferrari is attested to by the fact that Ferrari abandoned the Dutch Grand Prix and the German Grand Prix, although Ickx took part in the latter with a McLaren. In the Austrian Grand Prix, Ferrari was represented by Merzario alone and in the Italian race by Merzario and, for the last time, Ickx. Merzario took part in the last two GP races of the season (the Canadian and the American).

Once again the same situation which followed the loss of a driver of Surtees' caliber recurred. One party was no longer capable of meeting the requirements of the other. The fact that Ickx was not available as a test driver brought things to a head.

This was the year in which another celebrated driver, Jackie Stewart, also gave up racing after 99 world championship events and three titles.

312 B2 - 1972

312 B3 - 1973

312 B3 - 1974

The B3 took on a completely different appearance from the 1974 Dutch Grand Prix onwards as a result of the reinstatement of the engineer Mauro Forghieri as head of Ferrari's technical staff. The most salient feature of the new B3 was the forward position of the driving seat and the unusually high intake behind the driver. The 1974 B3 was much more compact than previous models with a wheelbase of 2.51 meters (8' 3''), a front track of 1.59 meters (5' 2.5''), a rear track of 1.62 meters (5' 4''), and a weight of 590 kg (1,327 lb).

This car marked the real comeback of Ferrari to the world championship scene, greatly boosting the close collaboration that existed between Forghieri, Rocchi, and Bussi, who were responsible for the "renaissance" of the single-seater. And results were quick to come in. The newly acquired driver, Niki Lauda, won the Spanish and Dutch Grands Prix, while Regazzoni won in Germany and came in second in the Brazilian, Spanish, Dutch and Canadian Grands Prix.

In that year Clay Regazzoni narrowly missed winning the title, mainly because of the age-old custom at Ferrari of not designating a team chief, not even as the racing season proceeded, showing the cumulative results of each driver. Lauda and Regazzoni did battle with each other throughout the season, and Fittipaldi clinched the championship title by just three points (55 to 52) from the Swiss driver, who truly missed a golden opportunity. He was never to have another one like it. The narrowly missed title was all the more irritating, because the championship was in fact decided in the last race of the season, the American Grand Prix, in which Ferrari should have focused on a sole tactic: keeping Fittipaldi in check and letting Regazzoni stay ahead of him, even if only by one place (before this race both drivers had the same number of points: 52). The edginess that was rife in the ranks of the Italian team was immediately evident. Regazzoni broke three engines in trials and came in eleventh, while Fittipaldi finished fourth.

312 T - 1975   312 T2 - 1976

After the "boxer"-type engine, the second major innovation of the Ferrari 312 was the transverse gearbox; in 1975 this gave rise to the first 312 T. At the same time, the engine had its power output increased once more to 500 hp at 12,200 rpm, with a weight: power ratio among the best going (3.12 kg [7.02 lb] / hp). The frame was also further modified, especially where size was concerned. In the T the wheelbase was 2.51 meters (8' 3") as it was in the 312 B3, but the front and rear tracks were reduced to 1.53 m (5' 0"). The overall weight rose slightly by 8 kg (18 lb) to 598 kg (1,345 lb).

The T was used earlier than planned (in the South African Grand Prix) because of the unsatisfactory performance of the B3 in the first two championship races of 1975 (in Argentina Regazzoni came fourth and Lauda, sixth; in Brazil Regazzoni was again fourth and Lauda, fifth).

In South Africa, Lauda came in fifth, and in the next race (the Spanish Grand Prix) the two Ferrari drivers damaged each other's cars at the start because of a rash maneuver by Andretti But from the fifth race, the Monaco Grand Prix,

Niki Lauda in the 312T with which he won the 1975 world championship.

312 T - 1975

Placings of Niki Lauda's 312 T in 1975

RACE	DATE	RESULT
Argentinian GP	January 12	6th
Brazilian GP	January 26	5th
South African GP	March 2	5th
Spanish GP	April 27	retired: accident
Monaco GP	May 11	1st
Belgian GP	May 25	1st
Swedish GP	June 8	1st
Dutch GP	June 22	2nd
French GP	July 6	1st
British GP	July 19	8th
German GP	August 3	3rd
Austrian GP	August 17	6th
Italian GP	September 7	3rd
American GP	October 5	1st

TECHNICAL DATA

Engine: Ferrari (''boxer'') Flat-12, rear
Cylinder capacity: 2992 cc
Bore $\times$ stroke: 80 $\times$ 49.6
Power output: 495 hp at 12,200 rpm
Carburation: injection
Gearbox: Ferrari 5-speed + reverse
Frame: monocoque
Wheelbase: 251.8 cm (8' 3'')
Front track: 151 cm (4' 11.5'')
Rear Track: 153 cm (5' 0.25'')
Weight: 575 kg (1,294 lb)

Lauda won a surprising number of races (in addition to winning at Monte Carlo, he also won in Belgium, Sweden, France and the United States) and thus won his first world title. Regazzoni placed fifth in the championship ranks, with one win in the Italian Grand Prix. The T's superiority was also demonstrated by the fact that Lauda often started in first position because of this car's exceptional road-holding qualities. The way the championship proceeded was also helped by the fact that there was no longer any rivalry between Lauda and Regazzoni; the Austrian was considered to be Ferrari's number-one driver and Regazzoni serenely accepted the role of second lead.

1976 saw the appearance of the T2, which was little different from the T. The body was modified, in accordance with the regulations, with the addition of a tubular structure in the front section. The rear suspension was rounded off by inverted lower wishbones, with a narrower base. When this car was shown off to the press, there was talk of a possible use of the De Dion axle, but this never actually materialized. The T2's wheelbase was lengthened to 2.56 meters (8' 5''), the front track was 1.40 m (5' 5'') and the rear track 1.43 m (5' 6''). With an overall weight of 575 kg (1,294 lb), there was a very positive weight : power ratio of 1.15 kg (2.58 lb) / hp.

The T2 was used for the first time in the Spanish Grand Prix, after Lauda had already won in Brazil (the first race of the season) and in South Africa, and Regazzoni had romped home first in the United States-West Grand Prix. In Spain, Lauda finished second. The season continued brilliantly, with two more wins for Lauda (in Belgium and Monaco), and a third place in Sweden. Lauda's success was interrupted in France, where he had to retire; but two weeks later he came back as strongly as ever in the British Grand Prix. At that point he was so far ahead of his rivals that it was more than certain that the second world title was his, but in the German Grand Prix at the Nürburgring he was involved in a very serious accident, which put even his life in danger. To everyone's surprise and admiration, he was back on the scene in time to take part in the Italian Grand Prix, where he came in fourth after missing only the Austrian and Dutch races. There were still three Grand Prix events to go. He came in eighth in Canada and fourth in the United States. The struggle for the title had narrowed down to a duel between Lauda and Hunt. In Japan the Englishman came in third, while Lauda retired: for the first time he had been afraid, possibly because of the bad weather conditions. James Hunt won the title by a single point.

312 T2 - 1976

312 T2 - 1977

The size of the 1977 T2 was completely revolutionized to comply with the new rules and regulations which had come into force since the 1976 Spanish Grand Prix. These changes took the form of an extended wheelbase (2.56 meters [8' 4.5"]) and shorter tracks (front: 1.40 m [4' 7"], rear: 1.43 m [4' 8"]); the maximum length was increased by 17 cm (6.7") (from 4.14 to 4.31 meters [13.5 to 14.1']); the width was reduced by 10 cm (4") (from 2.03 to 1.93 m [80 to 76"]); and the height by 15 cm [6"] (from 1.27 to 1.12 m [50 to 44"]). The T2 was to have adopted the De Dion rear axle with the tubular structure and fairings on the front wheels, but these two major innovations never actually materialized. Because of the 500 hp developed by the engine at 12,000 rpm, as opposed to the 495 hp of the T at the same speed, the T2 is reckoned to be the Formula 1 single-seater Ferrari with the best weight : power ratio (1.15 kg [2.58 lb] / hp).

The T2 made its debut with Lauda and Reutemann in the first race of the 1977 season, the Argentinian Grand Prix, with Reutemann coming in third. Lauda was forced to retire with engine trouble. Reutemann came in first in the next race (the Brazilian Grand Prix) and Lauda, third. The latter won the next Grand Prix, in South Africa, and in the latter half of the season went on to win in Germany and Holland. In addition he came in second on six occasions (USA-West, Monaco, Belgium, Britain, Austria, and Italy). By the end of the championship he had chalked up 72 points in all, against Scheckter's 55, thus winning his second world championship title. Reutemann placed fourth, with one win and two second places to his credit.

The T2 was a transitional car between the T and the revolutionary T3 of 1978.

312 T2 - 1977

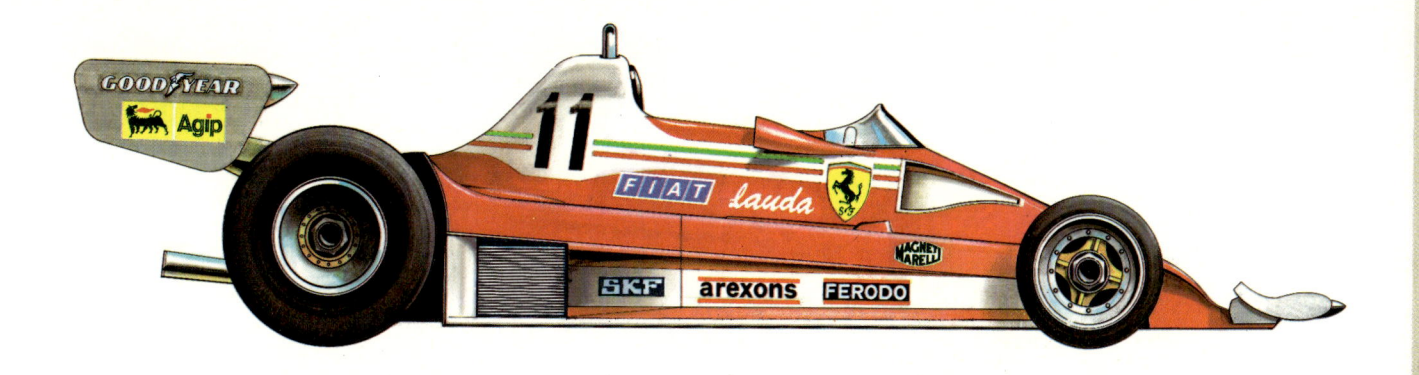

Placings of Niki Lauda's 312 T2 in 1977.

RACE	DATE	RESULT
Argentinian GP	January 9	retired: engine
Brazilian GP	January 23	3rd
South African GP	March 5	1st
USA-West GP	April 13	2nd
Spanish GP	May 8	did not race
Monaco GP	May 22	2nd
Belgian GP	June 5	2nd
Swedish GP	June 19	retired: road holding
French GP	July 3	5th
British GP	July 16	2nd
German GP	July 31	1st
Austrian GP	August 14	2nd
Dutch GP	August 28	1st
Italian GP	September 11	2nd
USA-West GP	October 2	4th
Canadian GP	October 9	did not race
Japanese GP	October 23	did not race

TECHNICAL DATA

Engine: Ferrari 12-cylinder ("boxer")
Cylinder capacity: 2991.8 cc
Bore × stroke: 80 × 49.6
Power output: 500 hp at 12,200 rpm
Carburation: injection
Gearbox: Ferrari 5-speed + reverse
Wheelbase: 256 cm (8' 4.5")
Front track: 140 cm (4' 7")
Rear Track: 143 cm (4' 8")
Weight: 575 kg (1,294 lb)

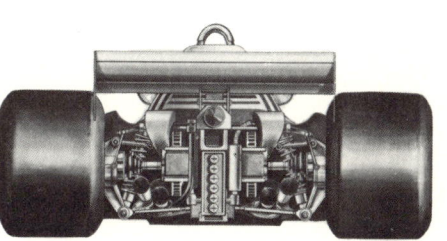

312 T3 - 1978

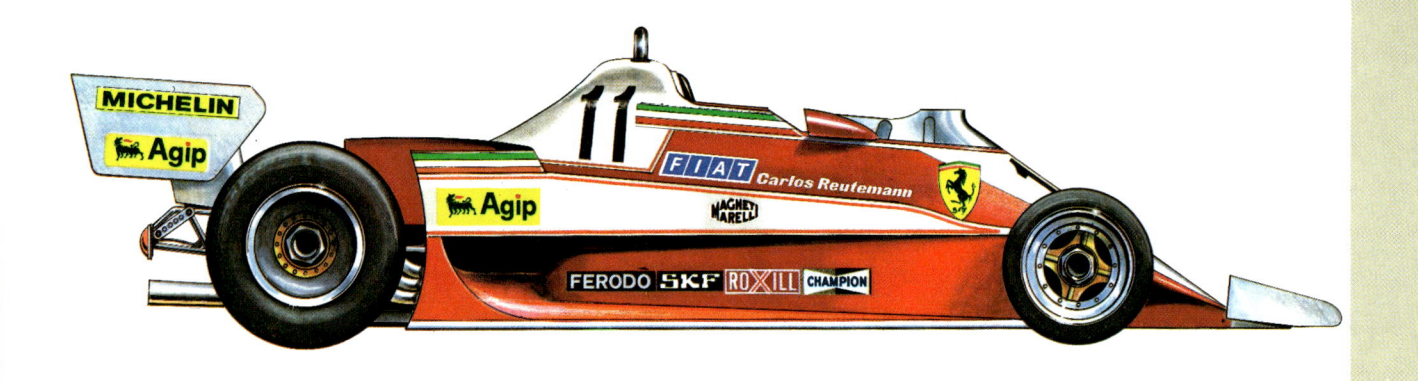

In the words of the Ferrari company itself, the T3 represented a development of the T series, which began in 1976 and was characterized by a "complete evolutionary independence from every group, in such a way that the research could be carried out virtually independently, sector by sector." The most obvious and striking feature was the aerodynamic aspect, in the fullest sense of the term. Tests in the Pininfarina wind tunnel and at Fiat underlined the importance of being able to carry out very accurate studies in the field of aerodynamic interactions.

The engine-gearbox complex was considerably modified in terms of various basic components and the frame-suspension layout was radically redesigned, taking into account the various aspects relating to the tires available in that year as well as those which appeared during 1977. In addition, the greatest importance was attached, in the T3, to the safety of the driver in the event of an accident, by increasing the impact-absorbent capacity of the cockpit unit under deformation. Lastly, the possibilities of fuel leaks from connections and tubing were reduced, making the most of results obtained in recent years in European and American races.

The power output of the engine was slightly raised (510 hp at the same 12,200 rpm, with an unchanged compression ratio of 11.5:1). The dimensions, on the other hand, were substantially modified when compared with the T2 (wheelbase: 2.56 - 2.70 meters [8' 5'' 8' 10'']; front track: 1.62 m [5' 4'']; rear track: 1.58 m [5' 2'']; length: 4.25 m [13.9']; width: 2.13 m [7' 0'']; height: 1.01 m [3' 4'']; weight: 580 kg [1,305 lb].

When Lauda moved to Brabham-Alfa Romeo, Ferrari's two drivers were Reutemann and Villeneuve. The T3 met the public for the first time in the South African Grand Prix, but both Reutemann and Villeneuve retired. Reutemann scored the first win soon afterwards, however, in the USA-West Grand Prix. Reutemann won the British and American Grands Prix, while Villeneuve came home first in Canada. Reutemann also won a fourth race (Brazilian Grand Prix) in 1978, but driving the T2.

312 T4 - 1979

In the year when all the builders of Formula 1 single-seater cars hurriedly adopted the aerodynamic principles proposed by Lotus with the "79" (1978), which subsequently gave rise to the "wing-cars," the T4 represented a halfway mark between past and present. The T4 is not a "wing-car," or not altogether, because of its "boxer" engine which prohibits the full application of the principles on which "wing-cars" are based. But Ferrari has called the T4 "the compendium of in-depth studies of *internal aerodynamics* carried out in the Pininfarina wind tunnel, on the basis of the recent research techniques, on a new model and on previous Ferrari cars."

The T4 has also been called "a car with an integral *internal flow* system, as indicated by the absence of air intakes and outlets. At the same

Jody Scheckter driving the 312T4 in the running for the 1979 world championship.

85

312 T4 - 1979

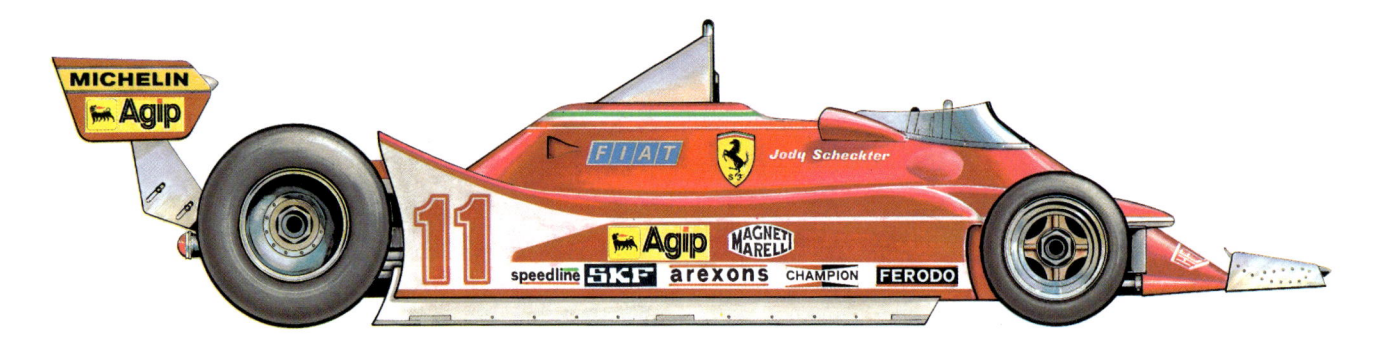

Placings of Jody Scheckter's 312 T4 in 1979

RACE	DATE	RESULT
Argentinian GP	January 21	retired: accident (T3)
Brazilian GP	February 4	6th (T3)
South African GP	March 3	2nd
USA-West GP	April 8	2nd
Spanish GP	April 29	4th
Belgian GP	May 13	1st
Monaco GP	May 27	1st
French GP	July 1	7th
British GP	July 14	5th
German GP	July 29	4th
Austrian GP	August 12	4th
Dutch GP	August 26	2nd
Italian GP	September 9	1st
Canadian GP	September 30	4th
USA-East GP	October 7	retired: flat tire

TECHNICAL DATA

Engine: Ferrari Flat-12 ("boxer"), rear
Cylinder capacity: 2991.8 cc
Bore × stroke: 80 × 49.6
Power output: 515 hp at 12,300 rpm
Carburation: injection
Gearbox: Ferrari 5-speed + reverse
Wheelbase: 270 cm (8' 10")
Front track: 170 cm (5' 7")
Rear track: 160 cm (5' 3")
Weight: 590 kg (1,327 lb)

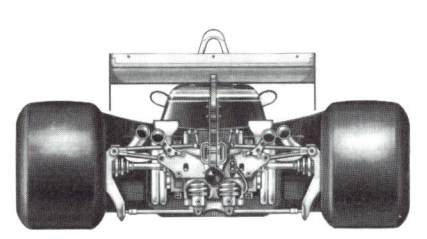

312 T4 - 1979

time, systems have been used which make it possible to increase the negative lift on the basis of the combined aerodynamic effects between body and ground. The moving and rigid bulkheads have, by harmonizing the two flows (internal-external), made it possible to obtain high negative vertical loads which act more efficiently on the car." The transverse gearbox stayed put, but the power output of the engine increased to 515 hp at 12,300 rpm. The T4's dimensions are, front track: 1.70 m (5' 7"), rear track: 1.60 m (5' 3"), length: 4.46 m (14.6'), width: 2.12 m (6' 11"), height: 1.01 m (3' 4"), wheelbase 2.70 m (8' 10"); weight: 590 kg (1,327 lb).

Driven by Scheckter and Villeneuve, the T4 made its debut at the South African Grand Prix (T3s were used for the first two races of the season), and over all won six races (Scheckter, three and Villeneuve, three) out of the fourteen in which it took part. It also came in second on seven occasions, thus enabling the two Ferrari drivers to end up first and second in the world championship ranks, and putting the F1 Constructors' Cup in the hands of the firm from Modena.

312 T5 - 1980

In the wake of the experience gained in 1979, the T5 is more of a "wing-car" than the T4 was, but it is not a thoroughbred in this sense; because the engine used is still the Flat-12, which has a considerable transverse bulk when compared with the Ford-Cosworth and Alfa Romeo 60° V-8.

In anticipation of a new "boxer"-type, 12-cylinder engine the heads have been altered, with a gain of 5 cm (2"); the suspension has been modified, as has the aerodynamic efficiency, by broadening the "wings" inside which the airflow passes and contracting the body.

TECHNICAL DATA
Engine: Ferrari Flat-12 ("boxer"), rear
Cylinder capacity: 2991.8cc
bore × stroke: 80 × 49.6
Power output: 515 hp at 12,300 rpm
Carburation: injection
Gearbox: Ferrari 5-speed + reverse
Wheelbase: 270 cm (8' 10")
Front track: 175 cm (5' 9")
Rear track: 165 cm (5' 5")
Weight: 595 kg (1,339 lb)

The T5 shown at Fiorano on November 26, 1979, bore number 42. This means that, on average, ten series T cars have been built a year.
Ferrari, incidentally, is still busy building and developing a 1500 cc V-6 car, powered by a turbo-compressor, similar to the Renault. Alfa Romeo-Autodelta is also following this path.

The Ferrari Drivers

A HUNDRED MEN IN SEARCH OF GLORY

There was a time when you had to line up if you wanted to drive a Ferrari racing car, whether it was Formula 1, Formula 2 or a sports model. There was a sort of employment office at Modena and Commendatore Enzo (he was not yet officially "Ingenere") took no small delight in keeping the applicant waiting, at times taking him on under precise conditions, and at others sending him away.

Nowadays things have changed. Drivers are offered hundreds of thousands of pounds or dollars, or hundreds of millions of lire. The participation of perfume and tobacco companies has spoiled the world of racing and put an old fox like Enzo Ferrari in a situation which is diametrically opposed to that of the past. Now it is Enzo Ferrari who awaits the answer to an offer, anxious to have the very best driver, but also worrying that at the last moment some meddling sponsor might send everything up in smoke.

Ferrari scored a bull's-eye with Lauda. When Regazzoni pointed out the Austrian to him, he was not a proven driver, rather just a hopeful. Lauda did not strike a truly hard bargain, and he amply repaid Ferrari for the trust he had in him by winning fifteen Grand Prix races in the four years in which they worked together (1974-1977 inclusive). In this sense Lauda was one of the best investments made by the old wizard of Modena, because Lauda's performance was consistent and, more importantly, he turned out to be a very valuable collaborator when it came to preparing the cars. After a settling-in period, he shed his apparent shyness and acquiescence and started to lay down the law, aware by now of his own power. The way in which he secretly handled his move to Brabham was cruel and disrespectful towards a man who had given him the chance of proving himself and of winning two world championship titles, which might well have been three had it not been for the almost-tragic accident at the Nürburgring in 1976 and the ill-fated day in Japan that same year.

In terms of ability and skill, but not of will-power and strength of character, Jacky Ickx can be compared to Lauda. When the Belgian went to Maranello in 1968 he was very young—twenty-three years old—but he already had an enviable store of experience behind him. Ickx can be called a natural talent. He started to race on two wheels at a very young age, like his father, the well-known Belgian journalist.

Jacky Ickx never danced attendance, which is possibly unique in the history of racing. He was discovered by that formidable talent scout, Ken Tyrrell, and started to earn big money from his very earliest races; and he never once considered buying a car directly for himself. There was a strange incident connected with the lucky way in which Ickx managed to push his way into the limelight. He took part in an uphill race in Belgium, when he was less than twenty years old, and crossed the finish with his wheels in the air—but he was not so much as scratched. The scene was filmed by TV cameras. The onlookers included the Belgian representative of Ford, who, far from dismissing Ickx as a daredevil, offered him a car for the next races. This was Ickx's lucky break. But his tricky character, his constant refusal to respect a certain degree of discipline, and his acute sense of privacy barred him from living up to his full potential, which is considerable.

First he broke with Brabham, who was the first to open the Formula 1 doors to him, and thence the path to the world championship; then he broke with Ferrari; and lastly with Chapman. He managed to get on fairly well with Porsche, with whom he coupled his own name on more than one occasion. Like his compatriot Olivier Gendebien, he won the Le Mans 24-hour race four times, and he could still be an extremely fine Formula 1 driver if he wanted to be, but it seems that he is already on the downward path (despite his youth—he was born in 1945). This is certainly not because of any premature physical deterioration; but, if anything, because of a blatant lack of interest in the racing world, where the atmosphere has become increasingly boisterous and gossip-ridden, thus forcing him to turn in on himself.

Ickx won six Grands Prix and a great many other races for Ferrari, and apart from his unavailability for trials—which was the main cause of his break with the Italian firm—he has left a good impression of himself behind.

If we travel back down the long list of drivers (a hundred or so in all) who have officially worn the Ferrari insignia, the next outstanding figure is John Surtees, an excellent driver and a skillful test driver. Surtees also left Ferrari because of a series of misunderstandings. The most deep-rooted reason was the suspicion that he was "stealing" ideas from the technical division with the intention of setting up in business on his own. In reality, however, once the contract with the Italian firm had been annulled amidst a very unpleasant atmosphere, Surtees did not set up his own firm; instead he raced for Cooper-Maserati and Honda. It was not until he had driven for the latter that he decided to build his own cars; but he was unlucky in this venture and eventually gave it up.

Going still further back in time, the figure of Luigi Villoresi summons up the image of a serious professional without any exceptional qualities, but a man who never provided any disappointments. Circumstances decreed that he should end up as Ferrari's "second" driver, although he had hoped to become number one. This caused him to become argumentative in his dealings with his boss, and he left of his own accord to go to Lancia. Villoresi was the commonly accepted mentor of Alberto Ascari because it was he who launched Ascari on his driving career; but at a certain point, as a result, Villoresi became jealous of him.

Alberto Ascari is still the best driver that Ferrari has had in the post-war period, in other words, without taking the Scuderia years into account. This man from Milan was truly endowed with everything it takes to be one of the world's great racing drivers: class, style, physical vitality, and determination. If he had a failing, and it was a fairly evident one, it was that he could only fight when he was in the lead. If he dropped back, he would let the wind go out of his sails, almost as if the race was no longer of any interest to him. Ferrari and Ascari held a sincere and honest affection for one another. Ascari started his career with Ferrari in 1940; and it was in a Ferrari that he died on the track at Monza in 1955 in an accident which is still shrouded in mystery and which has given rise to the most improbable conjectures.

Another driver who started and finished with Ferrari is Piero Taruffi, one of the most talked-about men in the world of automobile racing. Taruffi was a well-to-do engineer, with a passion for his trade, and he too can be listed among those who find it impossible to communicate with others. His sullen manner, the wide berth he gave to those around him, and his natural mistrust of others created awkward conditions for survival in all the teams of which he was a dominant member; but his expertise was beyond discussion. To his additional credit, he turned racing into nothing short of a research laboratory. In this respect he is one of the very rare people who personally drew useful lessons from racing, and transmitted those lessons to the builder of the car he was driving. In a word, he raced more with his head than his heart.

Clemente Biondetti rewarded Ferrari with two victories in the Mille Miglia, but Ferrari—so the story goes—never got round to thanking him. If that was the case, the reason possibly lies in the fact that Clemente Biondetti did not arouse much warmth or fondness in Ferrari. He was a poor devil, who was forever broke. And yet Biondetti left behind an indelible mark.

And so, step by step, we come to Ferrari's first drivers, not of the Scuderia, but of Ferrari as a make of car: Sommer, Nuvolari, Farina, and Cortese. To present a eulogy about Nuvolari would be out of place. But it must be said that when he took up racing again in the post-war years he was forty-six years old and not in good shape physically speaking; yet he achieved two memorable feats: in the Mille Miglia in 1947 with a Cisitalia 1100, and in the following year with a Ferrari, in the same race. In 1950 he took part in the Palermo-Monte Pellegrino uphill race with an Abarth 1100. It was the last race of his life. He died in his bed at the age of sixty-one. It was almost a mockery. He had played with death a thousand times on the track and almost sought it out after the death of his two children, and then he died that comfortable—some would say "bourgeois"—death.

Giuseppe ("Nino") Farina was another driver who was dear to Ferrari, because he drew his inspiration in everything from Nuvolari: his method of driving with his arms held straight (which was later to become universally adopted by racing drivers), the passion with which he drove, and the risks he ran. He was an instinctive driver, who used only one pedal—the accelerator.

Giuseppe "Nino" Farina    *Tazio Nuvolari*    *Franco Cortese*    *Raymond Sommer*

Froilan Gonzales    *Clemente Biondetti*    *Piero Taruffi* 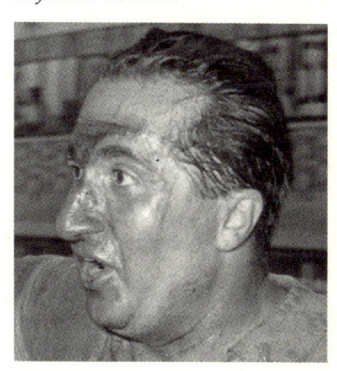   *Alberto Ascari*

89

Luigi Villoresi

Mike Hawthorn

Umberto Maglioli

Eugenio Castellotti

Phil Hill

Wolfgang von Trips

Peter Collins

Alfonso De Portago

Farina was the first world champion, but when Alfa Romeo withdrew from racing, he started to feel his age, and he became increasingly worried that he was being overshadowed by other drivers. He was a highly suspicious man with a great many complexes; but he was generous, spectacular, very daring, and devoured by an extraordinary passion for racing cars.

Franco Cortese was not a great driver, but he holds a particular place in the history of Ferrari, because he was the first professional driver of the new mark (1947). He was determined to finish every race, and this tactic earned him more than a little success.

Eugenio Castellotti came from the landed gentry, and on the track he displayed the brashness and over-confidence peculiar to those who have a lot of money and show it. But he was also a sensible young man, and he soon realized that there was more to automobile racing than money. He buckled down and managed to score some notable victories, including the Mille Miglia in 1956, which has gone down in history because of the impossible weather conditions in which it was raced. There is a splendid photograph which records this brilliant feat: Castellotti has left his car and is walking past the stands with Renzo Castagneto, peering into the crowd in search of his mother, whom he worshipped. Ferrari was fond of Eugenio Castellotti because, like Collins, he threw himself body and soul into the fray. Not for him any racing tactics or strategies. The race track was a do-or-die affair.

Luigi Musso, who belonged to quite another generation of drivers, was also liked by Ferrari. Ferrari compared him to Achille Varzi. Musso was likewise an all-round driver, but he never managed to bring off anything exceptional with the single-seater Ferrari, and only scored one world championship win, which he shared with Manuel Fangio (Argentinian Grand Prix of 1956).

The Marzotto brothers (Giannino, Paolo, Vittorio, and, to a lesser extent, Umberto) were all excellent drivers; and their passion for racing cars, which was lived out exclusively with Ferrari cars, brought a great deal of prestige to, and interest in, the rampant horse. Enzo Ferrari's great ambition has always been to show that a "man in the street" could win in one of his cars.

The most successful of the four brothers was undoubtedly Giannino, who won the Mille Miglia twice (1950 and 1953). The fact that he raced wearing a jacket and tie earned him the label of the "double-breasted" driver. It should be added that Giannino did not even wear a helmet. This was not a form of snobbery. It was simply out of scorn for any form of protection, and it corresponded to the way in which Giannino approached racing. For him, a racing vehicle was simply an automobile and in those days you drove automobiles in your jacket and tie.

Paolo was the most active of the brothers and possibly the only one who entertained the idea of becoming involved in racing on a more or less professional basis, though certainly not for the money. Like Giannino he was a magnificent driver and quite prepared to take any sort of risk. Vittorio raced for a certain period of time with some success and earned a place in the Monaco GP roll of honor by winning that race in 1952, the year in which it was limited to sports cars.

Umberto raced just a few times, and without a great deal of enthusiasm. But what he did achieve left those who saw

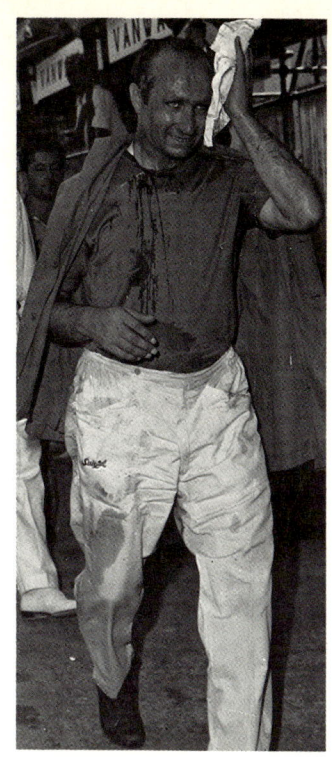

Juan Manuel Fangio  *Olivier Gendebien*  *Cesare Perdisa*  *Jean Behra*

Tony Brooks  *Giulio Cabianca*  *Dan Gurney*

him at the wheel with a sense of deep respect and sincere admiration.
If he had not died so young, after a terrible period of suffering, Lorenzo Bandini would undoubtedly have remained with Ferrari for decades. He had a difficult childhood, and only a great deal of determination and considerable sacrifices made it possible for him to enter the world of racing; so he was very appreciative of what the role of official Ferrari driver meant. He was spellbound by racing. In the few years that he was involved with Formula 1, he gave the impression that he would never reach the very top rung, but in the sports car field he was outstanding. Ferrari would certainly have kept him on, because he inspired confidence, and "the boss" greatly appreciated the effort he had made to get where he had.
Giancarlo Baghetti was the opposite of Bandini, a natural talent but a bad public relations man for himself. He forced his way into Formula 1 and set what is probably an unmatched record by winning a world championship race—the French Grand Prix in 1961—during his debut. If he had had more pluck, more strength of character, and more will-power he would have become a great Formula 1 driver. His move to ATS did him more than a little harm.
Lodovico Scarfiotti lies, as it were, halfway between Bandini and Baghetti: he had the former's love of racing, but the latter's sense of detachment. His well-born background showed in the way he treated those around him, but he enjoyed plenty of esteem and goodwill. No one has really been able to pronounce a verdict about his tangible potential as a driver. He was, beyond any doubt, an excellent sports car driver. In Formula 1 he has to his credit that victory in the 1966 Italian Grand Prix, although this was more than a little due to the conduct of that other great gentlemen, Mike Parkes.
The latter, an Englishman, (another lover of racing cars) is also hard to fit in to the overall picture of top drivers. He drove in Formula 1 so rarely that he does not really merit a place among the outstanding drivers in that class, but his contribution to Ferrari, and later on to Lancia, was greatly esteemed. It is rare when a technician soils his hand with the nonchalance and elegance with which Mike Parkes did. And people with style, who reach a high degree of competence in their trade, are unfortunately a dying breed.
Pedro Rodriguez, who was one of the official Ferrari drivers in 1965 and again in 1969, marks the watershed between the days of applicants lining up (to which we have already referred) and the period which saw the emergence of "sandwich-board" drivers who were prepared to advertise anything in order to pocket a little more money. In high South American style, Rodriguez lived far above his means, even driving around in a Rolls-Royce. Where racing was concerned, Pedro was an instinctive driver who would race brilliantly one day and in quite an average fashion the next; but he was a man on whom you could always count, and he had such a deep-seated love for Ferrari that, despite the harmless airs of a *grand seigneur* which he gave himself, he spent more time than most in the Ferrari waiting rooms, at Modena or at Maranello.
Like Scarfiotti, Umberto Maglioli was outstanding with sports models and not so strong with the single-seater. It was thus said that he disliked driving cars with open wheels, an observation that

91

Giorgio Scarlatti

Ritchie Ginther

Willy Mairesse

Pedro Rodriguez

Ricardo Rodriguez

Lorenzo Bandini

Lodovico Scarfiotti

would send the driver from Biella into a rage and elicit from him—quite rightly—the riposte that he had raced so little with single-seater cars that there could be no basis for such a statement. Umberto Maglioli, a stubborn, haughty, and not very sociable man, is another driver who gave a great deal to Ferrari and to Italy in sporting terms, but as far as his real worth is concerned he remains a mystery. If he had been easier to understand he could have been one of the all-time great drivers, despite his difficult character.

The last Italian member of the official Ferrari team was Arturo Merzario. Here we have another driver who had everything to gain by staying at Maranello. But, because of poor advice from others, he created a vacuum between himself and "the boss." That this was a mistake soon became evident: Merzario failed to achieve anything else afterwards, despite his determination to do so and the potential that could have allowed him to.

Clay Regazzoni worked hard for many years in the Ferrari team, but left virtually no trace, on the professional level, behind him. If we consider that he was with Ferrari for seven years (from 1969 to 1976, with the exception of 1973) and won only three Grand Prix races, it must be agreed that his achievement was a modest one. But his departure was greatly regretted at Maranello, because of his jovial nature.

Andretti could have gone very far at Ferrari (Formula 1, Indianapolis, Sport Class races), but just when all these possibilities could have been taken up, he was committed up to the hilt in the United States and undecided about whether to pursue the goal of becoming world champion or to remain for good on the other side of the Atlantic and look after his numerous activities in the USA. When Lauda decided to leave, Andretti was contacted, but it was too late in the day. He had become seriously involved with Chapman and had every intention of keeping to his word. It must have been very hard for Ferrari to say farewell to Andretti. He was always fond of the man because of the determination with which he raced: "He reminds me of Tazio Nuvolari," Ferrari said one day—words of praise which must sound sweet to the Italo-American.

Before the wind of advertising ruffled the motor-racing scene, Ferrari went through its American period, first with Phil Hill, followed by Ritchie Ginther and Dan Gurney. Phil Hill stayed with Ferrari the longest, and showed himself to be a splendid all-rounder (winning the Le Mans 24 hour race three times, numerous other sports car events, and the world championship in 1961). The Ferrari atmosphere as described by him in *Ferrari: The Man, The Machines* (published by Automobile Quarterly) is a masterly piece of writing which reveals the sensitivity and feelings that lay behind the rugged features of the Californian. Phil is a great lover of classical music and one of the few drivers to feel not only the brute force of the engine but also its "song," or should one say "melody"? (A well known English technician has called the "sound" made by the 12-cylinder engine of the Ferrari GT 250 "lyrical"). A man such as Phil Hill really had no option but to devote himself to the restoration of classic automobiles, a task which he carries on with great passion and skill in Santa Monica, California.

Ritchie Ginther did not stay long with Ferrari, but he lived through one of the most intense periods there, experienc-

Giancarlo Baghetti    *Jonathan Williams*    *Derek Bell*    *Vittorio Brambilla*

Jacky Ickx    *Brian Redman*    *Clay Regazzoni*    *Peter Schetty*

ing all the technical "labor pains" brought on by the change from front to rear engines. Ginther turned out to be extremely useful in this delicate phase. The extent of his moral stature and his close hold on reality (in contrast, he was physically a small man) were revealed on the day when (no longer with Ferrari) he had trouble finding a place in the starting line up at a race being held in the United States. The places were decided on the basis of lap times. On the spur of the moment he decided to give up racing.

Nor did Dan Gurney spend long with Ferrari; but he brought with him all the daring and open-mindedness typical of a marine, which he had formerly been. Here too it is difficult to pronounce a well-rounded verdict of him as a driver, but many people are of the opinion that he could have been one of the best. He has remained in the motor racing milieu as a successful builder of the Eagle, which has frequently acquitted itself well at Indianapolis.

Continuing through the various nationalities, Enzo Ferrari has had three Belgians (besides Ickx) on his team: Paul Frère, Willy Mairesse and Olivier Gendebien. Of the three, Gendebien made the major contribution, among other things by winning the Le Mans 24-hour race four times. This polished, distinguished, but terribly obstinate and particular driver was a tricky team member for Ferrari, even though he would also eventually do what had to be done. Gendebien, like a number of other Ferrari drivers, was not used in Formula 1 for a sufficiently long time to establish whether or not he was as good in that class as he was with sports cars. But even if he called himself a pure road racer, he nevertheless cut a fine figure whenever—and often it was with reluctance—Ferrari gave him one of his Formula 1 cars to drive. At Ferrari it has always been the rule that if a driver is taken on to drive one type of car, it is not easy for him to get the chance to broaden his horizons.

Willy Mairesse was a daring, whatever-the-cost driver, and his recklessness is amply attested to by the conspicuous number of cars he destroyed and by the injuries he suffered. Like all drivers who are capable, now and then, of grandiose feats, he was less than impressive on many an occasion. Paul Frère had a relatively modest career with Ferrari in terms of its scope, but it was a useful one. He always combined his job as a driver with that of journalist and technician. His relative unavailability as a full time driver had had its positive consequences; because he is one of the few men who, after having ended a working relationship with Ferrari, continues to have one which is hallmarked by mutual esteem and respect.

Wolfgang von Trips, Peter Collins, and Eugenio Castellotti can be grouped together for one specific reason: the affection which Enzo Ferrari had for them was no secret. Von Trips belonged to the category of the Scarfiottis and Gendebiens. He was a gentleman through and through and if Ferrari's version of the duel between von Trips and Taruffi in the final stages of the 1957 Mille Miglia is true, it must be said that the German was truly unselfish at the wheel as well as in life. In motor racing terms he was an all-round driver, i.e. as much at home in the sports car as in the single-seater. He would certainly have gone far, were it not for his untimely death at Monza in the 1961 Italian Grand Prix, after a collision with Jim Clark.

Peter Collins was a talkative, extrov-

93

Pedro Rodriguez: a very talented sports car driver.

erted, and gregarious Englishman whom people took to instantly. He was also a magnificent driver. He often pushed his driving to the limit but he did so with such a natural quality that it was not obvious to others. Like von Trips, he was at ease in any type of car. His finest race was probably the 1955 Targa Florio, which was battled out with Stirling Moss, who was at the wheel of a Mercedes. The spontaneous way in which he handed over his own car to Fangio in the 1956 Italian Grand Prix, thus enabling the Argentinian to win his fourth world championship title, has been described so often that there is no need to dwell on it here. But it should be added that generous gestures of this sort are virtually inconceivable in this day and age.

Mike Hawthorn won a world title for Ferrari in 1958, quite unexpectedly. This was a period when things were not going too well at Maranello. There was a crisis at the top of the technical division following the departure of Aurelio Lampredi. It was difficult to find a suitable replacement, and in fact, one did not materialize until the arrival on the scene of Chiti. (Vittorio Jano was no more than a consultant and already getting on in years.)

Hawthorn was one of Ferrari's few "ambidextrous" drivers, capable of a good performances in both the single-seater and the sports model. If Giannino Marzotto was a "double-breasted" driver, Hawthorn was "the driver with the bow-tie." He had a weak spot for bow-ties and there is more than one photo of him wearing this curious masculine accessory under his overalls or the leather jacket which was often worn in those days. Hawthorn had a great fighting spirit and was afraid of no one. In the 1953 French Grand Prix he led Fangio throughout the race and beat him at the finish by a hair (1.4"). He won the 1958 world championship title with a one-point lead over his compatriot Stirling Moss. In terms of racing, he did not really deserve the title, because he had won only one race as against the four wins chalked up by Moss. It was as a result of this that the organization of the world championship began to come under discussion; more points were awarded to first place and fewer to second place on down.

Hawthorn was among the very first men to bid a very early farewell to racing—he was 31 when he decided to quit. He announced this decision, which was taken for his mother's sake, late in 1958, shortly after winning the world title. In January 1959, he died in an automobile accident in England. It seems as if fate wanted to "punish" him for having abandoned such a risk-laden career and taken on the identity of an ordinary citizen.

Another small national group consists of the Argentinians Juan Manuel Fangio and Froilan Gonzales.

Fangio, the five times world champion, only stayed one year with Ferrari—1956. He could not have stayed any longer, because off the track there existed a sort of mistrust between him and Ferrari or mutual lack of esteem. Of his five titles, the one that Fangio earned in 1956 was certainly the hardest-fought, and, without that noble gesture by Peter Collins, the Argentinian would not have added it to his list, thus setting a world record. But in 1956, too, he lived up to his outstanding reputation, and all the more so because in that season Ferrari offered its drivers a hybrid car, the ex-Lancia D50, which suffered from not having been designed and built at Maranello.

It is in fact incorrect to talk in terms of an Argentinian group, because Froilan Gonzales was never in the team with Fangio. "El Cabezon," as he was called because of his obstinacy, was something of a "gorilla," driving very impulsively, head down and afraid of no one. He presented Enzo Ferrari with one of the finest successes of his life when he beat the Alfa Romeos at Silverstone in July 1951. This was the day when Ferrari felt matricidal and came out with the remark: "I killed my mother today."

Raymond Sommer was one of the most skillful and refined drivers ever produced by the French motor racing scene. Like his countryman Jean Pierre Wimille, he died in a minor race, driving a not very powerful car, a Cooper, because of a blocked wheel.

In 1979 Ferrari took on two men who, to start with at least, had the same qualities: drive, determination, and a disdain for danger. They were Jody Scheckter and Gilles Villeneuve. But once the former crossed the thirty-year-old mark he altered his racing style, or rather his racing conduct, radically; and he owes his world championship title precisely to his unsuspected powers of self-control. In the meantime, Villeneuve has also matured, although his distinctive characteristic is still his recklessness.

The list of drivers who have, on an official basis, driven Ferrari cars obviously includes many other names (for example, Jackie Stewart in 1967) not all of which can be mentioned here. Even those who did not get on well with "the boss" and left remember the years spent at Modena, because the atmosphere they breathed there was the feverish atmosphere of racing, it permeated everyone, from the mechanics to the technicians right on up to "the big boss." Ferrari's shrewdness has made an indelible mark on the world of motor racing.

As a personality, he might be remembered as a very beautiful woman with a temperamental nature, capable of kindling violent passions, but also deep hatred.

94

Mario Andretti

Ignazio Giunti

Arturo Merzario

Mike Parkes

John Surtees

Nino Vaccarella

Mario Casoni

Chris Amon

Andrea de Adamich

Ronnie Peterson

Helmut Marko

Tim Schenken

Carlos Reutemann

Niki Lauda

Gilles Villeneuve

Jody Scheckter

The Ferrari Racing Managers

ALL THE PRESIDENT'S MEN

Are they spokesmen and executors, with little or no personality of their own, or fully-fledged troop commanders? The figure of the racing manager at Ferrari has always been slightly blurred. Almost invariably he has been identified as a person at the beck and call of "the boss," careful not to contradict him and often unpopular with drivers.

In more than thirty years, at least a dozen middle-aged gentlemen (there have been very few young men) have held this post, starting with Nello Ugolini, whose name was almost without exception preceded by the title of "Maestro." It could be said that Maestro Nello Ugolini, a native of Modena, was a racing manager by profession, having worked actively as such both with Ferrari and with Maserati and the Serenissima group, where he also carried out other duties. He was a leader for another reason as well. Of all those who have had this job, he is the only one who knew how to handle the stopwatch with the proper skill. He demonstrated such ease and intimacy in his use of this instrument that, at one time or another, he landed the official timekeepers at almost all the world's racetracks in trouble. Another typical aspect of Nello Ugolini's character is the type of relationship that he managed to have with his drivers: confidential but detached, understanding but firm. While Stirling Moss was with Maserati he had total trust in and great admiration for the Maestro. This was when the Englishman was considered the infant prodigy of motor racing, and he was pampered and capricious.

Another racing manager who worked with Enzo Ferrari for many years was the engineer Mino Amorotti, a calm-headed country gentleman, not given to scheming. He was a close personal friend of Enzo Ferrari, a reserved man but one not averse to gossip. He would probably have kept his job much longer (he was with Ferrari for more than ten years) if his personal interests had not forced him to abandon racing. Once he had retired, he was never again seen at the race track.

With the arrival of Romolo Tavoni, the figure of the Ferrari racing manager started to become one of a man markedly under the thumb of "the boss." Tavoni trained with Ferrari and was promoted up through the ranks; but apart from the pleasure he found in travelling round the world—albeit fitfully—he suffered so many humiliations that his life was rendered virtually impossible. He left the firm with that group of "deserters" which included, among others, the engineer Carlo Chiti. Tavoni was a mild-mannered and highly respectful man, and, as such, he had to go beyond the threshold of his considerable tolerance in deciding to take such a sensational step.

With Eraldo Sculati and Franco Lini, Enzo Ferrari appointed to the job of racing manager two journalists who, both before and after their appointment, worked on a weekly paper called *Auto Italiana* which, in those days, was very popular. Sculati was an affable and fatherly figure, but he was not endowed with very much tolerance, and as a result he lasted just one year (1956). His reign was hallmarked by the fact that Manuel Fangio won his fourth world title in that year. Fangio too, of course, only stayed one year with Ferrari).

Franco Lini was the opposite of Eraldo Sculati, a man endowed with much verve, garrulous and egocentric; but he did not have much luck as the Ferrari racing manager either. His career, such as it was, was considerably affected by that sad day when Lorenzo Bandini was involved in the accident which claimed his life.

More recently, the reign of Franco Gozzi, who also came up through the ranks, was unexpectedly long. Gozzi could easily have ended up like Tavoni but unlike the man who had preceded him, Gozzi showed fairly exceptional talent as a navigator, and maneuvered skillfully between the ups and downs at Modena and the peace and quiet of far-off circuits, which were not watched over by the boss's eagle eye.

The Swiss, Peter Schetty is, not without reason, considered the most sharp-witted, scientific, and inflexible racing manager that Ferrari has ever had.

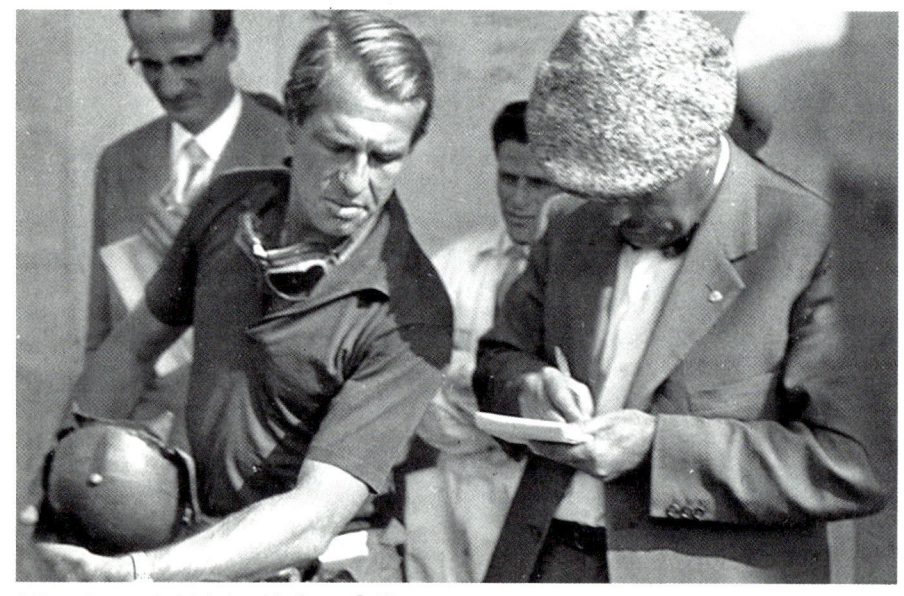

Mino Amorotti (right) with Peter Collins.

Mino Amorotti (second from the right) with Liugi Bazzi (right).
Nello Ugolini (wearing the cap) listening to Juan Manuel Fangio.

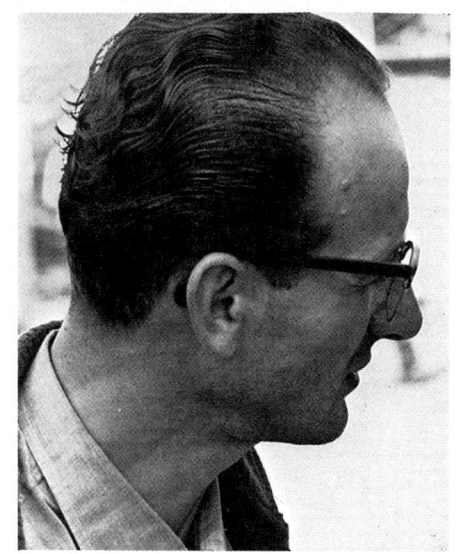

Romolo Tavoni

Eraldo Sculati

Franco Lini

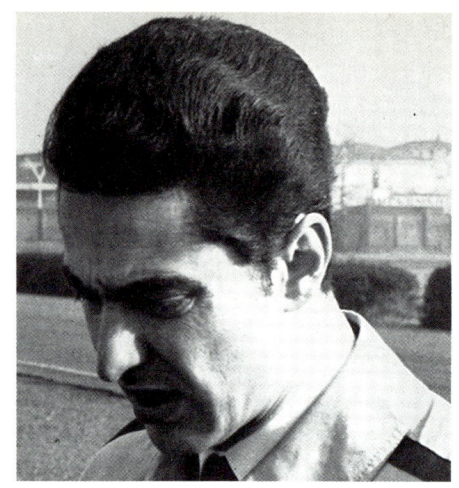

Peter Schetty

Franco Gozzi with Jacky Ickx

There can be no doubt that it was he who, both at the pits and elsewhere, instilled a sense of discipline and rhythm which had hitherto been unknown. The foreign press gave him much of the credit for the successes which the Italian firm chalked up in the period when he was in residence, both in Formula 1 and in the Sports championship. Some even likened him to the legendary Neubauer.

Like Mino Amorotti, Eugenio Dragoni was a racing manager who was also Enzo Ferrari's friend and confidant. An ambitious and enigmatic man, he had to bear the ambiguities and neuroses created by the conviction that Enzo Ferrari in no way wanted to open the doors of his Scuderia to Italian drivers. Dragoni was in no position to change Ferrari's attitude on this point. At best he was allowed to put one or two young Italians to the test, drivers like Bruno Deserti, who lost his life at Monza during a training session. It was Dragoni who showed John Surtees the door, thus depriving Ferrari of one of the best drivers of the day.

Ferrari's miraculous return to prominence, which coincided with the arrival of the 312 T, is also associated with the presence of Luca Cordero di Montezemolo, a gifted, dynamic and dazzling figure. Circumstances were certainly very much in his favor, but he was not endowed with great qualities as a technician or an organizer; he simply had an impressive human quality which earned him a great deal of affection. He was not, in fact, a racing manager. At Ferrari he represented the Fiat board, or, more personally, Gianni Agnelli himself. This was the first rung of his brilliant career which then took him to Fiat's Turin headquarters.

After Montezemolo, it was the turn of Daniele Audetto, who was followed by Roberto Nosetto, and then by Marco Piccinini, whose term of office has turned out to be unexpectedly long.

With one or two exceptions, the Ferrari racing managers have not handed in their resignations; rather, they have been invited to end their collaboration by "the boss." And the extraordinary personality of Enzo Ferrari has often put his racing managers in extremely uncomfortable positions.

Eugenio Dragoni

Luca di Montezemolo

The Ferrari Technicians

MANY MEN, SO MUCH HORSEPOWER

In more than thirty years in the business, Ferrari has built no less than 140 engines. The overwhelming majority of these have been 12-cylinder models. After his brief experience with the 815, Ferrari entertained the idea of setting up his own automobile factory. He turned to an old colleague, Gioachino Colombo, who had been at his side way back in the days of the Scuderia, and who, among other things, had designed the Alfa Romeo 158.

Born in Legnano in 1903, Gioachino Colombo was fourteen years old when he was taken on by Franco Tosi in 1917 as a draftsman. Five years later he had earned his engineer's "license." Two years after that, he presented a design for a three-stage piston supercharger and won a competition held by Alfa Romeo, which he had entered as a draftsman. He was immediately put to work on the new P2.

Colombo remained with Alfa Romeo until 1947, in constant contact, during this period, with Vittorio Jano, whom he helped with the design, development and planning of engines such as the P2 and P3 straight-8s, the 6-cylinder models, and the V-12s and V-16s. In 1945 he made his move to Ferrari. Colombo and Enzo Ferrari had gotten to know one another at Alfa Romeo and had become closer when they were at Modena with the Scuderia at the time when the Alfa Romeo 158 was on the drawingboard. It was the Lombard technician's view that this car should have had a rear engine, but Ferrari was fiercely opposed to the idea, being firmly convinced that this was not the right technical solution. He clung to this view for many years, in fact until the late '50s.

Gioachino Colombo designed the 12-cylinder engine for Enzo Ferrari in August 1945 at Legnano, drawing it on a sheet of wrapping paper, the only type of paper with the right texture and dimensions that he could lay his hands on at that time. When it came to the choice of a 12-cylinder engine, Enzo Ferrari and he were both heartily in agreement, because both were convinced that this was the best way to split up the cylinder capacity for a racing car. By September of that same year, the design was ready, but it could not be actually realized until 1946-47. This was a particularly fertile period in terms of ideas for Colombo, a designer who was fired by a tremendous zeal for his work, and Ferrari, a builder of cars whose highest aspiration was to make a name for himself after working for years for a large factory.

Gioachino Colombo stayed with Ferrari for a relatively short period of time. In 1951 he returned to Alfa Romeo, but he left that firm for good one year later because of a disagreement with the engineer Gallo, who was then chairman of the Milanese company. Gallo had accused Colombo of having designed, for Ferrari, an engine which was more or less identical to one designed for Alfa Romeo years earlier; Gioachino Colombo maintained steadfastly that there was no foundation to this accusation.

With the 12-cylinder engine, Colombo has left an indelible stamp of his presence at Ferrari, because the Ferrari production has always included a 12-cylinder model, although the forms and structures have differed. Colombo was also responsible for the 2000 cc engine, the 1500 cc engine with the two-stage supercharger, and the 2340 cc engine, but he has admitted candidly that the 12-cylinder induction engine which beat the Alfa Romeos for the first time at Silverstone was not his work, but that of Aurelio Lampredi, who had taken over from him.

Chronologically speaking, the first Ferrari was the 125 GT of 1946. In the following year, the vitality Enzo Ferrari infused into his technical division was clearly illustrated by the construction of two variants, the 125 S and the 159 S, the latter with an engine of about 2000 cc. Driven by Franco Cortese, the 125 S was the first Ferrari to appear in a race (on the Piacenza circuit); it was May 11, 1947. Cortese was forced to retire because of a broken fuel pump, but he stayed in the lead until three laps from the end. The first win by a Ferrari was chalked up at the Caracalla circuit some time later. In all, in the first real year of racing, the 125 S and the 159 S took part in fourteen races; they won seven, four of which were driven by Franco Cortese, two by Tazio Nuvolari, and one by Raymond Sommer.

The salient feature of the first Ferrari engines was the bore which was greater than the piston stroke; this explains the high rpm figure for those days (5600 in the GT, 7000 in the two S versions). In essence the 12-cylinder engine, set at an angle of 60°, corresponded in every way to a modern engine destined to undergo sharp increases in the rpm figure and the compression ratio, as in fact was the case. 1948 was the year of the first Formula 1 single-seater. It was entered for the Turin Grand Prix at the Parco del Valentino track. On that occasion Ferrari had three very renowned drivers in his employ: Raymond Sommer, "Nino" Farina, and Prince Bira, a wealthy Siamese who had made racing his raison d'être. This was the first official encounter between the Ferraris, the Alfa Romeos, and the Maseratis. Ferrari's best placing was Sommer's third, which he garnered after a thrilling duel with Luigi Villoresi, driving a Maserati, who beat Sommer by a car length. Jean Pierre Wimille driving an Alfa Romeo won the event. The engine of the Formula 1 Ferrari had the same stroke as the 125 GT. It was supercharged with a one-stage Roots supercharger and had a power output of 230 hp at 7,500 rpm, as opposed to the 275 hp at 8,000 rpm of the Alfa Romeo's straight-8 engine. Having collaborated with Jano in the drawing-up of the plans for the Alfa Romeo V-12 type A single-seater, the 1936 V-12 type C, the 12 C of 1937, the 1939 312, the prototype of a GT model in 1938, and a

99

Above: the V-8 engine and the Ferrari single-seater developed from the Lancia D50 designed by Vittorio Jano.

Below: Enzo Ferrari with some of the first rear-engined sports cars, at a press conference.

Enzo Ferrari with Liugi Bazzi.

125 GT

The ancestral engine of the entire Ferrari production: 60° V-12, 1496.77 cc, with a power output of 72 hp at 5,600 rpm.

sports model likewise with a V-12 engine, by 1939, Gioachino Colombo was already impressively familiar with engines using that arrangement of the cubic capacity. The modern form of that engine, i.e. with the bore greater than the piston stroke, corresponded to precise criteria of a practical nature: the potential possibility of increasing the maximum rpm, the reduced load on the bearings, the lower loss of power as a result of friction, the greater rigidity of the crankcase, and the lower weight and more compact dimension of the engine-block. The 125 single-seater appeared with one camshaft for each bank of cylinders and a 5-speed gearbox. Its first racing season, in 1948, ended rather badly with the retirement of Sommer and Farina in the Italian Grand Prix: the first because he felt out of sorts when he was lying in third position, the other because of broken transmission, when he was in fourth place. On top of this, three of the cars taking part in the Barcelona Grand Prix also retired, including Bira's and Farina's, once again because of transmission trouble, and the Spaniard Pola's, with a damaged engine. But Farina did manage to win at the Garda Circuit at the wheel of a 125.

The 1949 season was much more intense and rewarding. During the winter months, the 125 GP had been modified, particularly where its steering units were concerned. In addition, the arrival of two men of the caliber of Alberto Ascari and Luigi Villoresi had considerably reinforced the driving team. The sale of two cars, one to Peter Whitehead and the other to Tony Vanderwell, also gave the Ferraris a more powerful presence on the various race tracks. The clear proof that things had greatly improved over 1948 were the second and third places secured by Villoresi and Ascari respectively in the Belgian Grand Prix at Spa; the first and second places of Ascari and Villoresi in the Swiss Grand Prix at Berne; Villoresi's firsts in the French Grand Prix and in the Grand Prix held at Zandvoort; Ascari's first place, Cortese's fourth, and Whitehead's ninth in a race held at Lausanne; Ascari's first place and Sommer's fifth place in the Italian and European Grand Prix at Monza; and, lastly, Whitehead's win in the Czechoslovakian Grand Prix.

At the Italian Grand Prix there were not only five Ferraris taking part (Ascari, Villoresi, Sommer, and Bonetto, plus Whitehead in his own car), but two brand new models as well which were entrusted to Ascari and Villoresi, obviously enough. The main innovations, with regard to the single-seater used up to date, consisted in the Roots supercharger (two-stage) and the twin overhead camshafts for each bank of cylinders. The frame had been lengthened, the track widened, and the brakes improved. In its new version the engine produced a power output of 300 hp at 7,500 rpm. A further modification undergone by the revised single-seater was the adoption of the De Dion rear axle and the 4-speed gearbox. The 1950 season is particularly important in the Ferrari annals because a radical transformation was carried out in the Formula 1 sector: the supercharger was abandoned, and the induction engine adopted in its stead. Ferrari took this decision in light of the vain attempt to beat the Alfa Romeo 158 with a supercharged engine, even though it was more up-to-date. The Formula 1 Ferrari 125 of 1950 with a two-stage supercharger had a power output of 315 hp at 7,500 rpm and weighed 700 kg (1,575 lb); but although it dated back to 1937, the Alfetta had made such advances that in 1950, with two-stage carburation, it had a power output of 350 hp at 8,500 rpm. Nonetheless, Ferrari embarked on the season using first the single-stage, then the two-stage Formula 1 125. At Pau, for example, Villoresi and Sommer drove the one-stage version and came in second and fourth respectively. At San Remo, which saw the first clash of the season between Ferrari and Alfa Romeo, Ascari and Villoresi drove the one-stage version, while Sommer, Serafini, and Vallone drove the two-stage model, but victory still went to the Alfa. Of the Ferrari drivers Villoresi did best with his second place.

Ferrari did not take part in the first world championship meeting, the British Grand Prix. But he entered the second, the Monaco Grand Prix, which, as has already been mentioned, was marred by the accident caused by Farina (Alfa Romeo) which, in one fell swoop, and at the end of the very first lap, put the cars of Farina himself, Fagioli, Rosier, De Graffenried, Trintignant, Schell, Harrison, and Rol out of the race. Shortly afterwards Gonzales also retired because of damage suffered in the crash with Farina's car. At Monaco, the Ferrari driven by Ascari and Villoresi was the two-stage 125, while Sommer had to be content with a one-stage version. The results chalked up in that race are not that impressive or indicative, but Ferrari came out of it quite well, when compared with its rival, thanks to Ascari's second place and Sommer's fourth place. At the Swiss Grand Prix at Berne the Ferraris driven by Ascari and Villoresi had frames which were 18 cm (7") longer, the first having suspension by swing-axles and the second being fitted with a De Dion rear axle. Neither finished the race.

The really new feature of the season made its appearance in the Belgian Grand Prix at Spa where Ascari was given the 3300 Ferrari with an induction engine and Villoresi the two-stage version with the extended frame. Ascari placed fifth and Villoresi sixth. The 3300 which bore the marking "275," took part in the French Grand Prix trials at Rheims, but did not enter the race itself. The only Ferrari in the starting line up was Whitehead's privately entered one.

After a further increase of the cylinder capacity (4100 cc) achieved by increasing the bore from 72 mm to 80 mm (the stroke remained the same at 68 mm), the induction engine single-seater, in its final version—with the cylinder capacity at the upper limit permitted (4500 cc)—appeared at the Italian Grand Prix that year. Driven by Ascari it did not finish the race, but the signs were very promising. The Milanese driver clocked up a time in the trials which put him in second position after Fangio (driving an Alfa Romeo), and Ascari, in fact, led the field in the early stages of the race itself. In the final placings, Ascari came in second but driving Serafini's car (the drive-shaft of his own car had broken). The 4500 was successful in the Spanish Grand Prix held at Barcelona where Ascari and Villoresi secured first and second places, but the Alfa Romeos did not take part in the Spanish race, being quite content with the result of the Italian Grand Prix, which was the last race in the world championship. Taruffi drove the 4100 in the same race, one of the rare occasions on which this engine was used in a race—it was really a transitional model.

At this stage it is already possible to mark out a history of Ferrari from the technical point of view, or, at least, from the early stages of what was to be a very long road.

Gioachino Colombo had designed and planned the 125 GT in 1946 and its derivative versions, the 125 S and the 159 S, in 1947; 1948 saw the production of the Formula 1 125, the 166 S, the Formula 2 166, the 166 Inter and the 166 MM; and in 1949 there were the FL (Formula Libera) and the Formula 1 125 with the two-stage supercharger.

All these cars were fitted with the same V-12 engine, set at an angle of 60°, with minor variations in the bore and the stroke. Like the 125, the 166 is a founder in the genealogy of the Ferrari engines, because the Formula 2, Inter, MM and FL cars all followed an independent path in their evolution. The construction of the Formula 2 was probably motivated by the fact that Maserati had raised the cylinder capacity of its A6G from 1500 to 2000 cc. The Ferrari 166, in all its various forms, was planned and built in the winter of 1947-48, and it was an instant success. The FL used the same frame as the Formula 1 125, and supercharging was by a Roots one-stage supercharger. It weighed 740 kg (1,665 lb). The Argentinian Benedicto Campos put it to good use in the Temporada Argentina race in both 1949 and 1950, as did Ascari, Villoresi and Fangio in 1949, again in Argentina.

The engine of the first Formula 2 had the same characteristics as the FL engine and produced a power output of 155 hp at 7,000 rpm (it was obviously not supercharged) and 160 hp at 7,000 rpm in 1950-51. It weighed 610 kg (1,375 lb). This car was one which came up with instant results, which greatly pleased Enzo Ferrari: Ascari won at Modena, the Nürburgring and Garda, and Villoresi in the Autodromo Grand Prix. In all, Ascari won six races in 1950 with the Formula 2 and Villoresi won two.

In the meantime, there had been an important change at the head of the Ferrari technical division. Colombo's post had been taken over by a young (31-year-old) engineer by the name of Aurelio Lampredi, who was from Leghorn. He had completed his initial training in the Odero-Terni-Orlando shipyards in Leghorn and in the Piaggio works at Pontedera. From 1941 to 1945 he had designed engines with the Reggiane company in Reggio Emilia.

Soon afterwards he joined Ferrari, but did not stay long before moving to the Isotta Fraschini works in Milan. He went back to Ferrari in the winter of 1949 and was made responsible for both trials and testing.

Enzo Ferrari has himself called Lampredi "the most prolific of all my designers," and Lampredi stayed at Maranello until 1955, during which time he demonstrated a great deal of versatility. The change over, which was to be a decisive one, from the supercharged engine to the induction engine is to his credit. This change over took place in 1950 but did not actually bear fruit until 1951, the year when Ferrari put a stop to the Alfa Romeo supremacy in Formula 1. At the start of his productive career with Ferrari, Lampredi proceeded along the lines marked out by Gioachino Colombo, because the basic engine was still the 60° V-12. This engine was also used for a Formula 1 car, the 212, which never actually saw the light of day. The 212 was developed from the Formula 2 166; the cylinder capacity was 2562 cc, and the power output 200 hp at 7,500 rpm. Still in 1951, Lampredi designed four more cars: the 212 Export and the 212 Inter, both with the same engine as the Formula 1 212 but obviously with a lower power output (160 hp); the 195 Inter with the same engine as the 1950 195 S; and the 340 America with the same engine as the Formula 1 340 (4101 cc). This latter had made its debut, with Ascari at the wheel, in the Grand Prix des Nations at Geneva in July, 1950. The Formula 1 375 was also further improved (with dual ignition). But the Formula 1 375 driven by Froilan Gonzales, which beat Alfa Romeo at Silverstone for the first time had only single ignition.

It was, however, the 2000 cc, 4-cylinder engine made in 1951 which is considered to be Aurelio Lampredi's real masterpiece. Here, for the first time, he resolutely veered away from the guidelines provided by Colombo, to which he had remained more or less faithful, except that he had gotten rid of the supercharger. This engine, and the car in which it was mounted, are famous for two principal reasons: the very short time it took Lampredi to design the 4-cylinder engine, and its consistently sound performance throughout the period in which it was used. The 500 took part in 104 races, winning twenty-nine of them, and chalking up eighteen second places, nine third places, seven fourth places, four fifth places, five sixth places, two seventh places and one eighth place. In all, it retired on twenty-nine occasions, fifteen of which were due to engine breakdowns, two to transmission trouble and twelve to collisions. As we know only too well it was the 500 which enabled Alberto Ascari to win the world championship title in 1952 and 1953, when the title was a Formula 2 event. The 12-cylinder Formula 2 model, on the other hand, was entered in thirty-one races; it won fourteen of them, and came in second on three occasions and third on four. It retired in ten races, always because of transmission trouble. In other respects a further proof of the endurance of the Ferrari engines can be found by running through the curriculum vitae of the one-stage Formula 1 125 (which retired in eighteen out of fifty-two races), the Formula 1 212 (which retired once out of ten races), and the Formula 1 375 (retiring sixteen times in fifty-seven races). The track records of only two single-seater models fail to impress: the two-stage Formula 1 125 (retiring five out of eight races) and the Formula 1 340 (which retired in two out of four races).

With the 4-cylinder engine Lampredi obtained various major advantages over the 12-cylinder Formula 2 engine of the 166: an improvement of almost 30 percent in the power : weight ratio and of more than 9 percent in the specific power output; a reduction of the over-all weight of the engine calculated at 42 kg (94.5 lb) as opposed to 198 kg (445.5 lb) in the Formula 2 166 and 156 kg (351 lb) in the 500; a reduction of 60 percent and more in terms of the moving parts. The first 4-cylinder engine had a power output of 170 hp at 7,500 rpm in 1951, 175 hp in 1952, 180 hp in 1953 and 185 hp by the end of that same year.

The 4-cylinder engine gave birth to a whole series of other engines with the same cylinder arrangement: the 735 S (2941 cc), the 700 (2771 cc), the 500 Mondial (1984 cc) the 625 F1 (2498 cc), the 553 F2 (1997 cc), the 750 Monza (2999 cc), and the 625 S (2498 cc).

The extraordinary performance of the 500 was enough to convince Aurelio Lampredi that the 4-cylinder engine was also suitable for the new Formula 1 which provided for induction engines up to a maximum of 2500 cc and which was to come into effect on January 1, 1954.

Enzo Ferrari with his engineer Aurelio Lampredi (on the right). The car is a Squalo.

500 F2

The straight-4, 1984.85 cc. engine. Power output: 185 hp at 7,500 rpm. This was the first engine to break with the by-then-traditional 12-cylinder engine.

Before we discuss this new formula from the technical point of view, we would do well to take a look at what had happened to the large engines which had been virtually shelved by the premature end (in 1951) of the 1500 cc supercharged and 4500 cc non-supercharged Formula 1. A Formula 1 375 was bought by Tony Vanderwell and in 1951 became the third Thin Wall Special. Four Formula 1 375s finished the course at Indianapolis. One was entered by Johnnie Parsons, who called it the Grant Piston Ring Special. Another raced officially under the Ferrari colors driven by Alberto Ascari; it started in twenty-fifth position and, when it was forced to retire because of a broken wheel rim, it was lying in eighth position over-all. The third, entered by Howard Keek to be driven by Bill Vukovich, was not used for the race. The fourth was to have been driven by Johnny Mauro, but like the third did not take part in the race.

Ferrari was seriously tempted, on many occasions to take part in the Indianapolis 500-Mile Race, but conditions were somehow never favorable for this actually happening. Nor was there the time available to construct a car specifically designed for such a demanding race, so unlike the Formula 1 world championship events.

Nevertheless, the American agent for Ferrari, Luigi Chinetti, urged the Italian firm to make a showing at Indianapolis in 1953, and persuaded it to fit out a car for the race. It was more or less the same as the car driven by Ascari in 1952, but had a reinforced frame. The engine was also the same except for the inclusion of three four-barrelled carburetors. The car was not built with any particular driver in mind. In fact, it was available to any driver who wanted to take it on. One or two took the wheel but did not react positively to the car and decided not to carry the matter any further. The car was then offered to Bob Said for a race over the Daytona Beach Mile; the car exceeded 270 kph (168 mph), but more as a result of the driver's courage than the qualities of the vehicle. In 1954, after being modified by Chinetti, it appeared at Daytona once again. It was driven this time by Bill Holland but no tangible results were forthcoming. In the end, Chinetti offered it to Carrol Shelby who drove it to victory in two uphill races. It was then made available to Farina and relegated to the role of "work-horse" on the day when the driver from Turin—at the end of his career—wanted to try it out on the Indianapolis track. It then found its way back to Italy and was further modified so that it could take part in the Monza 500-Mile Race. It was driven by Harry Schell, but failed to finish. Nino Farina never gave up the idea of winding up his career at Indianapolis, and with the help of the Bardhal company he had Ferrari build an ad hoc car for the race. A 6-cylinder 4400 cc engine was chosen, but Ferrari soon lost interest in the project and it was taken up by OSCA of Bologna. Farina failed to qualify. He returned doggedly to Indianapolis the following year, but the car was totally written off in a serious crash, which took the life of the American driver, who was driving it. To complete the picture of Ferrari participation in races of the Indianapolis type, which include the Monza 500-Mile Race, we should add that for the 1958 event at Monza Ferrari prepared a 4100 with a 3-speed gearbox and De Dion rear axle, as well as a 3000 based on the 246 Dino, also with a De Dion rear axle. The first, driven by Luigi Musso, caused a sensation in the trials, but the other, in the hands of Phil Hill, did not finish the race. After three laps Musso made a pit-stop because he was in poor physical condition; Mike Hawthorn took over and, in turn, handed the car to Phil Hill (who had retired with his 3000), and he finished in third place.

The 4500 cars, which had earned Ferrari so much prestige in 1951 (by winning not only the British Grand Prix but also the Italian and Spanish Grands Prix), made a few further appearances in Europe. Villoresi raced in one in England (at Silverstone and Boreham). Two models were sold to Rosier and Landi who used them with only some success (Rosier won at Albi for example). In 1953, Ascari used a revised and updated 4500 in the Grand Prix at Buenos Aires but failed to finish the course. At Albi, the official 4500 driven by Ascari and the Thin Wall driven by Farina became involved in a thrilling duel, but in the end both had to retire, leaving the way ahead clear for Rosier. In effect the 4500 only won during one season. Then the premature end of the Formula 1 relegated it to the status of a display car at circuits of secondary importance. But for all that, it remains in Enzo Ferrari's heart one of the milestones in his bustling career as "trouble-maker."

The new 2500 cc Formula 1 came into effect on January 1, 1954. Ferrari was in something of a quandary about whether to use the 212, which had served him fairly successfully, driven by the Swiss driver Fischer (Dorino Serafini also used one in a few races), or to build a 4-cylinder version, in other words, a development of the 500 with which Ascari had won two world championships. In the end, the latter solution was chosen. The new car, which used a 4-cylinder engine with a 94 mm bore and a 90 mm stroke, as opposed to the 90 mm bore and 78 mm stroke of the 500, was called the 625. The 2500 cc engine made its first official run at the Bari Grand Prix in 1951, and Taruffi, at the wheel of the new model, placed third—an excellent result. It had dual ignition, a 4-speed gearbox, a De Dion rear axle, transverse leaf spring, and Houdaille shock absorbers. With a view to its being used on an official basis the 625 made its debut, in more or less finished form, at the Buenos Aires Grand Prix in 1952. The race ended with Farina, Villoresi and Hawthorn in the first three places. Ascari, who was driving a 4500 did not manage to finish. The 2500 had another showing in 1953 at the Susa-Mont Cenis uphill event; driven by Umberto Maglioli, it came in second. It made a third appearance at a Free Formula race at Silverstone, but Hawthorn, who was driving, was forced to retire.

The 2500 made another showing at Rouen in a Free Formula race in which Farina and Hawthorn came in first and second.

With this record, Ferrari embarked on the 1954 season with a well-prepared car which had been planned and designed way back in 1951, but the balance sheet of the 625 was far from glowing. From the French Grand Prix at Rheims on, the Mercedes entries came back with a vengeance, and not a single smaller car builder—not even Ferrari—was able to put up any real resistance to the Germans.

The first act of the championship was played out at the Grand Prix in Argentina, which was won by the indomitable Fangio in a Maserati, well ahead of Farina. Ferrari used its sound anchorman, Gonzales, who came in third, Ascari and Villoresi having moved over to Lancia in late 1953. Fangio also won the second Grand Prix in Belgium, easily outpacing Trintignant. He then transferred to Mercedes, after scoring two wins with his Maserati, which contributed more than a little to his third world championship.

The period in which this formula remained in force (1954-1960) can be considered as one of Ferrari's least fortunate. In the very first stages the 625 seemed inadequate for the onerous task that lay ahead of it, and before long Ferrari started work on another single-seater which was given the odd name of "Squalo" (meaning "shark"), or else bore the marking 553. The name was probably due to its shape (it had fuel tanks at the sides by the driving seat); but there was no apparent plausible reason for the number, unless the last two figures—53—stood for the year in which it was planned.

The Squalo 553 made its debut in the Grand Prix at Syracuse, driven by Gonzales, who won his own heat. But the car then refused to start for the final, so the Argentinian was given Trintignant's 625 which he drove to a resounding victory. The 553 was used in one championship event, the Belgian Grand Prix, with Farina and Gonzales, but both cars failed to finish because of engine trouble. It was also present in the line up at the Swiss Grand Prix at Manzon, but retired, although Maglioli came in seventh driving a similar car. In the Italian Grand Prix, Gonzales had to retire with a damaged gearbox; but in the Spanish Grand Prix, the Squalo, with Hawthorn at the wheel, won. In its modified version, called the 555 or Supersqualo the car was raced in 1955 at Bordeaux (Farina and Trintignant both retired); at Monte Carlo (where Schell and Taruffi both retired); in the Belgian Grand Prix (where Farina, Trintignant and Frère came third, fourth and seventh respectively); in the Dutch Grand Prix (where Castellotti, Hawthorn and Trintignant came in fifth, seventh and retired, respectively) and in the Italian Grand Prix (where Hawthorn retired and Trintignant, Maglioli and Castellotti came in eighth, sixth and third, respectively).

The somewhat obscure history of this car, which is only once mentioned in the list of engines compiled by Ferrari, as a Formula 1 and not as a Formula 2 model, came to a close at the Grand Prix in Argentina in 1956, where Collins and Piotti drove it in shifts but failed to finish the race.

The 625 won only two world championship races: the British Grand Prix with Gonzales at the wheel in 1954 and the Monaco Grand Prix in 1955, with Trintignant driving. It was powered by two different engines, both 4-cylinder types: one of 2497 cc the other of 2498 cc; the first with a bore and stroke of 100×79.5 mm; the second with a bore and stroke of 90×90 mm. It also won seven non-championship events, three with Trintignant at the wheel (Buenos Aires, Rouen, and Caen), three with Gonzales (Bordeaux, Silverstone, and Bari), and one driven by Farina (at Syracuse).

The active contribution made by Aurelio Lampredi to Ferrari ended with the 625, the 553 and the 555. In addition to the 4-cylinder models, he also built various sports cars and GT models; and before he left Modena, he took an active part in the planning of the 6-cylinder model which was officially attributed to Dino Ferrari in collaboration with Vittorio Jano.

In fact, when Lampredi had gone, the Ferrari works went through a confused period. The technical management was entrusted jointly to Vittorio Bel-

Vittorio Jano (third from right with cap) at Lyons in 1924. Liugi Bazzi is on the right. Giuseppe Campari is on Jano's right.

lentani and Alberto Massimino, the former being mainly in charge of the engine division, the latter of the frame and chassis unit.

Alberto Massimino's relationship with Enzo Ferrari was a long-standing one. He had taken a small part, in 1937, in the designing of the Alfa Romeo 158 at Scuderia Ferrari; and in 1939-1940 he had been totally responsible for the 815, the non-Ferrari Ferrari—the sports model with which Enzo Ferrari had made his sports car racing debut by giving two cars to Alberto Ascari and Lotario Rangoni for the 1940 Mille Miglia.

Vittorio Bellentani, who was born in 1906, had pursued his technical studies in Switzerland and, as a designer, had first earned a reputation in the world of motorcycling. He spent the war years with Ferrari, and the 1946-1952 period with Maserati. When he returned to Maranello, he found himself side by side with a young engineer called Andrea Fraschetti, for whom Ferrari had a great deal of esteem. Fraschetti was a thoroughly competent technician and took great pleasure in test driving the cars which he had built or helped to build. Sadly, he died in an accident at the Modena race track while he was testing out a car.

The first tangible fruit of the Bellentani-Fraschetti team was a new 4-cylinder car, the 354 S, which took the limelight, in the Ferrari motoring division, in 1956. Unlike the cars built up until that time, the 354 S had a bore (102 mm) which was smaller than the piston stroke (105 mm), but this did not make it a turning point. In fact, there was no follow-up to it. Bellentani and Fraschetti also worked on developing a 12-cylinder model, the 290 MM (Mille Miglia); but the task of developing the Formula 1 single-seaters fell almost exclusively to Vittorio Jano. This was principally because Jano had designed the Lancia D50 at Gianni Lancia's request; but the life of this car was very short. The death of Alberto Ascari caused Lancia to abandon racing with the same haste with which it had urged its technical division to become involved in that sector. This decision was accompanied by a truly altruistic gesture: the gift to Ferrari of all the racing equipment at Lancia. This gift made the "man in Modena" doubly happy: first, because his technicians were running short of ideas (the 625, the Squalo and the Supersqualo had all been something of a failure) and second, because he could thus get back in touch with Vittorio Jano, an old friend and an extremely gifted technician.

Born in San Giorgio Canavese on April 22, 1891, into a family which was probably of Hungarian origin, Vittorio Jano is now considered to be one of the most fertile and shrewd minds in the technical sector of international motor racing. At a very early age he worked at Giovanni Ceirano's Rapid company as a draftsman; subsequently he moved to Fiat, and contact was made between him and two of the most eminent technicians at the works in Turin: Guido Fornaca and Carlo Cavalli. Such was his dedication to his work and such his creativity that, six years after his transfer, Jano was already the chief draftsman. More importantly, he had also become one of the people in charge of the racing division at Fiat, which, in those days, was very active with cars such as the 6-cylinder 2000, which can be considered to be one of the milestones in the history of competitive motoring. Among other things, Fiat was the first to use the supercharger in racing cars.

It was Enzo Ferrari who persuaded Vittorio Jano to leave Fiat and join Alfa Romeo. Jano found the atmosphere congenial for developing, with complete freedom, all the technical projects which had been gradually maturing in his mind in Turin. His first car was the P2, which has gone down in history. Next came the 6-cylinder 1500 and 1750, the 8-cylinder 2300, and a long series of other cars powered by 12-cylinder engines. All these cars had their moments of glory, even though they often found their paths blocked by the extremely powerful Mercedes and Auto Union cars.

As was the case at a later stage with Enzo Ferrari, so Vittorio Jano's departure from Alfa Romeo was due to jealousies and misunderstandings. The then general manager of Alfa Romeo, Ugo Gobbato, considered Jano no longer capable of coming up with modern designs and projects for racing cars. The technician from Piedmont had ample opportunity, subsequently, to show how mistaken this verdict was, when he joined Lancia almost immediately and designed, among other cars, the D50, which would have become one of the most interesting Formula 1 single-seaters, had it not been for Gianni Lancia's sudden decision to quit racing.

The D50, bearing the famous rampant horse was to have made its debut in 1955 at the Italian Grand Prix, the last race of the 1955 season; but for purely commercial reasons (Lancia used Pirelli tires, and Ferrari, Englebert tires), the cars were not used until the following year.

Under the management of Bellentani,

156 F2

Another "founding father": the 65° 1498.35 cc. V-6 engine with a power output of 180 hp at 9,000 rpm.

Massimino, and Fraschetti, and the watchful eye of Jano, the ex-Lancias underwent various modifications in the winter of 1955-56 (rear transverse leaf spring, roll bar, and Houdaille shock absorbers at the front instead of the Lancia telescopic dampers, and fuel tanks at the sides built into the frame). A new 8-cylinder V-type engine was ready for the French Grand Prix (76 × 68.5 mm instead of the 73 × 73 mm [bore × stroke] of the V-8 Lancia). It was further altered in the winter of 1956-57 (80 × 62 mm). The car underwent additional modifications too, the major one being the elimination of the lateral fuel tanks; they were to come back into vogue at a later date and be adopted in all the Formula 1 models with the arrival of the rear engine. In this respect Vittorio Jano was a precursor. In its final version, the D50—which was later called the Ferrari-Lancia 801 F1—had a power output of 280 hp at 8,500 rpm and an over-all dry weight of 650 kg (1,460 lb) as compared with the 250 hp at 8,100 rpm and a weight of 620 kg (1,395 lb) in the original version.

Apart from the absence of the lateral fuel tanks (the most conspicuous modification effected on the D50), the different configuration of the engine, and the altered suspension, the ex-Lancia remained more or less like the initial conception designed by Vittorio Jano, and it acquitted itself very well in the 1956 racing season, at the end of which Juan Manuel Fangio—an official Ferrari driver for the first time—won his fourth world title. But it should be added that the fact that Mercedes retired from racing at the close of the 1955 season contributed more than a little to the Ferrari success. The D50—later called the 801—was one of the rare Formula 1 Ferrari single-seaters to be fitted with a V-8 engine, a type of engine which has evidently never been considered one of the best at Maranello, where the 12-cylinder engine has reigned supreme, except for various explorations into the realms of the 4- and 6-cylinder engine.

In fact Bellentani and Fraschetti turned their attention to the 6-cylinder engine after having worked on the 8-cylinder Lancia which Ferrari considered an out-of-date engine, even though it had enabled Fangio to win the world championship.

It is said that the idea of the V-6 engine was conceived by Dino Ferrari, but it was actually built by Aurelio Lampredi and then developed by Vittorio Jano. As was the case with the 2500 cc 4-cylinder engine, the V-6 was also mounted, to start with, in a Formula 2 car, which made its debut at the Grand Prix in Naples in 1957, driven by Luigi Musso, while his team-mates Collins and Hawthorn were driving Lancia-Ferraris. Musso finished in third place behind the two Englishmen, and the new car, with which the Roman driver was, incidentally, very satisfied, had a promising christening.

With the introduction of the new specification system the V-6 was called the 156 (the first two figures stood for the cylinder capacity of 1500 cc, and the last figure for the number of cylinders, 6) and had a power output of 180 hp at 9,000 rpm, with a compression ratio of 10:1; the rpm. and compression ratio figures were among the highest achieved up until then by the Ferrari engines. Apart from these characteristics the 6-cylinder engine had another special feature: the unusual angle of

107

65° for the V, designed to give the maximum amount of room for fitting the intake manifolds in the middle of the V. In every other respect, although on a reduced scale, the 156 F2 mirrored the form and shape of the Formula 1 Lancia-Ferrari with its tubular frame and the rear section of the engine set slightly to the left in respect to the axis of the vehicle; it had a 4-speed gearbox, suspension rounded off with Houdaille shock absorbers and rear brakes which were a combination of those of the 4-cylinder Supersqualo and the Lancia-Ferrari, and a De Dion rear axle. Another special feature of this car was the driver's seat which was set slightly to the right with the steering column almost straight.

The 156 got off to a good start. After its positive debut in Naples, it was taken to Monte Carlo, not so much to enter the Formula 1 race in a world championship event, but so that all the Ferrari drivers could try it out. This they did, pronouncing it very easy to handle, although it was less powerful and slower, especially on the uphill section of that race track. The 156 was later raced at Rheims in a Formula 2 event but Trintignant, who was at the wheel, did not have an easy time because of the tough resistance put up by the English Formula 2 cars. It was in a second version of this car, the main modification to which was the removal of the magnetos to the rear section of the camshafts which controlled the intake valves, that the engineer Andrea Fraschetti was killed on the track at Modena. "A young man of high caliber," Enzo Ferrari wrote of him, "who, in fact, combined the talents of a computer and a designer with those of an enthusiastic driver. On top of this, he was also a draftsman. It is not easy to come by designers-cum-engineers, because as a rule engineers are not designers. So what normally happens in the technical division is that the technician-cum-designer who designs the engines develops the idea conceived by the engineer. Fraschetti embraced all these talents."

The hopeful beginnings of the V-6 convinced Ferrari that this would be a good engine for Formula 1, and he urged his technicians progressively to increase the cylinder capacity which was raised to 1860 cc. Two cars powered by this engine made their debut at the Modena Grand Prix (driven by Collins and Musso) in a Formula 1 race won by Behra in a Maserati; but Musso came in second and Collins fourth. After two further improvements the cylinder capacity of the V-6 was increased to 2200 and then to 2417 cc.

In the Casablanca Grand Prix Collins had the 2400 and Hawthorn the 2200, but both had to retire. In any event the V-6 was to be the Formula 1 car for 1958 and in fact four 246s with 2417 cc engines (85 $\times$ 71 mm), at an angle of 65° and with a power output of 280 hp at 8,500 rpm were present at the Argentinian Grand Prix. The "Temporada" did not turn out well for Ferrari because the Argentinian Grand Prix was won by Moss in a Cooper (the beginning of the shift of emphasis in favor of the English teams in Formula 1), and the Grand Prix at Buenos Aires was won by Fangio in a Maserati. Hawthorn made up for things at Goodwood by winning the traditional opening race of the European Formula 1 season. In the second world championship race at Monaco, Ferrari fielded four cars, two of which were fitted with the new (more rigid) frame. But Trintignant won this race in a Cooper, once again, and a Ferrari driven by Musso secured second place.

The season proceeded badly with another defeat in the Netherlands and another win by Moss (this time driving a Vanwall); the best the Ferraris could boast was Hawthorn's fifth place. A fourth defeat followed in Belgium (where Hawthorn came in second); but Hawthorn drove to victory in the French Grand Prix at Rheims. As the season unfolded, the superiority of the English cars became more and more evident: Brooks won the German Grand Prix in a Vanwall, and Moss won the Portuguese and Moroccan Grands Prix. Ferrari scored its second success of the season when Collins drove to victory in the British Grand Prix, but it was Hawthorn's consistency—he came in second again in this race—in Portugal, Italy and Morocco that earned him the world title after a gruelling fight with Moss. It was truly astounding how, with just one win to his credit, Hawthorn managed to finish the season at the top of the world championship table, while Moss, who won four races, placed second.

The Ferrari 246 did not undergo any major modifications during the season apart from the alternate use of reinforced frames or Formula 2 frames, the use of larger fuel tanks mounted beside the driver's seat (in some races), and the frame of the 3000 cc car which had taken part in the 500 Mile race at Monza. In the Italian Grand Prix one Ferrari (Hawthorn's) was fitted with disc brakes and an engine with a cylinder capacity of 2451 cc (85 $\times$ 72 mm), called the 256, was used for the first time in Portugal. Between races changes were made to the suspension, which sometimes involved the use of coil springs.

The 1959 season was begun with more or less the same cars, but things improved from the aesthetic and aerodynamic viewpoint with the arrival, from Maserati, of Fantuzzi (who was responsible for the functional and elegant body of the Maserati 250 F). But the driving team was almost totally changed after the deaths of Luigi Musso and Peter Collins. They were replaced by Tony Brooks and Cliff Allison. Jean Behra also joined the Ferrari team, but after the French Grand Prix, this notoriously impatient driver rescinded his contract and was immediately replaced by Dan Gurney. The American should have been an additional driver, but, instead, he was a substitute. In addition, Phil Hill and Olivier Gendebien were promoted to Formula 1, although not permanently. At the close of the season, Gurney also left Ferrari and his place was filled by von Trips.

In view of the change which was to be made in Formula 1 in 1961, Ferrari took part in the 1959 and 1960 seasons with the same cars as in 1957–58. That they were by now no match for the onslaught mounted by the English cars is shown by the fact that in these two years they only won three races: the French and German Grands Prix in 1959 with Brooks driving and the 1960 Italian Grand Prix, with Phil Hill at the wheel. This latter race was boycotted by the English in protest against the way the whole circuit at Monza was organized, including the extremely unpopular high-speed ring. During this two-year period Ferrari, in turn, did not participate in the 1959 British

250 TR

The "Testa Rossa," a 60°, 2953.21 cc., V-12 engine with a power output of 290 hp at 7,500 rpm.

Grand Prix or the 1960 American Grand Prix. As the date approached on which the new Formula 1 was to come into effect, limiting the maximum cylinder capacity to 1500 cc, Ferrari changed everything: men and machines.

Bellentani and Jano—the latter stayed on as a consultant—had been replaced by Carlo Chiti, back in 1957. Chiti was born in 1924 in Pistoia; he obtained his engineering degree at the University of Pisa; and the year after, at the age of 28, he joined the Alfa Romeo racing division. This brilliant and gifted man is responsible for having persuaded Ferrari to abandon the front engine, once and for all, and to opt for the rear engine, as the English firms had already done. Chiti designed a car which was an instant winner, the Formula 1 156. It was with this car that Phil Hill won the world championship title in 1961 with his teammate von Trips, who lost his life in the last race of the season, the Italian Grand Prix.

With the help of Franco Rocchi and Walter Salvarani, Chiti modified the 65° V-6 Dino by reducing the cylinder capacity by altering the bore and the stroke (73 × 58.8 mm) and redesigning the cylinder head. The 156 had fuel tanks mounted beside the drivers seat, which was set further forward.

The Formula 1 156, developed from the Formula 1 246, had its first outing at the 1960 Monaco Grand Prix, driven by Ritchie Ginther, who pulled out in the seventieth lap, but the car was pushed across the finish line and placed sixth. In the Formula 2 version, again fitted with the 1500 cc engine, the car reappeared at the Solitude Circuit in July of that year, and von Trips won a promising victory by beating the Porsches on their home ground. Still in 1960, the 1500 rear engined model was also used at Monza and von Trips scored another win in the 1500 class.

A 120° V-6 model was developed at the same time as the 65° V-6, following the lead of an engine designed by Aurelio Lampredi in 1950–51 which had the same features. The initial power output of the 65° V-6 (150 hp at 8,000 rpm) was raised to 185 hp at 9,200 rpm, while that of the 120° engine increased from the 190 hp of the first version to 200 hp at 10,500 rpm. This latter engine was the one used for the 1961 races.

The success chalked up by the 156 in the 1961 world championship was undoubtedly due to the excellent characteristics of the car but, if the truth be told, it was made considerably easier by the fact that the English firms, in that first year of the new formula, did not have an engine to meet the situation and were forced to use the 4-cylinder Formula 2 Coventry-Climax engine, which turned out to be decidedly inferior to the Ferrari V-6.

But things were to change in the year following. From the 1961 German Grand Prix on, a new 8-cylinder Coventry-Climax engine was mounted on the Brabham Cooper (the Australian clocked up the third fastest time overall in trials). In the Italian Grand Prix in 1961, Graham Hill, for his part, had a completely new 8-cylinder BRM, but he only used it for the trials. The two 8-cylinder engines both had their teething troubles; but in 1962, after various improvements and changes, they were in a position to restore English motor racing to the prestigious position it had enjoyed in 1959 and 1960.

For Ferrari things were a little different. The 1962 season was a thorough

156 F1

The 120°, V-6 engine of the 156 F1; with a cylinder capacity of 1476.60 cc. It had a power output of 190 hp at 9,500 rpm. It was preferred to the 65°, V-6 engine.

Phil Hill during trials at Monza. On the left, engineer Carlo Chiti.

disappointment. Although mechanically improved by the adoption of a 6-speed gearbox and 4 valves per cylinder (actually, the 4-valves-per-cylinder innovation was announced by Ferrari at the traditional end-of-the-year press conference, but it never, in fact, materialized) and aesthetically up-graded with a more oblique windscreen, together with modifications to the geometry of the suspension, the Ferraris failed to win a single race; and their efficient performance of the previous year, culminating in winning the world championship title, was no more than a memory. A further revision of the Formula 1 156, which was presented at the German Grand Prix in 1962, was to no avail. The most conspicuous modification was the elimination of the pointed nose (the air intakes looked like two nostrils) which was replaced by a central oval-shaped air intake.
In addition, the driver's seat was set at a more marked angle, as it was in the English single-seaters. The frame of the car was also modified to make it less flexible, and allowed it to incorporate, in the lower section, the gearbox, which had been moved toward the

rear. The suspension and exhaust systems were also modified.

The lack of success which marked the 1962 season was undoubtedly due to the disastrous situation at Ferrari after the sudden departure of Carlo Chiti and various other senior figures. It would seem this defection was triggered by the intolerable meddling of Laura Ferrari, the boss's wife, who, at a certain stage, had started following the racing team wherever it went. This would have been all right—the point is made by several parties—if she had simply been a travelling companion. But she saw fit to become involved in every single decision, even those taken in the inflammable atmosphere of the eve of a race.

This difficult period was handled by Enzo Ferrari with his usual dexterity. He did not lose heart; and instead of resorting to outsiders, he promoted two young men already in his employ, Angelo Bellei and Mauro Forghieri. Bellei and Forghieri not only proceeded with the work that Chiti had walked out on, but each also designed a new engine under pressure from Ferrari. Ferrari put Forghieri in charge of the racing division, and despite the inevitable ups and downs that have occurred, he is still there.

Born in Modena in 1935, Mauro Forghieri earned a degree in mechanical engineering from the University of Bologna by the time he was twenty-four and has shown himself to be one of the most inspired and versatile of engineers. His natural vitality, typical of an Emilian, goes hand in hand with a solid background of experience, both in the workshop and on the race track. He joined Ferrari soon after graduating, taking on the job of liaison officer between the design office, then under the engineer Chiti, and the engine-testing section. Everything produced by Ferrari from 1962 on bears his stamp, even though, in practice, a sort of triumvirate (Enzo Ferrari has called it the "troika") was established at that time in the technical division. It was headed by Mauro Forghieri, who was flanked by Franco Rocchi, an engine specialist, and Giancarlo Bussi, also an engineer. The "troika" split up in 1978 when Rocchi retired after a serious illness, and Bussi was kidnapped in Sardinia—his whereabouts remain a mystery to this day.

Up until the expiration of the 1500 cc Formula 1 in 1965, the Formula 1 156 underwent mechanical improvements—a slight lengthening of the wheelbase (2.32m to 2.38m [7'7" to 7'10"]). The most important new feature of this car was introduced in 1962 in the form of a semi-monocoque frame, although this did not alter the weight which stayed put at 460 kg (1,035 lb), 1963 also saw the introduction of direct injection (Bosch) carburation which made it possible to raise the power output of the 120° engine to 200 hp at 10,200 rpm. But with the exception of the first year, the 156 did not turn out to be a successful and competitive car, a fact which is borne out, as already mentioned, by its failure to win a single race in 1962, and its paltry single win in 1963 (Surtees in the German Grand Prix).

In 1964, Ferrari changed tack some-

158 F1

The V-8 engine of the 158 F1, one of the few engines of this format used by Ferrari.

111

Ferrari technicians. From the left: Franco Rocchi, Walter Salvarani, Mauro Forghieri, Angiolino Marchetti, and Giancarlo Bussi.

what by fielding a 90° V-8 model (64 × 57.8 mm) with a maximum power output of 205 hp at 1,500 rpm. Surtees drove this car, fitted with this engine, to victory once more in the German Grand Prix. In 1964 Lorenzo Bandini also won his only Formula 1 race, the Austrian Grand Prix, but driving the Formula 1 156 (the 8-cylinder version took on the title of 158 F1 and in 1965 the power output of its engine was raised to 210 hp at 11,000 rpm).

His wins at the Nüburgring and in the Italian Grand Prix at Monza, plus his second place in Holland, the USA and Mexico (helped in the latter by Bandini) enabled Surtees to win the world championship title in 1964. This gave a shot of confidence to Ferrari which, in the winter of 1963-64, had built a 12-cylinder Formula 1 model with the aim of getting back to the top of the pack. The salient feature of this engine was the arrangement of the cylinders, which were horizontally opposed, (i.e., flat) and the carburation by indirect Lucas injection. The maximum power output was 255 hp at 11,500 rpm (the same rpm as the previous engine). The 512 F1 was christened by Lorenzo Bandini in the US Grand Prix in 1964. He retired in the fifty-ninth lap. For that race both John Surtees' 8-cylinder car and Bandini's 12-cylinder car wore the white and blue colors of the North American Racing Team under Luigi Chinetti, as a mark of protest by Ferrari towards the Italian Automobile Club, which had not recognized the 250 LM. In the next Grand Prix, in Mexico, three cars appeared in the line up: the 6-cylinder 156 (Pedro Rodriguez), the 8-cylinder 158 (John Surtees), and the 12-cylinder 512 (Lorenzo Bandini). 1965, the last year of the 1500 cc Formula, bore as little fruit as 1962 and 1963. Ferrari failed to win a race, but managed to clinch two second places (Surtees in South Africa and Bandini in Monaco).

During the period when the 1500 cc Formula 1 was in effect (from 1961 to 1965 inclusive), Ferrari made an essentially undistinguished showing, apart from the first year when the English were caught off-balance. But in that same period many changes and innovations were made on the domestic front: the abandonment once and for all of the front engine, except in some GT cars; the departure of Carlo Chiti and the rise of Mauro Forghieri; the adoption of carburation by injection, a task allocated in particular to the Swiss technician Michael May; the construction of an 8-cylinder and, more importantly, a 12-cylinder "boxer" type engine (the flat 12, with horizontally opposed cylinders) which was to play a decisive role in the history of Ferrari. If this five-year period did not add much to the fame of the Ferrari mark on the race track, it nevertheless laid the foundations for the advances subsequently achieved.

When it was made known that the new Formula 1 would raise the maximum cylinder capacity to 3000 cc, it seemed that Ferrari was in a position to vie with its opponents much more effectively than in the past. Once again, the English were without a suitable engine; but their ability to react to the situation was, in this instance, completely unforeseen. Ferrari fitted its new single-seaters with a 60° V-12 engine (77 × 53.5 mm), the 312, which had a maximum power output of 375 hp at 10,000 rpm, more than enough—it was thought—to match the British opposition; but no one suspected that the tough and taciturn Jack Brabham could manage to prepare a car which, because of its high efficiency, would meet the situation. The 312 Ferrari started off with two valves per cylinder, but this had been changed to three by the time the 1966 Italian Grand Prix was held. The season closed with two wins (Surtees in the Belgian Grand Prix and Scarfiotti in the Italian Grand Prix); but the driving team was taken considerably aback by the unexpected departure of John Surtees, who was sacked on the eve of the 24-hour race at Le Mans by the then racing manager at Ferrari, Eugenio Dragoni. Surtees was to some extent replaced by a fellow countryman, Mike Parkes. Parkes had been taken on with the specific task of supervising the development of the GT production and the possibility of taking part in one or two races with the sports models. The use of Parkes in Formula 1 deprived the Ferrari rearguard of a very valuable person. Ferrari took steps to remedy this by taking on a very promising young man from New Zealand, Chris Amon, a move which reconfirmed the positions of Lorenzo Bandini and Mike Parkes. But 1967 turned out to be one of the most ill-fated years for the Modena firm. It started the season by making few changes to the car fitted with a 36-valve engine dating back to the end of the previous season, although the power output was increased to 385 hp at 10,000 rpm. By using a fiberglass and aluminium body it was finally possible to reduce the over-all weight of the 312 to 550 kg (1,240 lb) from the 595 kg (1,340 lb) of the previous year, eliminating a defect which had plagued this car from the outset. In the Italian Grand Prix, faithful to the Ferrari tradition, an additionally modified version of the 12-cylinder 312 was presented. This had 4 valves per cylinder, the power output was raised to 390 hp at 10,500 rpm, and the maximum weight of the car dropped to 530 kg (1,195 lb).

But all these modifications were to no avail. 1967 was disappointing and even tragic. In the Monaco Grand Prix Lorenzo Bandini was horribly burned in the very serious crash which cost him his life. Mike Parkes ended up unconscious after an accident, in the Belgian Grand Prix, which virtually put an end to his career as a driver. Ferrari also lost the weighty presence of Lodovico Scarfiotti, who may not have excelled as a driver of single-seater cars but was outstanding with sports models, and a true gentlemen in the way he conducted himself. He had a fatal accident at the wheel of a Porsche during the trials for the Rossfeld uphill event in 1968. Not least because of the loss of its two official drivers, Ferrari failed to win a race in 1967. The void left in the team by the death of Bandini and the unavailability of Parkes was such that from the French Grand Prix on Ferrari only entered one car, the one driven by Amon. Unfortunately, Amon failed to live up to expectations as the season progressed.

Ferrari started the 1968 season with the same car used at the end of 1967, with improvements which made it possible to raise the power output to 408 hp at 11,000 rpm. The persistent weight-losing "diet" of the 312 bore fruit, however. In the third year of its life it weighed only 512 kg (1,152 lb). It underwent further modifications at the end of the year, as usual, to honor the Italian Grand Prix, the major change consisting of a new cylinder head. But the most important innovation, mechanically speaking, carried out that year by Ferrari was the use of the rear wing for the first time. This aerody-

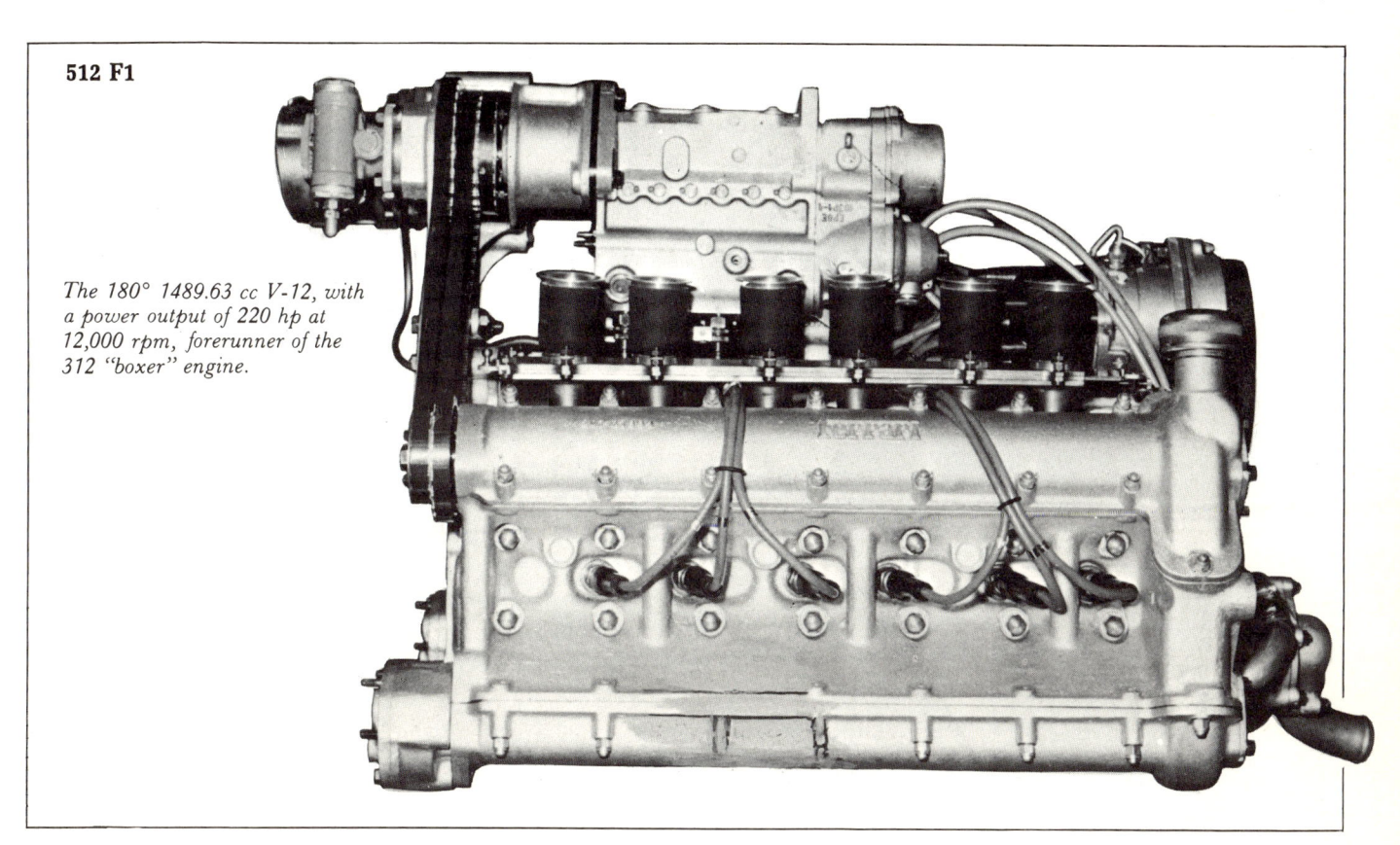

512 F1

The 180° 1489.63 cc V-12, with a power output of 220 hp at 12,000 rpm, forerunner of the 312 "boxer" engine.

113

namic addition appeared at the trials for the Belgian Grand Prix, which on those days were still held on the very quick Spa circuit. The purpose of the wing was to achieve better road-holding by the rear wheels. It was given such a positive verdict that, in no time at all, all the other builders, except Brabham, had followed suit. But some of the forms the new feature took were clumsy and off-the-cuff. The International Racing Committee was brought in to lay down rules about the dimensions and the method of fitting the wings, which then became a permanent fixture on all single-seaters.

In 1968 Ferrari called on two other young men, in addition to Amon: Jacky Ickx and Andrea de Adamich. But the latter was involved in an accident in the first trials of the world championship season, in the South African Grand Prix, and another in the Race of Champions at Brands Hatch. This put an end to his career with Ferrari.

1968 was, all in all, another rather inconclusive year, which earned just one win (Ickx in the French Grand Prix). And 1969 was little better. Ferrari once more fielded the 312 with the 60° V-12 engine, and increased the power output to 436 hp at 11,000 rpm, but the season produced poor results. Ickx went back to Brabham, and Amon was once again on his own to defend the name of Ferrari. From the British Grand Prix on, however, Pedro Rodriguez joined the team, a good reason it turned out for persuading Chris Amon to leave. Ferrari did not take part in the German Grand Prix and came back on to the scene for the Italian Grand Prix with just the Mexican driver, who stayed on until the end of the season. Things changed radically in 1970 with the use of the 12-cylinder "boxer" engine. The development of this engine was a somewhat laborious task. One of the reasons for Chris Amon's departure from Ferrari was his irritation over not being able to use an engine in which he clearly had confidence but whose use in racing was constantly delayed. It was finally ready for the first race of the 1970 drivers' world championship, the South African Grand Prix. The car was called the 312 B (B for "boxer"), and it marked a tangible leap forward in terms of quality. In its initial version

Mike Parkes

the new 12-cylinder engine (78.5 × 51.5 mm, giving a total cylinder capacity of 2991 cc) with 4 valves per cylinder produced 455 hp at 11,500 rpm. It was quick to show its potential, not least because of the return of Jacky Ickx to Ferrari, to drive the first 312 B. It took a while for the "boxer" to work as planned, but by the end of the 1970 season, Ferrari could once again draw up a favorable balance sheet with four wins, three of them by Ickx (the Grands Prix in Austria, Canada and Mexico), and the other by Clay Regazzoni (in the Italian Grand Prix). This was the latter's first year in Formula 1 and to begin with he and Ignazio Giunti drove alternately. At the Belgian Grand Prix Ferrari fielded two 312 Bs (one for Ickx and one for Giunti, making his Formula 1 debut). Two weeks later it was Regazzoni's turn to make his appearance on the world championship stage. It was not just the four wins which showed that Ferrari once more had a sound car, but also the three second places, the five pole positions, and the seven lap records. Ickx was poised to win the world championship title, but this was awarded, posthumously, to Jochen Rindt who had died in a crash in the trials for the Italian Grand Prix. It has never been possible to reconstruct the causes for this crash, although it was probably due to a broken suspension unit.

The 312 became the 312 B2 in 1971 and underwent a change of shape compared to the earlier model. The main concern of Forghieri, Rocchi, and Bussi was to improve the road-holding ability of the car by working on the aerodynamics of the body. The season got off to an excellent start with Andretti's win in South Africa. The Italo-American seemed to be the right man for Ferrari, but his numerous commitments in his adopted country made his full-time availability something of a problem. The year ended with another win, this time by Jacky Ickx in Holland. All things considered, 1971 marked another lull after the excellent performances of the 312 B in 1970. It was also the year dominated by Stewart and his impressive Tyrrell.

In 1972 the "boxer" engine was revised; both the bore and the stroke were altered to 80 × 49.6 mm, thus accentuating the characteristics of this "super-square" engine. The power output was raised to 480 hp at 12,500 rpm, but this started to pose lubrication problems, which rendered it very unreliable. In addition, Ferrari failed to solve the unsatisfactory road-holding of the car. After the promising year, 1970, Ferrari once more dropped back to the status of a second-rate mark in search of its identity. The scene was dominated by Tyrrell and Lotus.

1973 was another year without a single win, despite the construction of a third and fourth version of the 312 B, the first with an engine producing 485 hp at 12,500 rpm, the second with modifications to the monocoque frame, which had already been adopted in the first version of the B3. The frantic efforts to extricate Ferrari from its awkward situation ended with the construction of a car with a body which was totally different from the customary "boxer" body. Because of its bulky and prominent front section it was nicknamed "spazzaneve" ("snowplough"). It was never used. In fact its construction threw an even longer shadow over Mauro Forghieri, who risked being excluded from the "troika."

A major change in the situation came with the new version of the B3 in 1973; its line was a decisive break with the Ferrari tradition. The driving seat was pushed forward, which involved a

312 B   *The 1974 version of the 2991.80 cc, 180° V-12 engine. Power output: 495 hp at 12,600 rpm.*

complete reshaping of the body. It also made it possible to increase the capacity of the fuel tank mounted behind the driver. It was this car which allowed Ferrari to start on the upward path. Good results were soon forthcoming. In 1974 the newly recruited Niki Lauda won two races (in Spain and Holland) and Clay Regazzoni, one (in Germany). In 1975 the "T" (T standing for transverse, referring to the gearbox) replaced the "B". This new feature was introduced to concentrate the weight as much as possible around the driving seat. The "T" put Ferrari once more in the top Formula 1 bracket, with five wins by Lauda (Monaco, Belgium, Sweden, France and the USA) and one by Regazzoni in Italy. Lauda deservedly won the world title also.

By now the Ferrari-Lauda marriage seemed indissoluble. Had Ferrari made Lauda, or was it Lauda who had restored Ferrari to its former glory? The patience which the Austrian driver demonstrated in the preparation of the car was undoubtedly a decisive factor in the success of both parties.

In 1976 the engine of the T had its power output raised to 500 hp at 12,000 rpm. There was every reason to believe that in that year too Ferrari and Lauda would emerge victorious at the end of the season, but in the German Grand Prix the Austrian was involved in a very serious crash which might well have proved fatal. Up until that moment, it had been a triumphant year for him (first place in the Brazilian, South African, Belgian, Monaco, and British Grands Prix; second in the USA-West Grand Prix and in Spain; and third in Sweden). The most benevolent and optimistic forecast was that Lauda would be away from the race track for many months, possibly for good; but after missing just two Grand Prix races (in Austria and Holland), he made a comeback in the Italian Grand Prix, and finished fourth. His determination to continue was so strong that, despite the marks left by the burns he suffered on his face—scars which he has never tried to hide—he got back to work with all the grit and care of old. The courage which he had so valiantly displayed in the hospital failed him only in the last race of the season, the Japanese Grand Prix, where he retired in the second lap because of the precarious conditions on the track caused by the torrential rain which fell before and during the race. He lost the world title by one point. But he managed to win it back in 1977 with the T3 (with an improved body and suspension).

In 1979 it was Jody Scheckter's turn. With the T4; he won the title after winning three Grands Prix. An additional three were won by Villeneuve. If we retrace the history of the thirty world championships between 1950 and 1979 we find that Ferrari tackled them with six basic engines: the 60° V-12 in the supercharged and non-supercharged versions, the straight-4, the 65° V-6, the 120° V-6, the V-8 and the 12-cylinder "boxer." The 8-cylinder Lancia engine, after modification, was also used. If one bears in mind that this firm is the only one which has taken part in all the world championships, during which time, the formula has changed four times (plus a fifth time if we consider the fact that Formula 2 cars were used in the 1952 and 1953 races), the matériel developed by Ferrari, including the sports, GT, and Formula 2 cars, is vast. A table of power output shows that in these thirty years there has been a constant progression from the figure of 50 hp/liter to more than 170 hp/liter. The weight: power ratio, which was 3.11 kg (7 lb)/liter in the first single-seater, the Formula 1 125 of 1948-49, has dropped to 1.15 kg (2.58 lb)/liter in the 312 T4. With its range of engines Ferrari has undoubtedly been the most versatile

115

A family group. On the left, Peter Schetty; on the right, Clay Regazzoni. In the center, head and shoulders above the others, Mike Parkes.

Engineer Giancarlo Bussi, who disappeared in Sardinia in 1978, with Jacky Ickx.

and flexible of all car builders, thanks in large part to the fact that, by building them directly, they have always assembled and dismantled them at leisure; whereas their most relentless opponents, the English (with the exception of BRM) have always had to resort to the magnanimity and patriotism of Coventry-Climax and Ford-Cosworth. But to say that in thirty years Ferrari has built 140 different engines can be misleading, because the engine is an important part of the car, but by no means the whole story. In many cases, the unsatisfactory performance of a single-seater or sports model is not due to the engine, to which Ferrari has always attached a great deal of importance, but to the frame, suspension, and tires.

The presence of the Ferraris on the world's race tracks, which has gone uninterrupted for decades, has been made possible by the vitality and enthusiasm of the man who created them, but also by the spirit of cooperation of so many people working for him, from the racing division mechanics on up.

We have mentioned the best-known technicians and those who have played the most active part in the designing and building process, but we should not forget the contributions made by Gianni Marelli, Stefano Jacoponi, Angiolino Marchetti, Alessandro Colombo, Gianandrea Bianchi, Antonio Cocozza, Giacomo Caliro, Ferrari's own Son, Dino, who shared his father's devouring interest in racing, and Antonio Tomaini. Cocozza and Bianchi died in a road accident on Octobr 20, 1969 in a Daytona driven by the former. In particular we should not omit Luigi Bazzi, that most loyal of colleagues, who has been alongside Enzo Ferrari throughout his extraordinary rise to fame. For very many years Bazzi was one of the authors of the successes of Ferrari. His extremely impressive skill with engines was not the result of degrees and diplomas but of practice. The development of the 12-, 4-, 6-, and 8-cylinder engines invariably fell to him, and we all know what a demanding task this was. The idea of the twin-engined Alfa Romeo was his too, back in the days of Scuderia Ferrari. Enzo Ferrari recalls him as "the founding member of the old guard of collaborators." Over eighty, he finally left Ferrari, but only for reasons of health.

The seventy-nine victories chalked up by Ferrari in the world championship for drivers (from 1950 to 1979 inclusive) serve to show the magnitude of the contribution to motor sport made by the Italian firm simply in Formula 1. Its history unfolds as if choreographed, without changing a jot over the years. Why? because Enzo Ferrari has remained faithful to his principles and practices and never left his Modena and his Maranello. His world exists in those places. But it is an extraordinary and inimitable thing that his presence at the various race tracks has always been such that it has seemed that he has actually been following his team.

If we retrace the history of Ferrari, four out of the host of technicians who have lived the Maranello experience have really left their mark: Gioachino Colombo, Aurelio Lampredi, Carlo Chiti and Mauro Forghieri—and the latter still has his job.

Gioachino Colombo is five years younger than Enzo Ferrari; like his ageing employer, he also shows a great deal of lucidity. What is more he is extremely active and, when I visited him in his handsome house on the Piazzale Bacone in Milan, he was about to go to Switzerland to file an application for a patent for a "rolling" (not a "rotary") engine. First of all he showed me a copy of Luigi Fusi's book, *Tutte le vetture Alfa Romeo dal 1910* ("All the Alfa Romeos since 1910"). From the P2 on, each model bears the handwritten name of the designer, the draftsman, and the various other parties involved. As a result his own name recurs constantly beside that of Vittorio Jano, and later on we find those of Capritti, Roselli, Barletta, Taverna, Molino, and others.

Why was it he who designed the Alfa Romeo 158 at Scuderia Ferrari in Modena, and not Vittorio Jano? The question is a legitimate one, since Colombo was Jano's junior, and Jano was in charge of the Alfa Romeo projects.

Colombo explains unhesitatingly that at that time (1937), relations between Enzo Ferrari and Vittorio Jano were in a bad way. Also, Ferrari, in all probability, thought that the charges levelled by the Alfa Romeo management at Jano had some foundation—namely that the technician from Piedmont had run out of steam.

Jano's last design dates back to 1937. It involved the 4495 cc V-12 12C racing single-seater. It was Jano himself who recommended that Colombo should take on the 158.

Jano was replaced in 1937 by the air force major, Bruno Trevisan. In 1919, at the age of twenty-eight, he had been taken on by Fiat as a designer and assigned to the Avio Technical division. In 1934 he followed in Jano's footsteps and moved to Alfa Romeo; there he worked in the automobile design department and was put in charge of developing the V-12 engine planned by Jano.

This helps explain one of the most blurred aspects of the relationship that existed between Enzo Ferrari, Vittorio Jano, and Gioachino Colombo. Once that awkward patch was past, Ferrari and Jano became friends once again, as shown by the constant presence at Maranello of the former chief designer of Alfa Romeo and Lancia in the period which saw the development of the V-6 model desired by Dino Ferrari. Another unclear point that was cleared up for me after talking with Gioachino Colombo concerns the decision taken by Ferrari in 1949 to bid farewell to the (Formula 1) supercharger and to back the construction of an induction engine. This step was taken just as Colombo was leaving Ferrari, to be replaced by Aurelio Lampredi. The job of building the supercharger had in fact been given to Giuseppe Busso because Colombo had, temporarily, gone back to Alfa Romeo.

The 12-cylinder Ferrari was not intended to be supercharged, and it was very difficult to find adequate space to fit either the one-stage or two-stage supercharger. Back at Maranello, Colombo tried to round off Busso's work by using a two-stage type. But this was still a compromise and failed to produce satisfactory results. It was at this point that it was decided to abandon the idea altogether and invest in the induction engine. This was the first task for which Aurelio Lampredi assumed full responsibility.

But it is hard to trace the exact outlines of this particular period. When Lampredi arrived at Ferrari at the recommendation of Professor Carlo Ruini (a physicist and mathematician from Modena), Enzo Ferrari introduced him to Busso who was, as it happened, working on the supercharger. Lampredi suggested redesigning the head and took it upon himself to do so. In an experimental 2000 cc engine the two-stage type worked, in his view.

If the induction engine was preferred, it was, by and large, because its fuel consumption was much lower. One good way of beating Alfa Romeo was to do away with the refuelling stops that cars with superchargers had to make. It should be remembered that the 158 had a very high rate of consumption: it covered 980 meters (3,215') on one liter of 100 percent methyl alcohol. The 300 liters of fuel which it carried with it at the start were topped off with a liter of distilled water and 3 liters of castor-oil. 300 liters may seem a lot. But in those days the Grand Prix races were held over much longer distances than they are today.

The crucial factor which helped Ferrari in its duel with Alfa Romeo was, therefore, the lower consumption of the 4500 cc induction engine, but it should also be added that this engine ran at much lower speeds. At Barcelona, in the last race of the world championship of 1951, Ferrari made the mistake of using the same tires as at Monza in the Italian Grand Prix (a mistake which led to a tire "massacre"). It would otherwise have won its first world championship title in that year. To begin with the catastrophe was put down to the suspension, but this was not the problem.

Aurelio Lampredi was a hotbed of ideas at Ferrari and he was given carte blanche most of the time, to the point where he was also given authority to design a 2500 cc 2-cylinder car, the Formula 1 252.

Planned for use on twisting circuits, the individual cylinder capacity was about 1247 cc, not unlike the engines made at the beginning of the century. The crisis that led to the break between Ferrari and Lampredi occurred in 1955 in the days of the Formula 1 246 and 256. In a factory building racing cars the designer is like the trainer of a football team. He is always to blame when things are not going right. Lampredi was completely in charge of the entire sector: design, tests, trials, and production, with righthand-man Rocchi, supervising the engines, and Salvarani in charge of the frames, gearboxes, and differentials. He was often forced to work after hours at night.

Lampredi maintains dialogue had become difficult between Ferrari and himself. "We didn't understand one another any longer." At a certain point Lampredi had received enticing offers from Lancia, but he did not take them up. By mutual agreement, both men decided on a separation. Someone at Fiat had already offered Lampredi a job to suit his seniority the day he stopped working with Ferrari. And, in fact, twenty-four hours after leaving Modena, Lampredi had walked through the gates at Mirafiori.

Lampredi considers his time with Ferrari to have been extremely useful, just as he sees the experience at Fiat as an essential one: he designed 150 engines there. Lampredi, who sees Ferrari as a real magnetic force, says, "He manages to fill even a curbstone with enthusiasm." But he is a solitary man, too solitary. When ill-advised, his decisions sometimes reflect the thoughts of others rather than his own. Without his elan the Ferrari mark would certainly never have existed, Lampredi says, and he recalls the failure of all similar undertakings of the past in Italy.

If the relationship between the two men broke up it was largely because Lampredi saw completely eye-to-eye with the racing press. He was often discussed in very glowing terms. And it could not have been otherwise in view of Lampredi's contribution to the success of Ferrari.

In addition Lampredi enjoyed a very warm and truly affectionate bond with the drivers. He was inconsolable at the funeral of Alberto Ascari: It was 25 years ago, but I remember it clearly. His sobs also possibly had something to do with his sorrow at having to leave Ferrari. The decision was in the air. An important page was about to be turned, forever. But another was also about to be opened, and it was to be no less brilliant.

Today Enzo Ferrari and Aurelio Lampredi both live in the shadow of the same firm: Fiat. They often bump into one another, their friendship runs deep, as do their mutual esteem and admiration. In the words of Lampredi: "Anyone coming from Ferrari has a guaranteed position, as long as he was there for a good few years. If he did not stay long at Maranello, beware."

The job of head of the technical division at Ferrari was taken over by Carlo Chiti, a very talented designer, and also an extroverted, talkative and energetic man who had started out at the Montecatini research center in 1952. He stayed there for eight months. Before 1952 was through, he joined the experimental division at Alfa Romeo for a short period. Chiti's first task at

Engineer Aurelio Lampredi, today.

Engineer Carlo Chiti (on the right). His latest brainchild is the Alfa 179 "wing-car."

118

Engineer Mauro Forghieri (left) with Daniele Audetto and Niki Lauda.

Maranello was to redesign the 65° 6-cylinder model. He introduced a major modification by replacing the leaf springs with coil springs. As already mentioned, it was he who persuaded Enzo Ferrari of the advantages of the rear engine. Ferrari did not want to hear about it, but he had to give in when faced with the success achieved by the English cars.

Apart from this fundamental innovation, which soon bore fruit, enabling Ferrari to win the world championship in 1961, Chiti concentrated in particular—during his time with Ferrari—on designing the 120° 6-cylinder model which, at a certain stage, was preferred to the 65° version. This latter had the drawback of having a very heavy crankshaft with a distinct moment of inertia, and an excessive number of crank-pins (6). The 120° model, with just 3 crank-pins, was 10-15 cm (4-6 ″) shorter than the 65° version, as well as being lighter and giving a more all-round performance (on the test-bench its power output of 190 hp was 10-12 hp higher than that of the other engine).

But Chiti recalls that the 120° version brought to light a defect which was fairly widespread at the time, known as "barbotage," or, in English, "chattering" or "clattering." This barbotage became a considerable problem: much of the oil remained in the crankcase,

119

and thus failed to do its duty completely. This was remedied by using a larger number of scavenge pumps. Chiti maintains that barbotage was a "virus" which affected all the engines of that period. It was Keith Duckworth who introduced a far-reaching cure with his V-8 Cosworth. From then on, the virus has been kept under control thanks to a different internal structure which has been universally adopted.

In addition to the rear-engined cars, of which there were several, including the 1960 246 P, Chiti also designed for Ferrari a car with a transverse engine, but this model never left the drawing-board.

At the end of 1961 Chiti left Maranello, followed by a group of other managers and employees of Ferrari. He was one of the founders of ATS and, in 1964, of Autodelta, with Ludovico Chizzola. Chizzola had also been with Ferrari for a while. Autodelta moved from Udine to Milan in 1965 and became a stepping-stone for Alfa Romeo. In the last fifteen years Carlo Chiti has provided ample proof of his abilities by assuming responsibility for the excellent sports cars produced by the Milanese firm, including the model powered by the 12-cylinder "boxer" engine and, more recently, the 177 and 179 single-seaters. The transformation of the 12-cylinder engine from "boxer" to 60° V-type, necessitated by the arrival of the new "wing" structure on the body, was achieved in the record time of five-and-a-half months.

Although he left Ferrari in an unfortunate manner, Carlo Chiti now talks in glowing terms of his old boss, and, among other things, recognizes in him a strength of purpose and a fount of determination which are unmatched. This, according to Chiti, is where Ferrari's greatness lies: "He is a genius in economy," in the way he runs his firm. The selection of the best people, be it technicians or drivers; the way in which he has managed to maneuver through the slippery twists and turns of racing rules and regulations; the intuition shown by his association with Michelin, which would have been a major risk if it had not worked: all these things—in Chiti's eyes—make Ferrari a phenomenon in his own right.

With a sincere admiration for the man and the "trouble-maker," he recalls the period he spent with him by admitting that his methods of squeezing the best from his men were extremely intelligent, because they were based on a strong practical sense as well as a great deal of intuition. Men are judged by their deeds, Chiti asserts. By this yardstick, the achievement of Enzo Ferrari is unprecedented in the history of the automobile. And what he had achieved is the fruit of his "peasant" mentality, his strategy, and his "craft." In a world dominated by hysteria he is completely at ease and manages to bring out the best qualities in those around him.

Chiti is sure that one of the reasons for the success of Ferrari cars is that Enzo Ferrari never leaves Modena. And woe if he had. His constant presence at the place of work, his personal involvement in the racing division, his interest in the smallest details (which is shown by his detailed daily lists, jotted in a notebook, regarding "things to do"), all instill fear but also respect among those working for him.

Considering the way in which Carlo Chiti left Maranello, we might conclude that it would be hard to find better words uttered about Enzo Ferrari. To sum up, Chiti expresses his regret at having failed to adopt "his methods" and adds that "he was the one who was right."

It is certainly true that Enzo Ferrari gives more credit to his cars than to the merits of his drivers. There was only one moment when it looked as if the cars were beaten and that was when the rear engine was introduced. He tried to draw strength from his old conviction that, with the world the way it is, "it's the horse that draws the cart, and not the other way round."

Mauro Forghieri has practically been at Ferrari since the day he was born. The son of a Ferrari employee, he joined the technical division after graduating in mechanical engineering. In practical terms, everything that has been done since Chiti bears his signature. This is a long period of time; the twenty-year mark is about to be crossed. Forghieri's balance-sheet shows four world championship titles (Surtees in 1964, Lauda in 1975 and 1977 and Scheckter in 1979) and at least five world championships for builders (in 1963, 1964, 1965, 1967, and 1972). Since he has been in charge of the Ferrari technical division, with varying fortune, certain fundamental landmarks have been set, such as the "boxer" engine, the transverse gear-box, and the in-depth research in the aerodynamic sector carried out in collaboration with Pininfarina, using the latter's wind-tunnel. Because of this research work, Forghieri has been able to completely alter the appearance of the Ferrari single-seaters and create an extremely compact and balanced car. Because of his typically Emilian vitality, his dynamism, and the way in which he handles those working with him, Forghieri is another of the leading personalities in the "club." This is what Niki Lauda says of him in his book *I miei anni con Ferrari*: "The presence of Forghieri is a major contributive factor to the anxiety among the team. He has such faith in himself and in his ideas that he forces them on others without considering the drawbacks. In conditions of this sort it is perfectly normal that, at a certain point, a driver should want to have a technician who does not turn every test session into a tragedy and with whom it is possible to work together on a rational and non-emotional basis towards a common goal. But I must repeat for the umpteenth time that I believe in the ability of Mauro Forghieri. He is a genius and it is my bad luck that I don't know how to deal with geniuses."

SPORTS CARS

The 125 S has an important place in the history of Ferrari, having been the first car to bear the name of the constructor from Modena. It was powered by a 60° V-12 engine with a cylinder capacity of 1496.77 cc (55 mm bore, 52.5 mm stroke), a power output of 72 hp at 5,600 rpm, and a compression ratio of 8:1. Single camshaft; cylinder block of light alloy; hemispherical combustion chambers; 7 engine mountings; 2 valves per cylinder; chain-driven cams; carburation by 3 Weber 30 DCF carburetors; 5-speed gearbox, 3rd and 4th synchromesh; frame with tubular members; independent front suspension: lower transverse leaf spring, oleodynamic shock absorbers; rear suspension with rigid semi-floating axle, longitudinal leaf springs, stabilizer bar and hydraulic shock absorbers; drum brakes. Wheelbase: 2.42 meters (7' 11"), front track: 1.25 m (49"), rear track: 1.20 m (47"), weight: 750 kg (1,690 lb), fuel tank capacity: 75 liters.

It was with this car, on May 11, 1947, that Franco Cortese took part in a race on the Piacenza circuit, and, for the first time, broadcast the name of Ferrari as a builder. The car behaved very well, but, although it was in the lead, it failed to finish the course because of fuel pump trouble. Some time later, again with the 125 S, Cortese won the Roman Grand Prix on the built-up Caracalla circuit.

Starting what was subsequently to become a typical feature of the Ferrari system, the 125 was almost immediately joined by a sister model, the 159 S. The markings took on a precise meaning: 125 stood for the unitary cylinder capacity: 124.73 cc, and 159 for 158.57 cc. On this basis, the 159 was a 12-cylinder model with a cylinder capacity of about 2000 cc (1902.84 cc.), bore: 59 mm, stroke: 58 mm., power output: 125 hp at 7,000 rpm. On August 16, 1947, with the 159 S, Franco Cortese won at Pescara. In all, seven 125 S cars were built.

This car hallmarked the start of the third year of activity at Ferrari. It was also a 12-cylinder model of about 2000 cc. (bore: 60 mm, stroke 58.8 mm, giving a total cylinder capacity of 1995.02 cc); power output: 150 hp at 7,000 rpm, compression ratio: 8.5:1. It is worth noting that in just three years Ferrari was already on its second 2000 cc. engine, sure proof of the dynamism of the small Maranello works, which was to be amply demonstrated in the years to come.

The 166 S is a famous car in the Ferrari family tree, because it developed into various types (S, F2, Inter, MM, and FL), all, it goes without saying, with the same engine, the power output of which increased from the 150 hp at 7,000 rpm in the S type, to the 160 hp at 7,000 rpm in the F2 model, but with a high compression ratio of 10:1. It was also, and above all, famous because it gave Enzo Ferrari his first really satisfying results. At the wheel of a 166, Clemente Biondetti won his third Mille Miglia in 1948, teamed up with the mechanic, Navone. This was Ferrari's first success in the extremely prestigious endurance race across half of Italy. As a result, his name acquired international stature virtually overnight. In the following year, again driving a 166, Clemente Biondetti won the same race, his fourth. In 1950 it was Giannino Marzotto's turn, at the wheel of a composite car. This was the combination of a 166 frame and a 195 engine, again a 12-cylinder model, but with the cylinder capacity raised to 2341.02 cc, giving a total power output of 170 hp at 7,000 rpm, and with a compression ratio of 8.5:1.

The 166 MM scored another major victory: the win by Luigi Chinetti and Lord Selsdon in the first 24-hour race at Le Mans in 1949. They averaged 132.420 kph (82.76 mph) over a distance of 3,178.299 km (1,986.437 miles). What is more, in 1948 and 1949 Biondetti won the Targa Florio and the Giro di Sicilia, the first with Igor and the second with Benedetti.

125 S - 1947

166 S - 1948

With the 375, which developed into four models (F1, MM, America, and Plus), Ferrari went back to the large engine, a theme he had tackled in the 275 in 1950, then in the 340, and finally in the 375 F1.

The 375 MM was powered by a 60° V-12 engine, with an 84 mm bore and a 68 mm stroke, giving a total cylinder capacity of 4522.9 cc, which was slightly larger than that of the Formula 1 single-seater (4493.73 cc). The power output was 340 hp at 7,000 rpm; the compression ratio 9:1; the cylinder head of light alloy had pressed-in liners; 1 camshaft per bank of cylinders; 7 mountings; feed by 2 diaphragm pumps and 1 electric pump, 3 inverted four-barrelled Weber 40 IF/4C carburetors; magneto ignition; 4-speed gearbox; frame with tubular and transverse members, transverse leaf springs, stabilizer bar and Houdaille shock absorbers; rigid rear axle, longitudinal leaf springs and Houdaille shock absorbers; drum brakes. Wheelbase: 2.60 meters (8' 6"); front track: 1.32 m (4' 4"); rear track: 1.32 m (4' 4"). Weight: 900 kg (2,025 lb), fuel tank capacity: 180 liters.

In the Plus version the cylinder capacity of the engine was raised to 4954.34 cc by increasing the stroke to 74.5 mm and leaving the bore unchanged. The power output rose to 330 hp at 6,000 rpm, with a compression ratio of 9.2:1.

The 375 and the models derived from it chalked up plenty of wins: in 1953 Villoresi won the Giro di Sicilia with the 4500, Giannino Marzotto and Crosara won the Mille Miglia with the 4500, Farina and Hawthorn won the 1,000-kilometer (621.37 miles) Spa-Francorchamps also with the 4500, and Ascari won the Nürburgring 1,000-kilometer race with the 4500. In 1954 Farina-Maglioli won the Buenos Aires 1000-kilometer race with the 4500; Gonzales-Trintignant, the Le Mans 24-hour race with the 4954 cc; and Magioli won the Carrera Panamericana with the 4954. In 1955 Saenz Valiente-Ibanez won the Buenos Aires 1000-kilometer race in the 4954.

Apart from the engine of the 252 Formula 1, a two-cylinder, one-off engine which was the outcome of the extraordinary mind of Aurelio Lampredi, the engine of the 750 Monza is the model with the largest bore (103 mm) of all the Ferrari engines ever built.

The 750 Monza was a 4-cylinder model with a cylinder capacity of 2999.6 cc (stroke: 90 mm), a power output of 260 hp at 6,500 rpm, and a compression ratio of 9:1. The crankcase and engine block were of light alloy; 5 mountings; 2 overhead camshafts; carburation by mechanical pump and 2 Weber 58 DCO A/3 carburetors; dual ignition; 5-speed gearbox situated at the rear together with the differential; frame with tubular members and cross members; deformable structures; independent front suspension, with coil springs and stabilizer bar; rear suspension with De Dion rigid axle, transverse leaf spring and hydraulic shock absorbers, drum brakes; wheelbase: 2.25 meters (7' 4.5"), front track: 1.27 m (4' 2"), rear track: 1.28 m (4' 2.5"); weight: 760 (1,710 lb); fuel tank capacity: 150 liters.

Although it was fairly successful, the 750 Monza was a car which left behind some ugly memories: it was in a car of this type that Alberto Ascari was killed on May 26, 1955, at Monza in an accident which will never be properly explained. As mentioned elsewhere, Olivier Gendebien blames the 750 for the accident in which he was involved during the trials for the 1956 Tourist Trophy. According to Gendebien, the basic flaw of this car was the fact that it simply did not "take corners," because it suffered from considerable understeering, and this could well explain both accidents.

But Mike Hawthorn gave another explanation of Ascari's crash; and this, from the technical point of view, was more detailed and convincing than Gendebien's. The 750 Monzas were naturally enough modified, but, by that time, they were stuck with their bad reputation.

375 MM - 1953

750 Monza - 1954

125

With the 290 MM, Ferrari returned to the traditional 12-cylinder model. This move earned the firm more than a little success, because the car was a very lucky one. The engine had a bore of 73 mm and a stroke of 69.5 mm, giving a total cylinder capacity of 3490.62 cc, and a power output of 330 hp at 8,000 rpm, with a compression ratio of 9:1. The engine block, crankcase, and head were made of light alloy; the combustion chambers were hemispherical; 7 mountings; 2 valves per cylinder with one camshaft per bank of cylinders; carburation by 2 mechanical pumps and 3 twin-barrelled downdraft Weber 46 TRA carburetors; dual ignition; 4 coils; 4-speed gearbox en bloc with the differential; tubular frame; independent front suspension with deformable structures, coil springs, transverse anti-roll bar, and hydraulic shock absorbers; rear suspension with De Dion axle, transverse leaf spring and hydraulic shock absorbers; drum brakes. Wheelbase: 2.35 meters (7' 10.5"), front track: 1.31 m (4' 3.5"), rear track: 1.28 m (4' 2"). Weight: 880 kg (1,980 lb); fuel tank capacity: 190 liters.

The 290's debut exceeded all expectations, with Fangio-Castellotti winning the Sebring 12-hour race in 1956, and Castellotti coming in first in the Mille Miglia that same year, in what was possibly the young driver from Lodi's finest feat. In 1957, Gregory, Castellotti, and Musso won the 1000-kilometer event at Buenos Aires (Castellotti took turns at the wheel with De Portago and Collins, which is why he was placed first and third). The 3500 also scored a very special victory because it enabled Piero Taruffi to win the 1957 Mille Miglia, which was the last of the series and also the Roman driver's last race.

The 290 was the only 3500 cc, 12-cylinder car built by Ferrari. There was another 3500 model, but it had a 4-cylinder engine: This was the 354 S (3431.93 cc), with a power output of 280 hp at 6,000 rpm and a compression ratio of 8.5:1.

Another highly renowned Ferrari Sport model is the 250 TRS. The name might seem enigmatic, but is in fact easily explained: 250 stands once again for the unitary cylinder capacity of 246.95 cc, and TRS for "Testa Rossa" ("Red Head") Sport. The nickname has lent itself to some wild interpretations. It was coined quite simply because at a certain moment the cylinder heads, with twin overhead camshafts, were painted red, probably on the spur of the moment by one of the mechanics, who was a fan of that type of car.

The 250 was also a 12-cylinder model with a bore of 73 mm and a stroke of 58.8 mm, giving a total cylinder capacity of 2953.21 cc, a power output of 290 hp at 7,500 rpm, and a compression ratio of 9.8:1. The engine block, crankcase and head were of light alloy; 7 mountings; 2 valves per cylinder, single camshaft for each bank of cylinders; carburation by 6 twin-barrelled downdraft Weber type 40 DCN carburetors; ignition by coil and two distributors; 4-speed gearbox; self-locking differential; frame with members reinforced by struts; independent front suspension, large coil springs, deformable structures, telescopic shock absorbers; rear suspension by De Dion axle, telescopic springs and shock absorbers; wheelbase: 2.35 meters (7' 10.5"); front track: 1.31 m (4' 3.5"); rear track: 1.30 m (4' 3"). Weight: 800 kg (1,800 lb).

Like the 290 MM, the 250 TRS was an instant winner. Driven by Peter Collins and Phil Hill, it came in first in the Buenos Aires 1000-kilometer race in 1958, and followed that win by another in the Sebring 12-hour event. Musso-Gendebien in turn won the Targa Florio, and Gendebien-Phil Hill their first 24-hour race at Le Mans.

In 1959 Ferrari was virtually guaranteed the world championship title. The 250 TRS again won the 12-hour race at Sebring, driven by four men: Gendebien, Phil Hill, Gurney, and Daigh, one Belgian and three Americans.

290 MM - 1956

250 TRS - 1958

As its name indicates, the 400 Superamerica was not meant to be a sports car, but merely a deluxe GT model. Enzo Ferrari cleverly used the high-falutin' name he had dreamed up and used the 400 for both purposes. It was powered by a 12-cylinder engine with a bore of 77 mm and a stroke of 71 mm, giving a total cylinder capacity of 3967.44 cc, a power output of 340 hp at 7,000 rpm, and a compression ratio of 8.8:1. The engine block and crankcase (all in one) were of light alloy with pressed-in liners of cast iron; the cylinder head was also of light alloy; hemispherical combustion chambers; 7 mountings; 2 valves per cylinder driven by one camshaft per bank of cylinders; carburation by 3 Weber 46 DCF/3 carburetors; ignition by coil; 2 distributors; 4-speed gearbox; frame with tubular members and cross members; independent front suspension with deformable structures, telescopic springs and shock absorbers; rigid rear axle, rear leaf springs and telescopic shock absorbers. Wheelbase: 2.60 meters (8' 6''); front track: 1.39 m (4' 7''), rear track: 1.38 m (4' 6.5''). Weight: 1,280 kg (2,880 lb); fuel tank capacity: 100 liters.

The above data refer in particular to the GT version, but for the Le Mans 24-hour race in 1962 a sports model was fitted out. This was called the 330 LM and, with the team of Gendebien-Phil Hill at the wheel, it won the classic French race at the average speed of 185.469 kph (115.918 mph) over a distance of 4451.255 km (2,782.034 miles). It was Ferrari's sixth success in this race and Gendebien's fourth win. That year's race was nothing less than a triumph for the Italian firm, with Guichet-Noblet coming in second at the wheel of a GTO, and another GTO, driven by Eldé-Buerlys coming in third. To illustrate the superior quality of their car, it is worth mentioning that Gendebien and Phil Hill were at the wheel for 19 out of the 24 hours, including the second 12 hours at a stretch.

The 246 is another founding-father of a new technical concept developed by Ferrari. In fact it was the first sports model built by the Emilian factory with a rear engine—a close relative of the Formula 1 156. As all those who follow the goings on in the world of motor racing know, Enzo Ferrari was not at all happy about the rear engine, and he hesitated for some time before mounting it on one of his cars, but once the Rubicon had been crossed, there were no second thoughts. The 246 P had a 6-cylinder 2417.33 cc engine (bore: 85 mm, stroke: 71 mm), with a power output of 280 hp at 8,500 rpm, and a compression ratio of 9.8:1. This was a 65° V-6 engine. The block, crankcase and head were made of light alloy; hemispherical combustion chambers; 4 mountings; 2 valves per cylinder driven by twin overhead camshafts per bank of cylinders; carburation by 3 twin-barrelled downdraft Weber carburetors, type 42 C; coil ignition, 2 distributors and 2 coils; 2 plugs per cylinder; 5-speed gearbox en bloc with the differential, frame tubular with small-diameter tubing; independent front and rear suspension, deformable structures, large coil springs and telescopic shock absorbers; disc brakes all round. Wheelbase: 2.32 meters (7' 7''), front track: 1.31 m (4' 3.5''), rear track: 1.30 m (4' 3''). Weight: 750 kg (1,690 lb); fuel tank capacity: 120 liters. This car made a very successful debut by winning the Targa Florio in 1961, driven by the von Trips-Gendebien team.

As has always been the case with the house of Ferrari, the 246 P was not an end in itself but gave rise to various combinations: it was fitted with both 8- and 12-cylinder engines. The Le Mans 24-hour race in 1963 was won by a 250 P with a `12-cylinder 2953.21 cc engine, with a power output of 300 hp at 7,800 rpm and a compression ratio of 9.8:1.

400 Superamerica - 1960

246 P - 1960

In the varied and often changeable list of names of the different Ferrari engines, one finds the mark GTO, which, for a long time, caused many people to scratch their heads. It was finally decided that it stood for Gran Turismo Omologata ("Classified Grand Touring"). In reality, it would seem that the "O" was a redundant letter, slipped in inadvertently by a typist and never amended.

To return to the story, however, what really matters is that the 250 GTO was one of the most impressive cars of the entire range of Ferrari production, and it remains one of the last examples of a front-engined Ferrari. It was powered by a 60° 2953.21 cc V-12 engine, with 73 mm bore and a 58.8 mm stroke, giving a total power output of 290 hp at 7,400 rpm, with a compression ratio of 9.8:1. The cylinder block, crankcase, and head were of light alloy with pressed-in liners of cast iron; 7 mountings; 2 valves per cylinder, single overhead camshaft per bank of cylinders; carburation by 6 twin-barrelled downdraft. Weber 38 DCN carburetors; coil ignition with 2 distributors; 5-speed gearbox en bloc with the engine; frame with tubular members and cross-members; independent front suspension with deformable structures, large coil springs, transverse stabilizer bar and telescopic shock absorbers; rear suspension with rigid axle, coil springs and telescopic shock absorbers. Disc brakes all round. Wheelbase: 2.40 meters (7' 8.5"); front and rear track: 1.35 m (4' 5"). Weight 1,060 kg (2,385 lb), fuel tank capacity 130 liters.

The GTO won an impressive number of races, starting with the classic win by Phil Hill and Gendebien in the 12-hour race at Sebring in 1962; then the 1962 and 1963 Tourist Trophies, driven by Ireland and Graham Hill respectively. Pedro Rodriguez won the 2,000-kilometer (1,242.74 miles) race at Daytona in 1963, and Guichet-Behra won the Tour de France the same year.

Winning a 24-hour Le Mans meeting against all the predictions and odds was the highest success of this car, which, in theory, was to have been a quiet GT model. But, the 250 LM fitted with an engine of about 3300 cc took part in the French race. It was driven by Jochen Rindt and Masten Gregory, having been entered by Luigi Chinetti. The two drivers started the 24-hour race at a gentle pace and were lying in fourteenth position after 8 hours. Victory seemed out of the question, but little by little they moved up steadily through the field, to everyone's considerable surprise. After 11 hours they were lying third; after 12, second; and after 21, they had secured the lead, which they did not relinquish from then on.

The 250 had a 60° V-12 engine with a 73 mm bore and a 58.8 mm stroke, giving a total cylinder capacity of 2953.21 cc, and a power output of 300 hp at 7,500 rpm, with a compression ratio of 9.2:1. The all-in-one engine block and crankcase and the cylinder head were made of light alloy. The car had polyspherical combustion chambers, 7 mountings, 2 valves per cylinder, single camshaft for each bank of cylinders, carburation by dual pump, 2 twin-barrelled downdraft Weber 38 DCN carburetors, coil ignition, 2 distributors, 5-speed gearbox en bloc with the self-locking differential and engine, tubular frame, independent front and rear suspension, deformable structures, coil springs, stabilizer bars, telescopic shock absorbers, and disc brakes all round. Wheelbase: 2.40 meters (7' 10.5"), front track: 1.35 m (4' 5"), rear track: 1.34 m (4' 4.5"). Weight: 850 kg (1,915 lb). Fuel tank capacity 130 liters.

The 250 was rear-engined, and, because it was an enclosed car, Pininfarina, to whom Ferrari now turned constantly to add the body to its frames, did not find it an easy task to solve the various problems which the engine—housed in a single unit—caused.

250 GTO - 1962

250 LM - 1964

131

The series of sports cars with the P marking is undoubtedly one of the most handsome and efficient of the entire Ferrari production. The letter P was first used on a 250 built in 1963 (2953.21 cc cylinder capacity; total power output of 300 hp at 7,800 rpm; compression ratio of 9.8:1). Prior to this there had been a 246 SP in 1961 (2417 cc; 270 hp at 8,000 rpm; compression ratio of 9.8:1); a 196 SP in 1962 (1983 cc, with a power output of 210 hp at 7,500 rpm, and a compression ratio of 9.8:1), plus another 246 SP (2417 cc; 265 hp at 7,000 rpm; compression ratio of 9.6:1); and lastly, a 268 SP in 1963 (2953 cc; power output of 210 hp at 7,500 rpm; and a compression ratio of 9.6:1).

With the 250 P, Ferrari went back to 12-cylinders which were retained for the next series too—the 275 P, the 330 P, the 250 LM, the 275 P2, the 330 P2, the 365 P, the 330 P3, the 330 P4, and the 412 P coupé, better known as the 330 P3/4. Lastly, 1965 and 1966 saw the 206 SP, the 206 S and, once more, the 206 SP, all with 65° V-6, or Dino, engines.

The 330 P2 had a 60°, 3967.44 cc V-12 engine (77 mm bore, 71 mm stroke) with a power output of 410 hp at 8,200 rpm and a compression ratio of 9.8:1. The engine block, crankcase, and head were of light alloy with pressed-in liners of cast iron; 7 mountings; two valves per cylinder for each bank; carburation by 6 twin-barrelled downdraft Weber 42 DCN 2 carburetors; coil ignition with two double distributors and 4 coils, 2 plugs per cylinder; 5-speed gearbox en bloc with the engine; self-locking differential; tubular frame with struts; independent front and rear suspension with deformable structures, stabilizer bar, coil springs and telescopic shock absorbers; disc brakes all round. Wheelbase: 2.40 meters (7' 10.5"); front track 1.35 m (4' 5"); rear track 1.34 m (4' 4.5"). Weight 820 kg (1,845 lb).

The 206 Dino was the most complete expression of Enzo Ferrari's wish to remember his son "Alfredino" who died in 1956. Dino Ferrari, backed up by Vittorio Jano who, after leaving Lancia, had become an official consultant at Ferrari, had urged his father to build a V-6 engine.

The Dino engine enabled Ferrari to win two world championships in 1958 with Hawthorn (2500 cc) and in 1961 with Phil Hill (1500 cc). The 206 S version was also successfully used in a sports model for the European hill-climb championships. This car had a 1986.61 cc, engine with an 86 mm bore and 57 mm stroke, a power output of 205 hp at 8,000 rpm, and a compression ratio of 11:1. The V was set at an angle of 65°; the engine-block, crankcase and head were of light alloy, pressed-in liners in cast iron; hemispherical combustion chambers; 4 mountings; two valves per cylinder, driven by twin overhead camshafts per bank of cylinders; carburation by three twin-barrelled downdraft Weber 40 DCN 2 carburetors; coil ignition with a single distributor; 5-speed gearbox and self-locking differential en bloc with the engine; tubular frame; front and rear independent suspension with transverse deformable structures, coil springs, stabilizer bars and telescopic shock absorbers; disc brakes all round. Wheelbase 2.28 meters (7' 6"); front track 1.36 meters (4' 5.5"); rear track 1.35 meters (4' 5"). Weight 580 kg (1,305 lb). Fuel tank capacity: 110 liters.

At the wheel of a Dino 206, Lodovico Scarfiotti won the European hill-climb championship in 1965. It was, moreover, the Dino engine which paved the way for negotiations to begin between Fiat and Ferrari. In order to build a Formula 2 car which he wanted to make, Ferrari had to produce 500 engines of the same type. It was Fiat who undertook to do this, and the end product was a sports model called the Fiat-Dino.

330 P2 - 1965

206 Dino - 1965

The 330 P4 is a close relative of the P2 and P3, but with a slightly increased maximum cylinder capacity (3989.56 cc as opposed to 3967.44 cc). It has a power output of 450 hp at 8,200 rpm and a compression ratio of 10.5:1. Compared with the P3, the P4 had modified tracks (they were widened) and, more importantly, a revised engine, which had 3 valves instead of 2, although it retained the 2 plugs per cylinder. The tires were also changed from Firestone to Dunlop.

The P4 won a magnificent victory on its first outing, the Daytona 24-hour race in 1967, driven by Amon and Bandini. It was followed by Parkes-Scarfiotti in a similar car, with Pedro Rodriguez and Guichet coming in third in a P3/4. The three cars crossed the finish abreast, as Fords had done the year before at Le Mans. The P4s were not entered for the Sebring 12-hour race, but Bandini and Amon once again won at Monza in the 1,000-kilometer event. Scarfiotti and Parkes were second.

By now the season was abuzz with the renewed duel between Ferrari and Ford. The American firm, with a 7000 cc car, had won the 1966 meeting at Le Mans (the 24-hour race), bagging the first three places. Ferrari tried to keep pace with Ford in 1967, but the latter won again with Gurney-Foyt at the wheel of the 7000 cc car. But this time Ferrari acquitted itself far better, managing to secure second and third places, with Scarfiotti-Parkes and Mairesse-Beurlys respectively. Both the driving teams had the P4 which Ferrari had conscientiously prepared, forsaking the 1000-kilometer (621.37 miles) race at Spa-Francorchamps to do so. It should be mentioned that both the winning Ford and the two Ferraris on its tail achieved an average speed that has not since been touched at Le Mans, as well as covering more kilometers than in any other Le Mans meeting.

Because of an absurd and much-criticized decision by the International Racing Committee, the 1970 championship (for cars, not drivers) involved 5000 cc cars which had a production total of at least 25. Enzo Ferrari appeared to dissociate himself from the IRC decision, but in the end he agreed to build 25 models, which he tried to sell as quickly as possible to private buyers and scuderias, keeping back the absolute minimum number for himself. The 512 S had a 60° V-12 engine with a cylinder capacity of 4993.53 cc (87 mm bore, 70 mm stroke), giving a total power output of 500 hp at 8,500 rpm with a compression ratio of 11.5:1. The engine block and head were in light alloy, with cast iron pressed-in liners; flat combustion chambers; 7 mountings; 4 valves per cylinder driven by two camshafts per bank of cylinders; carburation by direct Lucas injection; electronic ignition; 5-speed gearbox en bloc with the engine and differential; mixed frame (box and tubular); independent front and rear suspension; coil springs and telescopic shock absorbers; disc brakes all round. Wheelbase: 2.40 meters (7′ 10.5″), front and rear track: 1.51 m (4′ 11″). Weight 820 kg (1,845 lb). Fuel tank capacity: 120 liters.

The 512 S was not a lucky car, not least because the men who built it were well aware of the absurdity of making cars with such a large cubic capacity. It won the 1970 12-hour race at Sebring, driven by Giunti, Andretti, and Vaccarella. A new version christened the SM and driven by Ickx and Giunti, won the Kyalami 9-hour race. The 512 was finally put to one side, but a new version, the 512 M, with its power output raised to 610 hp at 9,000 rpm, caused something of a stir. In its original version the 512 S came in fourth and fifth in the 1970 24-hour race at Le Mans with the teams Posey-Bucknum and Walker-De Fierlandt, and third and fourth in the 1971 Le Mans meeting, with Posey-Adamovicz and Craft-Weier.

330 P4 - 1967

512 S - 1970

FORMULA 2 FERRARIS

The Formula 2 cars only make rare appearances in the family tree of Ferrari production. In fact with the exception of the 500, which became a leading player in the world championship stakes, the races for these "junior" cars never greatly interested Enzo Ferrari. But for all that, the Formula 2 Ferraris have always been important because they have often preceded the Formula 1 models of the same period.

The first Formula 2 Ferrari was the 166 of 1948, which can therefore be considered, in an absolute sense, as the forebearer of all the single-seaters of this type which were fielded by the Modena firm. What is more, it was a part of Enzo Ferrari's program. When he announced the birth of the 125 (his first car), he specified that he would make a sports model, a competition model, and a Grand Prix model. These each had a 1500 cc. 60° 12-cylinder engine. The 166 was inspired by the competition type, and started to be discussed in 1948.

The 166 differed from the 125 competition in as much as it had a 12-cylinder engine of about 2000 cc with a bore of 60 mm which was slightly higher than the stroke of 58.8 mm; the compression ratio was 10:1; and the power output was 160 hp at 7,000 rpm. The performances of Alberto Ascari and Luigi Villoresi, and, less regularly, of Felice Bonetto, Chico Landi, Franco Cortese, Roberto Vallone, Piero Taruffi, and Nando Righetti provided Ferrari with the first truly satisfying results.

In 1950-51, the 166 underwent certain major modifications, the main one being the "transaxle" arrangement, i.e., the transferral of the gearbox unit to the rear en bloc with the self-locking ZF differential. The De Dion rear axle was another fundamentally new feature introduced to these cars. The Formula 2 with the De Dion axle made its debut, on a purely experimental basis, at Pau, driven by Ascari in 1950, in a race for Formula 1 and other cars. Although it was very quick, it revealed several defects which forced Ascari to retire. It was, however, a profitable experiment, because, from then on, the 166 turned out to be virtually unbeatable. In 1950, driven by Ascari, it won at Modena, Mons, Rome, Rheims, the Nürburgring, and Garda. With Villoresi at the wheel it won at Monza and Erlen; and Sommer drove it to victory in Switzerland. In 1951, Villoresi won at Marseilles, Ascari at Monza and Naples, Raffaeli at Rome, and Giannino Marzotto at Rouen.

The announcement that the 1954-1960 Formula 1 was to admit engines up to 2500 cc induced Ferrari to consider an engine different from the 12-cylinder model, and a 4-cylinder was chosen. The development of this engine and the now legendary 500 single-seater in which it was to be used, diverted Aurelio Lampredi from further improving the 166. This car was to have gotten a new engine with twin overhead camshafts, derived from the Formula 1 supercharged model, with a bore of 63.5 mm and a stroke of 57.8 mm.

All in all, the Formula 2 166 produced good results for Ferrari. It won fourteen out of thirty-one races, came in second in three, third in four, and retired in ten (all because of transmission problems). The history of the 4-cylinder engine of the 500 is too familiar to be retold here, but it must be emphasized that this was one of the most successful cars of the entire Ferrari production line, possibly because of its very simplicity.

It is also true that in that period Ferrari did not come up against any real opposition, with the exception of the Maserati A6GCS, which, in fact, put up valiant resistance to the 4-cylinder car in 1953. If there had not been a change in the formula in 1954, it is possible that the 500 would have ceased dominating the scene. But the fact remains that no other model of Ferrari has had such a rich roll of honor (twenty-nine wins out of 104 races, eighteen second places, nine third places, seven fourth places, four fifth places, five sixth places, two seventh places, and one eighth place). In all, it retired on twenty-nine occasions: fifteen times because of engine trouble, twice because of transmission problems, and twelve times because of collisions or going off the track. It is also worth noting that the 500 did not undergo any substantial modification in the two years (1952 and 1953) in which it was used, and this demonstrates its ability to meet the requirements laid down for it.

The third Formula 2 model built by Ferrari was the Squalo ("Shark"), also known as the 553, which was built in 1953. Were it not for the fact that the 553 was the precursor of the 555 Formula 1 model, it would probably have gone unnoticed, because it does not have its own tale to tell. It had a 4-cylinder engine that was structurally different from that of the 500: bore 93 mm, stroke 73.5 mm, giving a total cylinder capacity of 1997.11 cc and a power output of 180 hp at 7,200 rpm with a compression ratio of 12:1. As in the 166 and the 500, the 4-speed gearbox was fitted at the rear en bloc with the self-locking ZF differential. Here too the rear axle was of the De Dion type. The total weight of the Squalo was 575 kg (1,295 lb).

Three more years were to slip by before there was discussion at the Ferrari works of a new Formula 2 car; but the successor to the 553 was, like the 166 and the 500, a car which has a significant place in the history of the firm because of the numerous models to which it gave rise. The new "junior" car, called the 156, had a 65° V-6 engine, a type that was particularly dear to Enzo Ferrari because his son Dino had followed its progress through the planning stages while he was ill. In fact Enzo Ferrari writes in his 1974 book: "I and my dear friend Jano spent many an hour at his bedside discussing the plans for a 1500 cc. engine. There were various solutions: 4-cylinder, straight-6, 65° V-6, or 8-cylinder. I well remember the insistence and sound

The 1967, 166 F2 Ferrari had an engine with 6 cylinders mounted in a 65° V. Its power output was 210 hp.

knowledge with which Dino discussed and listened to all the memos I brought him each day from Maranello. In the end, we chose the V-6, for mechanical reasons and also because of its dimensions. So the famous 156 was born, and it uttered its first cries in November 1956, five months after Dino's death."
The 156, mounted in a Formula 2 model, developed a power output of 180 hp at 9,000 rpm, with a compression ratio of 10:1. The construction of this engine went along with the first research in placing it at the rear of the car. This research, the story goes, was carried out on a Cooper frame belonging to the Scuderia Centro-Sud. The first trials took place on the Modena track, with the then chief test-driver, Martino Severi, driving. The racing debut of a rear-engined Ferrari (driven by Ritchie Ginther) took place in the Monaco Grand Prix in 1960.
While Vittorio Jano went ahead with the development of the 65° V-6 engine (the design was by Aurelio Lampredi, however), Carlo Chiti, who had taken Lampredi's place, designed another V-6 engine, but with a 120° angle, a bore of 73 mm and a stroke of 58.8 mm, giving a total cylinder capacity of 1476.80 cc and a power output of 190 hp at 9,500 rpm. In the same period, a 60° V-6 engine was also developed (73 × 58.8 mm, total cylinder capacity: 1476.60, power output: 150 hp at 8,000 rpm); but the 65° version was preferred to it (70 × 64.5 mm, total cylinder capacity: 1489.35 cc, power output: 180 hp at 9,000 rpm). In 1961, when the new 1500 cc Formula 1 came into effect, the 156 was promoted to play a leading role.
Starting with the 206, or Dino, of 1966, Ferrari resumed its Formula 2 activities. In 1967, after adapting the engines to the new limit on cylinder capacity, a 65° V-6 engine was fitted in a Formula 2 car (86 × 45.8 mm, giving a total cylinder capacity of 1596.25 cc, and a power output of 210 hp at 10,500 rpm).

In 1968 the 65° V-6 had a bore of 79.5 mm and a stroke of 53.5 mm (total cylinder capacity of 1593.60 cc, giving a power output of 225 hp at 10,500 rpm). In 1969, the last year in which Ferrari took an active part in this formula, the power output of the 65° V-6 engine of 1968 was raised to 232 hp at 11,000 rpm. It is worth mentioning that the 1967 Formula 2 Dino (1596.25 cc) had three valves per cylinder and the 1968 Formula 2 Dino (1593.60 cc) had 4 valves per cylinder.

THE HILL-CLIMBING FERRARIS

212/E "boxer."

From 1957 to 1969, in other words from the year when the European Hill-Climb Championship was established until the last year when Ferrari took part in this championship, the Italian firm officially entered the championship four times, and won it three: Scarfiotti in 1962 and 1965, and Schetty in 1969. Scarfiotti came in second in 1966 behind Mitter (Porsche). In 1962 the Italian driver, who won three trials out of seven (coming in second in another) drove a sports model with a 2000 cc V-6 engine at the rear, for the Scuderia Sant'Ambroeus. In 1965 the winner of the championship was a 2000 cc Dino rear-engine (power output: 218 hp at 9,000 rpm), used initially in a berlinetta and later in a spider. Scarfiotti won four trials out of seven, after a gruelling duel with Mitter (Porsche). Of the seven trials in the 1966 championship, Mitter won five against Scarfiotti's two, the latter driving the same car as the year before, but with fuel injection. Peter Schetty was the unrivalled master of the 1969 championship, winning all seven events. The most important feature of that year was the use of a 12-cylinder "boxer" engine, the 212/E, with a power output of some 300 hp. A few years later, with the cylinder capacity raised to 3000 cc, this was to be one of the Formula 1 strong points, the 312/B.

The Ferrari 212/E. It was with a car like this that Schetty won the 1969 hill-climbing championship.

The Ferrari Body Designers

FROM TOURING TO PININFARINA

The first official Ferrari auto body builder was Touring of Milan, which was responsible for the outer shell of the 125. This was derived from the shell of the 815. The first Ferrari coupé was produced by Allemano of Turin, and, at a later stage, on an industrial scale, by Touring once again, and by the Stabilimenti Farina, which went out of business in 1950.

In that same year the Carrozzeria Ghia of Turin, then headed by Luigi Segre and Mario Boano, started to work with Ferrari. Ghia specialized in luxury automobiles with a special emphasis on coupé and cabriolet models. A special direction in terms of style and inventiveness came from another Turin designer, Alfredo Vignale, often assisted in the design room by Giovanni Michelotti.

In 1952, when the association between Enzo Ferrari and Alfredo Vignale started to wane (it ended altogether in 1954), it was the turn of Pininfarina. The first Ferrari body designed by the latter—a cabriolet mounted on a 212 Inter frame—appeared at the Paris Salon in 1952 and was followed in early 1953 by convertibles and coupés on 250 Europa and 342 America frames.

From 1952 on Pininfarina has continued to be Ferrari's official body designer, and certainly his most distinctive one, developing many projects which have ended up in small series of cars, built either directly by Pininfarina or by the Modena firm, Scaglietti and Fantuzzi, or by Mario Boano of Turin, once he had parted company with Luigi Segre.

Pininfarina has been both the most prolific and the most versatile Ferrari designer, both in terms of units produced and in terms of design studies which are ends in themselves, such as the amazing Modulo made in 1970, a very advanced design which represents a major turning-point in the history of body design.

Up until 1979, Pininfarina produced more than 100 prototypes for Ferrari and built more than 6,000 cars (in small series of 100-150 units each). At the same time, Scaglietti has produced more than 10,000 Ferrari cars in eighteen different models designed by Pininfarina.

In 1973, Ferrari asked Bertone to work on the body of the 308 GT 4. Their association had lain dormant since 1952. Zagato of Milan was another auto body firm which worked for Ferrari. Zagato and Ferrari had known one another back in the days when both were working at Alfa Romeo.

Individual cars on Ferrari frames, which have had no practical followup, have also been proposed by Giovanni Michelotti and by other builders and stylists.

From the beginning, Enzo Ferrari saw that the continual overhauling and alteration of models—a feature peculiar to his firm—was a bad policy from the industrial viewpoint; but it was the only way he could satisfy his deep desire to modify, up-date, and improve. On this subject he has written: "Every morning I felt like putting something new into my cars and this terrified the people working with me, who hastened to point out to me that this would be tantamount to rendering a service to tomorrow's client, but that it would certainly halt production."

This continual progress, regardless of the cost, has given Ferrari a record which it will be hard to match or overtake: the number of new models offered to the public during the period of time the Ferrari works has been in operation. Even General Motors, with all its five divisions, has probably not produced as many.

Not everything—insofar as the lines of their cars are concerned—that the Ferrari team has designed and built can be said to be completely satisfactory. The intriguing feature of the Touring "barchetta" was its simplicity and the fact that the first chapter of Ferrari history was written by those cars, in which the driver sat perched with a good view of the road ahead. This position was gradually modified for aesthetic and aerodynamic reasons.

The models which bear the Pininfarina mark have a certain something which time has not marred, a sort of regal quality, a sense of proportion, and purity, which recurs throughout the production range of this famous designer and builder, whose creations, it has rightly been remarked, never age. The cars designed by Pininfarina for Ferrari have been so numerous and, in many cases, so varied that it is a hard task to list the most handsome. But the 250 GT certainly numbers among those that one recalls with nostalgia. Here we have another living example of how the essential quality of the line, stripped of all decorative or ornamental gimmicks, has produced a car which remains unaltered by time because of the harmony of the concept of the whole.

Many of the cars signed by Pininfarina have been one-of-a-kind models made for special clients. It was possible to do this for a certain number of years. There were customers who clung to the idea of having an exclusive model, even if the model cost a small fortune.

Among the competition models one of the most successful all-round cars is the 500 TRC Roadster of 1957, produced by Franco Scaglietti, together with the 500 Testa Rossa with the 12-cylinder engine and "pontoon" type fenders, also made by Scaglietti in 1957. These cars are much sought after on the classic car market and are more costly than older models.

Pininfarina

1952 - 212 Inter cabriolet 2-seater

1953 - 212 Inter coupé 2 + 2

1953 - 212 Inter coupé 2 + 2

1953 - 342 America berlinetta 2-seater

1953 - 342 America coupé 2-seater

1953 - 342 America coupé 2-seater

1953 - 342 America cabriolet 2-seater

1953 - 250 MM berlinetta 2-liter

Pininfarina

1953 - 375 MM Mexico coupé

1953 - 375 MM Mexico coupé racer

1953 - 375 MM Le Mans spider

1953 - 250 Europa coupé 2 + 2

1953 - 250 Europa coupé 2 + 2

1953 - 375 America coupé 2 + 2

1953 - 500 Mondial spider 2-seater

1954 - 375 MM Le Mans spider 2-seater

Pininfarina

1954 - 250 Europa coupé 2-seater

1954 - 250 Europa cabriolet 2-seater

1954 - 250 GT coupé 2-seater

1954 - 375 America coupé 2-seater

1954 - 375 America berlinetta 2-seater

1954 - 375 MM coupé racer

1954 - 375 MM berlinetta 2-seater

1954 - 375 MM coupé racer

Pininfarina

1954 - 375 MM spider 2-seater

1955 - 250 GT coupé racer

1955 - 250 GT coupé 2-seater

1955 - 250 GT coupé type 375 MM

1955 - 375 MM coupé racer

1955 - 375 America coupé 2-seater

1955 - 375 America cabriolet 2-seater

1956 - 410 Superamerica Superfast coupé

Pininfarina

1956 - 250 GT spider 2-seater

1956 - 250 GT coupé 2-seater

1956 - 250 GT coupé 2-seater

1956 - 250 GT coupé 2-seater

1957 - 250 GT cabriolet 2-seater

1957 - 250 GT spider racer

1957 - 250 GT coupé special 2-seater

1956 - 410 Superamerica coupé 2-seater

Pininfarina

1957 - 250 GT spider 2-seater

1957 - 250 GT spider 2-seater

1958 - 250 GT coupé 2-seater (1st prototype)

1958 - 250 GT coupé special 2-seater

1958 - 250 GT coupé special 2-seater

1957 - 410 Superamerica coupé 2-seater

1958 - 410 Superamerica coupé 2-seater

145

Pininfarina

1958 - 250 GT coupé special

1959 - 410 Superamerica coupé 2-seater

1959 - 250 GT coupé special

1959 - 410 Superamerica coupé special (1st version)

1959 - "Testa Rossa" spider racer

Another best-selling model was the "Testa Rossa". It made its debut on May 26, 1957, in the 1000-kilometer race at the Nürburgring driven by Masten Gregory and Olindo Morolli. A "Testa Rossa" with a 3100 cc. engine took part in the Le Mans 24-hour race that same year driven by Olivier Gendebien and Maurice Trintignant.

1960 - 250 GT coupé 2 + 2 (1st prototype)

1960 - 250 GT coupé 2 + 2 (2nd prototype)

Pininfarina

1960 - 400 Superamerica cabriolet 2-seater

1960 - 410 Superamerica Superfast II coupé 2-seater

1960 - 250 GT cabriolet 2-seater

1960 - 250 GT cabriolet 2-seater with hardtop

1960 - 250 GT California spider 2-seater

1960 - 410 Superamerica cabriolet special 2-seater

1960 - 250 GT coupé 2 + 2

1960 - 400 Superamerica coupé special (streamlined)

Pininfarina

1961 - 250 GT cabriolet 2-seater hardtop

1961 - 250 GT coupé 2-seater special

1958 - 250 GT berlinetta 2-seater

1961 - 250 GT Le Mans berlinetta (experimental).

Pininfarina

1961 - 400 Superamerica coupé special 2-seater

1961 - 400 Superamerica cabriolet hardtop

1962 - 250 GT berlinetta

1962 - 400 Superamerica cabriolet 2-door special

1962 - 400 Superamerica Superfast IV coupé 2 + 2

149

Pininfarina

1963 - 250 GT coupé 2 + 2

1963 - 250 GT berlinetta (one model only)

1963 - 250 GT berlinetta special 2-seater

1963 – 400 Superamerica Coupé special 2 + 2

1963 - 250 Le Mans berlinetta

The Le Mans berlinetta has an important win to its credit, the victorious drive in 1965 by drivers Masten Gregory and Jochen Rindt in the most famous of French races. Hence the name of the car which, while being built, posed serious problems to Pininfarina because of the rear engine.

Pininfarina

1964 - 275 GTS spider 2/3-seater hardtop

1964 - 500 Superfast coupé special 2-seater

1964 - 275 GTB berlinetta special 2-seater

1964 - 330 GT coupé 2 + 2

1964 - 330 GT coupé 2 + 2

1965 - Dino berlinetta special

1965 - 275 GTS spider 2/3-seater

Pininfarina

1966 - 330 GTC coupé 2-seater

1966 - 330 GTS spider 2/3-seater hardtop

1966 - 365 P California cabriolet special 2-seater ▶

1966 - 365 P berlinetta 3-seater (central driving position)

Pininfarina

1967 - Dino berlinetta racer

1968 - Dino 246 GT coupé 2-seater

1967 - 330 GTC coupé special

1967 - 365 coupé 2 + 2

1968 - 365 GTB/4 Daytona coupé

Pininfarina

1968 - P6 berlinetta special

1968 - 250/P5 berlinetta special (prototype)

1969 - 312/S berlinetta special

Pininfarina

1969 - 365 GTB/4 coupé special

1969 - 365 GTS/4 Daytona spider

1969 - 365 GTS spider

1970 - PF Modulo ▲▼

155

Pininfarina

1971 - 365 GTC/4 coupé

1971 - BB Boxer berlinetta

1972 - 365 GT/4 coupé 2 + 2 ▲

1972 - 246 GTS spider 2-seater ▼

Pininfarina

1974 Studio Cr 25

As indicated by the name and number ("25" stands for the coefficient of resistance), this model was a simple exercise built with the secret hope—nurtured by Pininfarina—that it might be powered by a suitable Ferrari engine. In fact there was no further development of it, but it is nevertheless still thought of as a good prototype. Pininfarina exhibited it in 1979 at a motor show in Helsinki.

1975 - 308 GTB coupé 2-seater

Pininfarina

1976 - 512 BB Boxer berlinetta

1976 - 308 GTB coupé 2-seater

1976 - 400 coupé 2 + 2 automatic

Pininfarina

1977 - 308 GTB (study)

1977 - 308 GTS spider 2-seater

Bertone

1973 - Dino 308 GT 4

The Dino 308 GT was, according to Bertone, to be a car created from the "Ferrari experience in small series GT cars." Slightly longer than the Dino 2400, it is a 4-seater with a central engine, this being a 3000 cc. 8-cylinder model (power output: 255 hp at 7,700 rpm), which is remarkably compact because of the good ratio between the dimensions of the car and the cubic capacity.

Bertone

1950 - Bertone

1962 - Bertone

1962 - 250 GT

1962 - 250 GT

1974 - Rainbow

The Rainbow was proposed by Bertone in 1974. It used the mechanical parts of the Dino 308 GT 4. A specific and patented device made it possible to slide the roof completely behind the seats, thus turning it into a convertible.

161

INDEX

Numbers in bold type refer to illustrations.

A

Abarth 1100, 89
Abate, 38
Acerbo, Giacomo, **10**
Adamovicz, 134
Agnelli, Gianni, 98
Aldrighetti, Giordano, 47
Alessi, Davide, 23
ALFA (Anonima Lombarda Fabbrica Automobili), 12
— 4500, 11
Alfa Romeo, 10-11, **11**, 12-14, 18, 29, 33, 36, 44, 47-49, 52, 56, 60, 90, 94, 99, 103, 106, 109, 117, 120, 139
— ES, **9**
— P2, 12, 99, 106, 117
— P3, 99
— P3 type B, **29**
— RL, 12
— V 12 type A, 99
— V 12 type C, 99
— 12 C, 101, 117
— 158 (Alfetto), 12, 32, 99, 102, 106, 117
— 159, 13
— 312, 99
— 1500 6-cylinder, **31**, 106
— 1750 6-cylinder, 106
— 2300 8-cylinder, 106
Allemano, 139
Allison, Cliff, 108
America (Ferrari 340), 103, 124
America (Ferrari 342) berlinetta, 15, 139, **140**
— cabriolet, **140**
— coupé, **140**, **141**
America (Ferrari 375), 122
— berlinetta, **142**
— cabriolet, **143**
— coupé, **142**, **143**
Amon, Chris, 38, **95**, 113-114, 134
Amorotti, Mino, 19, 96, **96**, **97**, 98

Andretti, Mario, 38, 74, 92, **95**, 114, 134
Anonima Lombarda Fabbrica Automobili (ALFA), 12
Arcangeli, Luigi, 12, 31
Ascari, Alberto, 13, 14, **14**, 15, 16, 20, 30, 35-36, **36**, 43, 47, 56, 58-60, 64, 89, **89**, 104-106, 118, 124, 136
Ascari, Antonio, 30, 101-102
Astori, Fulvio, 27
ATS, 26, 91, 120
Audetto, Daniele, 98
Auto Avio Costruzioni, 47
Autodelta, 120
Auto Union, 106

B

Baghetti, Giancarlo, 25-26, 37, **39**, 69, 91, **93**
Balbo, Italo, **10**
Bandini, Lorenzo, 38, 69, 91, **92**, 96, 112-113, 134
Banquo, 36
Bardhal, 104
Barletta, 117
Bazzi, Luigi, 12, 32, **97**, **100**, **106**, 116
Behra, Jean, 23, 35, **91**, 108, 130
Bell, Derek, 38, **93**
Bellei, Angelo, 111
Bellentani, Vittorio, 105-107, 109
Benedetti, 122
Bertone, 139, 160-161
— Rainbow, **161**
Beurlys, 128, 134
Bianchi, Gianandrea, 116
Bianchi, Luciano, 39
Bignami, 30
Biondetti, Clemente, 19, 89, **89**, 122
Biro, Prince, 99, 101
Boano, Mario, 139
Bonetto, Felice, 30, 101, 136
Bordino, Pietro, 30-31, 43
Borzacchini, Mario Umberto, 12, 30-31
Bosch (injection), 69, 111

Boschi, Severo, 29
Bottasso, **15**
Brabham, Jack, 72, 109, 112, 114
Brabham, 88, 114
Brabham-Alfa Romeo, 27, 84
Bracco, Giovanni, 33-34
Brambilla, Tino, 38
Brambilla, Vittorio, **93**
Brilli-Peri, Gastone, 30-31, 42
Brivio, Antonio, 12, 33
BRM, 14, 109, 116
Brooks, Tony, 67, **91**, 108
Bucknum, 134
Bugatti, Ettore, 17, 25, 43
Bussi, Giancarlo, 78, 111, **112**, 114, **116**
Busso, Giuseppe, 117

C

Cabianca, Giulio, **91**
Caliro, Giacomo, 116
Campari, Giuseppe, 12, **16**, 30, **31**, 32, **106**
Campos, Benedicto, 102
Capritti, 117
Caracciola, Rudolf, 43
Carrozzeria Scaglietti, 49, 139
Casoni, Mario, **95**
Castagneto, Renzo, 10, 90
Castellotti, Eugenio, 15, 22-24, 36, **37**, 90, **90**, 93, 105, 126
Casucci, Piero, 38
Cavalli, Carlo, 43, 106
Ceirano, **49**
Ceirano, Giovanni, 106
Cévert, 39
Chapman, Colin, 24, 88, 92
Chevrolet, 43
Chinetti, Luigi, 104, 112, 122, 130
Chiron, Louis, 12, 35
Chiti, Carlo, 94, 96, 109, **110**, 111-112, 117, 118-120, 137
Chizzola, Ludovico, 120
Cisitalia 1100, 89
Clark, Jim, 21, 24, 34, 43, 93
CMN (Construzioni Meccaniche Nazionali), 10, 18, **31**

162

Cocozza, Antonio, 116
Collins, Peter, **19**, 20, 22, 23, 24, 30, 34, 36-37, **37**, 39, 67, 90, **90**, 93-94, **96**, 105, 107-108, 126
Colombo, Alessandro, 116
Colombo, Gioachino, 12-13, 56, 99, 101-103, 116-117
Compagnia Nazionale Aeronautica, 12
Cooper, 24, 94, 108-109
Cooper-Maserati, 88
Cortese, Franco, 12, 14, 30, 33-34, 89, **89**, 90, 101, 122, 136
Costantino di Grecia, **11**
Costruzioni Meccaniche Nazionali (CMN), 9-10, 17, **31**
Coventry-Climax, 109, 116
Craft, 134
Crosara, 124

D

Daigh, 126
Da Zara, 10
de Adamich, Andrea, 39, **39**, **95**, 114
De Dion (car), 9
De Dion (axle), 56, 62, 64, 66, 81, 102, 104, 105, 108, 124, 126, 136
De Dion-Bouton, 11
De Fierlandt, 134
De Graffenried, 102
Della Stufa, **29**
De Portago, Alfonso Cabeza de Vaca, 16-17, **90**, 126
Deserti, Bruno, 98
Diatto, 9
Dino Ferrari berlinetta racer, **153**
Dino Ferrari berlinetta special, **151**
Dino Ferrari 206, 132, **133**, 138
Dino Ferrari 206 S, 132
Dino Ferrari 206 SP, 132
Dino Ferrari 246, 104
Dino Ferrari 246 GT coupé, **153**
Dino Ferrari 308 GT 4, 15, 139, **160**, 161
Dragoni, Eugenio, 98, **98**, 113
"Drake", 45
Duca degli Abruzzi, **10**
Duckworth, Keith, 120
Duesenberg, 43
Dunlop (brakes), 67, 71
Dunlop (tires), 134

E

Eagle, 93
Eldé, 128
Englebert (tires), 16, 65, 106

Europa (Ferrari 250), 15, 139
— cabriolet, **142**
— coupé, **141**, **142**

F

Fagioli, Luigi, 12, 24, 33, 102
Fairman, 60
Fangio, Juan Manuel, 13-15, 22-23, **23**, 24, **25**, 29-30, 36, 60, 62, 64, 90, **91**, 94, 96, **97**, 102, 105, 107-108, 126
Fantuzzi, 108, 139
Farina, Giuseppe ("Nino"), 14, **17**, **22**, 33, **33**, 60, 89, **89**, 99, 101-102, 104-105, 124
Farina, Giovan Battista (Pininfarina), 15, 139, 140-159
Federazione Italiana Scuderie Automobilistiche (FISA), 26
Ferrari, 16, 20, 24, 26, 28, 30, 37-40, 43-44, 47, 49-51, **51**, 53-54, 59, 62, 64, 68, 70-72, 76, 78, 84-85, 87-93, 96, 98-99, 102-104, 107-120, 122, 124, 126, 128, 130, 132, 134, 136, 139, 157
— 125 C, 136
— 125 F1, **14**, 56, **57**, 101-103, 116, 139
— 125 GP, 101, 136
— 125 GT, 12, 14, **14**, 99, 102
— 125 S, 99, 102, 122, **123**, 136
— 156 F1, 68-70, **68**, **69**, 108-112, 128
— 156 F2, 107-109, 136
— 158 F1, 70, **70**, **71**, 111-112
— 159 S, 99, 102, 122
— 166 F2, 102-103, 122, 136-137
— 166 FL (Formula Libera), 102, 122
— 166 Inter, 102, 122
— 166 MM, 102, 122
— 166 S, 102, 122, **123**
— 177, 120
— 179, 120
— 195 Inter, 103
— 195 S, 103
— 196 SP, 132
— 206 Dino, 132, **133**, 138
— 207 S, 132
— 206 SP, 132
— 212/E, **138**
— 212 Export, 103
— 212 F1, 103, 105
— 212 Inter, 15, 103, 139
— 212 Inter cabriolet, **140**
— 212 Inter coupé, 15, **140**
— 246 Dino, 104
— 246 F1 (156 F2), 66, **66**, 67, **67**, 68, 108-109, 117
— 246 GT Dino coupé, **153**
— 246 GTS spider, **156**

— 246 P, 120, 128, **129**
— 246 SP, 132
— 250 Europa, 15, 139
— 250 Europa cabriolet, **142**
— 250 Europa coupé, 15, **141**, **142**
— 250 GT, 92, 139, **142**, **161**
— 250 GT berlinetta, **148**, **149**, **150**
— 250 GT berlinetta special, **150**
— 250 GT cabriolet, **144**, **147**, **148**
— 250 GT California, **147**
— 250 GT coupé, **143**, **144**, **145**, **146**, **147**, **148**, **150**
— 250 GT coupé racer, **143**
— 250 GT coupé special, **144**, **145**, **146**
— 250 GT coupé type 375 MM, **143**
— 250 GT spider, **144**, **145**
— 250 GT spider racer, **144**
— 250 GT Le Mans berlinetta, **148**, **150**
— 250 GTO (Gran Turismo Omologata), 128, 130, **131**
— 250 LM, 112, 130, **131**, 132
— 250 MM berlinetta, **140**
— 250 P, 128, 132
— 250/P5 berlinetta special prototype, **154**
— 250 TRS, 126, **127**
— 252 F1, 124
— 256 F1, 117
— 268 SP, 132
— 275 F1, 13, 56, 102, 124
— 275 GTB berlinetta, **151**
— 275 GTS spider, **151**
— 275 P, 132
— 275 P2, 132
— 290 MM, 126, **127**
— 306, 13
— 308 GT spider, **159**
— 308 GTB coupé, **157**, **158**
— 312 B, 74, **75**, 114-115, 138
— 312 B2, 74, 75, 76, **77**, 114
— 312 B3, 76, **77**, 78, **78**, 79, 114-115
— 312 F1, 71-72, **73**, 79, 113
— 312/S berlinetta special, **154**
— 312 T, 79, **79**, 80, **80**, 81-82, 98, 115
— 312 T2, **39**, 81, **81**, 82, **82**, 83-84
— 312 T3, 82, 84, **84**, 115
— 312 T4, 85, **85**, 86-87, 116
— 330 GT coupé, **151**
— 330 GTC coupé, **152**
— 330 GTC coupé special, **153**
— 330 GTS spider, **152**
— 330 LM, 128
— 330 P, 132
— 330 P2, 132, **133**, 134
— 330 P3, 132, 134
— 330 P3/4 (412 P), 132, 134
— 330 P4, 132, 134, **135**

163

- 340 America, 103, 124
- 340 F1, 13, 56, 103
- 342 America berlinetta, 15, 139, **140**
- 342 America cabriolet, **140**
- 342 America coupé, **140**, **141**
- 354 S, 106, 126
- 365 coupé, **153**
- 365 GT4 BB, 15
- 365 GT/4 coupé, **156**
- 365 GTB/4 coupé special, **155**
- 365 GTB/4 Daytona coupé, **153**
- 365 GTC/4 spider, **156**
- 365 GTS spider, **155**
- 365 GTS/4 Daytona spider, **155**
- 365 P, 132
- 365 PF berlinetta, **152**
- 365 P California cabriolet, **152**
- 375 America, 124
- 375 America berlinetta, **142**
- 375 America cabriolet, **143**
- 375 America coupé, **142**, **143**
- 375 F1, 13; 43, 56, **57**, 103, 104, 124
- 375 Formula Libera, 56
- 375 MM, 124, **125**
- 375 MM berlinetta, **142**
- 375 MM coupé, **142**, **143**
- 375 MM Le Mans, **141**
- 375 MM Mexico coupé, **141**
- 375 MM Mexico coupé racer, **141**
- 375 MM spider, **143**
- 375 Plus, 122
- 400 coupé, 158
- 400 S/A cabriolet hardtop, **149**
- 400 S/A coupé special, **149**
- 400 Superamerica, 128, **129**
- 400 Superamerica cabriolet, **147**, **149**
- 400 Superamerica coupé special, **147**, **150**
- 400 Superamerica Superfast IV coupé, **149**
- 410 Superamerica cabriolet special, **147**
- 410 Superamerica coupé, **144**, **145**, **146**
- 410 Superamerica coupé special, **146**
- 410 Superamerica Superfast coupé, **143**
- 410 Superamerica Superfast II coupé, **147**
- 412 P, (330 P3/4), 132, 134
- 500 F2, 14-15, **34**, **58**, 59, **59**, 60, **60**, 61, **61**, 62, 103, 105, 136
- 500 Mondial, **141**
- 500 Superfast coupé special, **151**
- 500 TRC Roadster, 139
- 500 TS, 139
- 512 BB Boxer, **158**
- 512 F1, 71, 112
- 512 M, 134
- 512 S, 134, **135**
- 512 SM, 134
- 625 F1, 60, 62, **63**, 64, 105-106
- 750 Monza, 15, 20, 36, 124, **125**
- 815 (Alfa Romeo 158), **14**, 47, 99, 106, 139
- BB Boxer, **156**
- Dino 308 GT 4, 15, 139, **160**, 161
- Dino berlinetta racer, **153**
- Dino berlinetta special, **151**
- Ferrari-Lancia 801 F1 (D 50), 64, **64**, 65, **65**, 94, **100**, 107-108
- P6 berlinetta special, **154**
- PF modulo, **155**
- Studio Cr 25, **157**
- Studio su 308 GTB, **159**
- Squalo (553), 62, **63**, 64, 103, 136
- Supersqualo (555), 62, 64, 108, 136
- Testa Rossa, 146, **146**

Ferrari (engines)
- 125 GT, **101**
- 156 F1, **110**, 137
- 156 F2, 107, **107**
- 158 F1, **111**
- 206 Dino, 132, 137
- 212/E, 138, **138**
- 250 TR, **109**
- 252 F1, 117
- 256, 108
- 290 MM, 106
- 312, 112-113
- 312 B, 74, **115**
- 500 Fé, **104**
- 500 Mondial, 103
- 512 F1, **113**
- 553 F2, 103
- 625 F1, 103
- 625 S, 103
- 700, 103
- 735 S, 103
- 750 Monza, 103

Ferrari, Alfredo, 8, 16
Ferrari, Alfredino (Dino), 9, 16, 27, 50, 66, 105, 107, 116-117, 132, 136-137
Ferrari, Enzo, 9, 10, **10**, 11, 13, **13**, 14-15, **15**, 16-17, **17**, 18-22, 24-29, **29**, 30-31, **31**, 32-36, **36**, **37**, 38-40, 47-50, **50**, 51, 54, 56, 60, 65-66, 74, 88-94, 96, 98, 99, **100**, 102, **103**, 103-106, 108, 110-112, 114-120, 123-124, 126, 128, 132, 134, 136, 139
Ferrari, Laura, 111
Ferrari-Ford, 51-52
Fiat, 10, 12, 17, 28, 49, 54, 84, 98, 106, 117-119, 132
- Dino 132
Firestone (tires), 134

FISA (Federazione Italiana Scuderie Automobilistiche), 25
Fischer, 105
Fittipaldi, Emerson, 21, 24-25, 39, 76, 78
Florio, Vincenzo, 11, **21**
Ford, 17, 38, 50-51, 54, 88, 134
— T, 46
Ford, Henry, 25
Ford-Cosworth, 72, 74, 116, 120
Ford-Ferrari, 51-52, 54
Forghieri, Mauro, 78, 111-112, **112**, 114, 117, 120
Fornaca, Guido, 106
Foyt, A.J., 134
Franco Tosi, 99
Fraschetti, Andrea, 106-108
Frère, Paul, 37, 93, 105
Fusi, Luigi, 47, 117

G

Galli, Nanni, 38-39
Gallo, 99
Gardini, 23
Gendebien, Olivier, 19-20, **21**, 26, 36-37, 88, **91**, 93, 108, 124, 126, 128, 130, 146
General Motors, 139
Ghia, 139
Giaccone, Enrico, 30
Giambertone, Marcello, 22-24, 30, 36
Ginther, Ritchie, 37, 92-93, **92**, 109, 137
Girling (brakes), 72, **74**
Giunti, Ignazio, 39, 74, **95**, 114, 134
Gobbato, Ugo, 106
Goethe, 45
Gonzales, Froilan, 13, **22**, 36-37, 56, 62, **89**, 94, 102, 103, 105, 124
Gozzi, Franco, 96, **98**
Grant Piston Ring Special, 104
Gregory, Masten, 126, 130, 146, 150
Guichet, Jean, 38, 128, 130, 134
Gurney, Dan, 37, **91**, 93, 108, 126, 134
Guzzi, 29

H

Hailwood, Mike, 39
Harrison, 102
Hawkins, Paul, 38
Hawthorn, Mike, 14, 20, 36, 60, 62, 66-67, **90**, 94, 104-105, 107-108, 124, 132
Henri, Ernest, 43
Hill, Graham, 24, 109, 130
Hill, Phil (Philip), 19, **19**, 20-22, 25-26,

164

37, 67, 69, **90**, 92, 104, 108–109, **110**, 126, 128, 130, 132
Holland, Bill, 104
Honda, 88
Houdaille (shock absorbers), 56, 59, 62, 66, 105–107, 108, 124
Hulme, Dennis, 39, 76
Hunt, James, 81
HWM, 24

I

Ibanez, 124
Ickx, Jacky, 28, 38, 72, 74, 76, 88, **93**, **98**, 114, **116**, 134
Igor, 122
Isotta-Fraschini, 11, 103
Issigonis, 46

J

Jacoponi, Stefano, 116
Jaguar, 36
Jano, Vittorio, 12, 16, 43, **50**, 64, 94, 99, 105–106, **106**, 107, 109, 117, 132, 136–137
John Player, 76

K

Keek, Howard, 104
Klass, Gunther, 38

L

Lampredi, Aurelio, 13, 59, 94, 99, 102–103, **103**, 105, 107, 109, 116, 118, **118**, 124, 136–137
Lancia, 14–16, 20, **34**, 36, **49**, 88, 91, 105, 106, 107, 115–117, 132
— D 50, 15, 36, 62, 64, 94, 106–107
— dampers, 106
Lancia, Gianni, 15, 64, 106
Lancia, Vincenzo, 10
Landi, Chico, 105, 136
Lang, 24
Lauda, Niki, 14, 21–22, 26–28, 39, **39**, 78–84, 88, 92, **95**, 115, 120
Lini, Franco, 96, **97**
Lockheed (brakes), 74
Lotus, 22, 24, 76, 114
Lucas (injection), 71, 74, 112, 134

M

Macbeth, 36
Maggi, 42
Maglioli, Umberto, 20, 37, **90**, 91–92, 105, 124
Mairesse, Willy, 37, **92**, 93, 134
Mambelli, Paride, 31–32
Marchand, 9
Marchetti, Angiolino, **112**, 116
Marelli (ignition), 74
Marelli, Gianni, 116
Marko, Helmut, **95**
Marzotto, Giannino, 90, 94, 122, 124, 136
Marzotto, Paolo, 90
Marzotto, Umberto, 90
Marzotto, Vittorio, 90
Maserati, 14, 22–23, 43, 96, 99, 102, 105, 106, 108
— A6G, 102
— A6GCS, 136
— 250, 62
— 250 F, 108
Masetti, Giulio, 30–31, 42
Massimino, Alberto, 106–107
Mauro, Johnny, 104
May, Michael, 112
Mayer, Teddy, 24
Mazzotti, 42
McLaren, 39, 76
Mendíteguy, 22
Mercedes, 12, 15, 22, 24–25, 33, 94, 105, 106, 107
— W 196, 62
Merzario, Arturo, 24, 76, **95**
Metternich, 22
Michelin, 120
Michelotti, Giovanni, 139
Miles, John, 24
Minoia, Nando, 30
Mitter, 39, 138
Molino, 117
Moll, Guy, 12, 32–33
Montezemolo, Luca Cordero di, 98, **98**
Monza (Ferrari 750), 15, 20, 36, 124, **125**
Morolli, Olindo, 146
Moss, Stirling, 22–25, **25**, 39, 62, 94, 96, 108
Musso, Luigi, **21**, 22, 24, 30, 36, **36**, 90, 104, 107–108, 126

N

Nallinger, Fritz, 43
Navone, 122
Nazzaro, Felice, 10, 30–31, 38, 43
Nelson, 16

Neubauer, Alfred, 24, 98
Nibel, Hans, 43
Niccoloni, 42
Noblet, 128
Nosetto, Roberto, 98
Nuvolari, Tazio, 12, 24, 30–33, **33**, 39, 43, **49**, 89, **89**, 92, 99

O

Oldsmobile (engines), 72
Orlando, Vittorio Emanuele, 11
Orsi, 43
OSCA, 104

P

Packard, 12
Paganini, 22
Parkes, Mike, 37–38, 72, 91, **95**, 113, **114**, **116**, 134
Parsons, Johnnie, 104
Perdisa, Cesare, **91**
Peterson, Ronnie, **95**
Piccinini, Marco, 98, **98**
Pininfarina, 130, 157
Pininfarina (Farina Giovan Battista), 15, 120, 139, 140–159
Pintacuda, Carlo, 12, **29**, 33
Piotti, 105
Pirelli, 15
— tires, 65, 106
Poli, prof., **15**
Porsche, 38, 88, 109, 113, 138
Porsche, Ferdinand, 43
Posey, 134

R

Raffaeli, 136
Rainbow (Bertone), **161**
Ramponi, **31**
Rangoni, Lotario, 14, 47, 106
Ranier of Monaco, **22**
Rapid, 106
Redman, Brian, **93**
Regazzoni, Clay, 21, 38, 74, 78–79, 81, 88, 92, **93**, 114–115, **116**
Reggiane, 102
Repco (engines), 72
Reutemann, Carlos, 82, 84, **95**
Revson, Peter, 39
Ricart, 12, 18
Righetti, Nando, 136
Rimini, Giorgio, **11**, 18
Rindt, Jochen, 24, 39, 74, 114, 130, 150

165

Rocchi, Franco, 78, 109, 111, **112**, 114, 117
Rodriguez, Pedro, 37, 91, **92**, **94**, 112, 114, 130, 134
Rodriguez, Ricardo, 37, **92**
Rol, 102
Rolls-Royce, 91
Romeo, Nicola, **11**, 12
Roots (superchargers), 56, 99, 102
Roselli, 117
Rosemeyer, Bernd, 33, 43
Rosier, 102, 105
Rubinstein, Arthur, 18
Ruini, Carlo, 117

S

Said, Bob, 104
Salamano, Carlo, 30-31
Salvarani, Walter, 109, **112**, 117
Scaglietti, 49, 139
Scala, Delia, **37**
Scarfiotti, Lodovico, 37-38, 72, 91, **92**, 113, 132, 134, 138
Scarlatti, Giorgio, **92**
Scheckter, Jody, 82, 86-87, 94, **95**, 115, 120
Schell, Harry, 102, 104
Schenken, Tim, **95**
Schetty, Peter, 38, **93**, 96, **98**, **116**, 138
Scuderia Centro-Sud, 137
Scuderia Sant'Ambroeus, 26, 138
Sculati, Eraldo, 24, 96, **97**
Segre, Luigi, 139
Selsdon, 122
Serafini, Dorino, 102, 105
Serenissima, 96
Severi, Martino, 137
Shelby, Carrol, 104
Siena, Eugenio, 13
Siffert, 39
Simon, 62
Sivocci, Ugo, 10
Solex (carburetors) 40 PII, 64
Sommer, Raymond, 10, 12, 89, **89**, 94, 99, 101, 102, 136
Squalo (Ferrari 553), 62, **63**, 64, 103, 105-106, 136
Superamerica
— Ferrari 400, 128, **129**
— Ferrari 400 cabriolet, **147**, **149**
— Ferrari 400 coupé special, **147**, **150**
— Ferrari 400 Superfast IV coupé, **149**
— Ferrari 410 cabriolet special, **147**
— Ferrari 410 coupé, **144**, **145**, **146**
— Ferrari 410 coupé special, **146**
— Ferrari 410 Superfast coupé, **143**
— Ferrari 410 Superfast II coupé, **147**
Supersqualo (Ferrari 555), 62, 64, 105-106, 108, 136
Stabilimenti Farina, 139
Stewart, Jackie, 24, 39, 43, 76, 94, 114
Surtees, John, 38, 69-72, 76, 88, **95**, 98, 111-113, 120
Sutcliffe, John, 38

T

Tadini, Mario, 12
Taruffi, Isabella, 34-35
Taruffi, Piero, 14, 34, **34**, 35, **50**, 59, 89, **89**, 102, 105, 126, 136
Taverna, 117
Tavoni, Romolo, 24, 96, **97**
Testa Rossa (Ferrari 250 TR), **109**
Testa Rossa spider (Ferrari), 146, **146**
Testa Rossa Sport (Ferrari 250 TRS), 126
Thin Wall Special, 104, 105
Tomaini, Antonio, 116
Touring, 139
Trevisan, Bruno, 117
Trintignant, Maurice, **22**, 35, 62, 102, 105, 108, 124, 146
Trossi, Carlo Felice, 33, 42
Tyrrell, 114
Tyrrell, Ken, 24, 88

U

Ugolini, Nello, 22, 96, **97**

V

Vaccarella, Nino, 37, **95**, 134
Valiente, Saenz, 124
Vallone, Roberto, 102, 136
Vanderwell, Tony, 101, 104
Vanwall, 108
Varzi, Achille, 12, **29**, 30-33, 37, 43, **50**, 90
Vignale, Alfredo, 139
Villeneuve, Gilles, 84, 87, 94, **95**
Villoresi, Luigi, 14, 30, 34, 88-89, **90**, 99, 101-102, 105, 124, 136
Voeler, Herbert, 26
Volkswagen Beetle, 46
von Trips, Wolfgang, 21, 24, 34-35, 37, 69, **90**, 93, 108-109, 128
Vukovich, Bill, 104

W

Wagner, Louis, 30-31
Walker, Rob, 24, 134
Weber (carburetors)
— 30 DCF, 122
— 38 DCF, 56
— 38 DCN, 130
— 40 DCF, 56
— 40 DCN, 126
— 40 DCN 2, 132
— 40 DCS, 65
— 40 DO3C, 56
— 40 IF/4C, 124
— 42 C, 128
— 42 DCN 2, 132
— 45 DOE, 60
— 46 DCF/3, 128
— 46 TRA, 126
— 50 DCO, 59, 62
— 50 DCOA, 60, 62
— 58 DCO A/3, 124
Weier, 134
Whitehead, Peter, 101-102
Williams, Frank, 24
Williams, Jonathan, 38, **93**
Wimille, Jean Pierre, 35, 94, 99

Z

Zagato, 139

BIBLIOGRAPHY

BOOKS

Mille Ruote, Editoriale Domus-Quattroruote Milano, Istituto Geografico De Agostini, Novara
The Ferrari, Hans Tanner, G.T. Foulis and Co. Ltd.
Tutto Fangio, Severo Boschi, Edizioni Calderini, Bologna
Ferrari, Enzo Ferrari
La mia vita a 300 all'ora, Fangio-Giambertone, Aldo Palazzi Editore
La storia delle Ferrari e Alfa Romeo campioni del mondo, Casucci-Tommasi, Arnoldo Mondadori Editore, Verona
Ferrari, Jonathan Thompson, Edita-Vilo
Ferrari Sport et Prototypes, Antoine Poiret, epa, Paris
Ferrari The Man the Machines, Stan Grayson, Dutton
A Turn at the Wheel, Stirling Moss, William Kimber, London
Challenge me the Race, Mike Hawthorn, William Kimber, London
Quatre fois vainquer au Mans, Oliver Gendebien, Flammarion, Paris
Bandiera a scacchi, Piero Taruffi
Le Ferrari, Gianni Rogliatti, l'Editrice dell'Automobile, Roma

PERIODICALS

Année Automobile, Edita, Lausanne
Quatroruote, Editoriale Domus, Milano
Autosprint, Editoriale Il Borgo, Bologna
Autosport, Haymarket Publishing Ltd., London
Autocar, IPC Transport Press Ltd., London

METRIC CONVERSIONS

1 millimeter (mm) = .03937 inch
1 centimeter (cm) = .3937 inch
1 meter (m) = 39.37 inches or 3.28 feet
1 kilometer (km) = .62137 mile

1 liter = .264 U.S. gallon or .220 Imperial gallon

1 cubic centimeter (cc) = .0610 cubic inch

1 kilogram (kg) = 2.2046 pounds